Thinking Whole

Rejecting Half-Witted Left & Right Brain Limitations

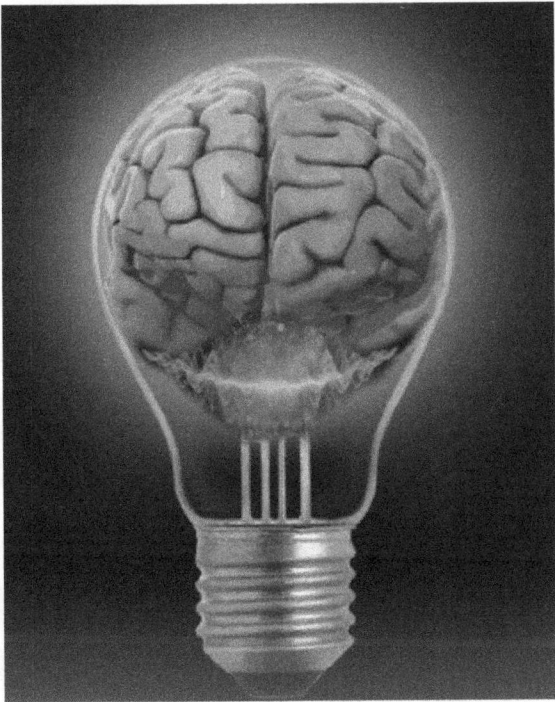

Larry Bell

Thinking Whole: Rejecting Half-Witted Left & Right Brain Limitations

Other books by Larry Bell:

Scared Witless: Prophets and Profits of Climate Doom
Climate of Corruption: Politics and Power behind the Global Warming Hoax
Cosmic Musings: Contemplating Life beyond Self
Reflections on Oceans and Puddles: One Hundred Reasons to be Enthusiastic, Grateful and Hopeful

STAIRWAY PRESS—Apache Junction

Book Cover Art: Suzana Bianco
Cover Design by Chris Benson
www.BensonCreative.com

STAIRWAY≡PRESS

www.StairwayPress.com
1000 West Apache Trail, Suite 126
Apache Junction, AZ 85120

Dedication

Dedicated to our whole-brained Paleolithic Homo sapiens ancestors who recorded pragmatic hunting survival interests, artistic animal depictions, and even self-aware hand stenciled selfies on Eurasian and Indonesian cave walls around 40,000 years ago.

Introduction: Becoming More Mindful

CHANCES ARE THAT you may have bought into a popularly accepted notion that divides personality types into predominate logically-analytical and technically-oriented left-brained thinkers versus more creative right-brained free spirits, and that these are mutually exclusive traits.

Perhaps you may have even taken a purportedly science-based aptitude test that placed you in one of those categories.

If you are perfectly content with viewing yourself as one or the other, then don't change a thing. If, on the other hand, you feel unnecessarily limited by such stereotypic labels, why settle for being unnecessarily half-witted?

For American science fiction writer Robert Heinlein, thinking whole is more than a way to enable a full and effective life—it's a requirement for one. He proposed an ambitiously comprehensive range of expectations in his book, *Time Enough for Love*...

> *A human being should be able to change a diaper, plan an invasion, butcher a hog, conn a ship, design a building, write a sonnet, balance accounts, build a*

wall, set a bone, comfort the dying, take orders, give
orders, cooperate, act alone, solve equations, analyze a
new problem, program a computer, cook a tasty meal,
fight efficiently, die gallantly. Specialization is for
insects.[i]

Whole brain thinking is evidenced in everyday life through our awareness of surrounding environments. It is expressed through curiosity which compels our interest in how and why natural and man-made things work the way they do...interconnected relationships between ourselves and others...patterns and rhythms observed in nature...spiritual lessons and explorations that motivate higher purposes and values...inspirations experienced through image forms, literature and stories of the past...music...everything combined that our whole minds can contemplate.

Whole brains serve to contemplate our personal potentials as well. As British-born neurologist and science writer Oliver Sacks instructed in a 2012 *New Yorker* magazine article:

To live on a day-to-day basis is insufficient for human
beings; we need to transcend, transport, escape; we need
meaning, understanding, and explanation; we need to
see over-all patterns in our lives. We need hope, the
sense of a future. And we need freedom (or, at least, the
illusion of freedom) to get beyond ourselves, whether
with telescopes and microscopes and our ever-
burgeoning technology, or in states of mind that allow
us to travel to other worlds, to rise above our immediate
surroundings.[ii]

Sacks further observes that this often requires peaceful minds:

We may seek, too, a relaxing of inhibitions that makes

it easier to bond with each other, or transports that make our consciousness of time and mortality easier to bear. We seek a holiday from our inner and outer restrictions, a more intense sense of the here and now, the beauty and value of the world we live in.

And as American neurologist physician, philosopher and poet Debasish Miridha advises:

Let your thoughts, intentions, imaginations, and dreams fly under a clear blue sky with a spring breeze floating like a butterfly from flower to flower. See the beauty of mankind. Enjoy the nectar of life. It will shift your awareness to a higher consciousness.

The ultimate benefit of thinking and living whole is realized through expanded and strengthened connections to life experiences. Writing in *The New Yorker*, David Brooks summed this up eloquently:

I've come to think that flourishing consists of putting yourself in situations in which you lose self-consciousness and become fused with other people, experiences, or tasks. It happens sometimes when you are lost in a hard challenge, or when an artist or a craftsman becomes one with the brush or the tool. It happens sometimes while you're playing sports, or listening to music or lost in a story, or to some people when they feel enveloped by God's love. And it happens most when we connect with other people.

Brooks concludes:

I've come to think that happiness isn't really produced

by conscious accomplishments. Happiness is a measure of how thickly the unconscious parts of our minds are intertwined with other people and with activities. Happiness is determined by how much information and affection flows through us covertly every day and year.[iii]

Pursuing passions stimulates our curiosity, inciting us to courses of inquiry and action that reveal unexpected possibilities. We should appreciate them, nurture them and enjoy them.

Have fun with your passions, and yes, apply them for good. A whole-lived life deserves no less.

---

[i] *Time Enough for Love*, Robert A. Heinlein, GP Putman's Sons, 1973.

[ii] *Altered States: Self-Experiments in Chemistry*, Oliver Sacks, *The New Yorker*, August 2012.

[iii] *Social Animal*, David Brooks, The New Yorker, Annals of Psychology, January 17, 2011.

Thinking Whole

Table of Contents

1

Larry Bell

Thinking Whole

Larry Bell

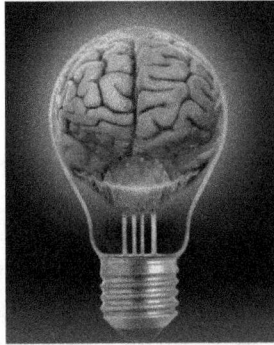

Part One: The Anatomy of Thought

ACCORDING TO POPULAR left-brain vs. right-brain theory, each side of the brain separately controls different types of thinking. In reality, each of our two brain hemispheres share and support both of these intellectual capacities.

While it is true that each side performs a variety of discrete roles and functions, both sides collaborate in surprising ways to fill in perceptual gaps. For example, since the left hemisphere controls the muscles on the right side of the body, damage to that side also affects that other side of the body. Studies show that for the general population, both hemispheres are equally functional.

Using instrument measurements of electric or magnetic fields, studies by a UC Santa Barbara research team headed by Michael Gazzaniga observed that subjects were able to distinguish real words from random strings of letters in nonsense words better than when the same information was fed directly to the left hemisphere via the right eye than from the left eye.

This led the research team to theorize that the brain has difficulty processing information that travels long distances.[1]

The Split-Brain Myth

Distorted notions stressing lateralized brain function originated with and exaggerated conclusions of 1960s "split-brain" research conducted by neuropsychologist Roger Sperry at the California Institute of Technology and his former doctoral student—again, Michael Gazzaniga. Early studies revealed that cutting corpus callosum fibers connecting two hemispheres of monkey brains resulted in unawareness of each side regarding what was going on in the other. Gazzaniga later found a similar, but more subtle effect in people whose neural corpus callosum bridge was severed in an operation called a "calloscotomy" to eliminate extreme epileptic seizures.

When the two sides of human brains were unable to communicate with each other, they responded to different stimuli. Many became unable to name objects that were processed by the right side of the brain, but were able to name objects that were processed by the left side.

One patient, a World War II veteran, was shown a square shape in his left visual field which connected to his right hemisphere. He recognized and articulated the item as a "box," yet when the item was shown on his right side, he was unable to name it. Such observations led to a conclusion that language is controlled by the left side of the brain, a concept that became widely popular in the 1970s.

Paul S., a child patient, had fully functional language centers in both hemispheres that enabled researchers to question each side. Sometimes the answers that came back were very different. For example, when they asked the right side of Paul what he wanted to be when he grew up, he replied "an automobile racer." When the same question was posed to the left, that side wanted to be "a draftsman."

Another subject pulled down his pants with his left hand at

the same time that his right hand struggled to pull them back up. On another occasion, the same patient's left hand attempted to strike his unsuspecting wife just as the right hand tried to grab and stop this from happening.

This dichotomous over-simplification got a big boost from a 1973 *New York Times Magazine* article, which began:

> *Two different persons inhabit our heads, residing in the left and right hemispheres of our brains. The twin shells that cover the central brain stem. One of them is verbal, analytic, [and] dominant. The other is artistic.*

Other influential stories soon trumpeted left vs. right-brain disconnects in *Time* magazine, *Harvard Review* and *Psychology Today*. Sperry's 1981 award of a Nobel Prize in Psychology enshrined that mischaracterized mental tug-of-war concept.

Sperry himself warned in an essay published in the journal *Neuropsychologia*:

> *Experimentally observed polarity in right-left cognitive style is an idea in general with which it is very easy to run wild...it is important to remember that the two hemispheres in the normal intact brain tend regularly to function closely as a unit.* [2, 3, 4]

Later studies indicate that right-left brain hemisphere dichotomy isn't nearly that simple because both function as a partnership. While the left hemisphere does tend to specialize in picking out sounds that form words and working out syntax for phrases, it does not monopolize language processing. It coordinates with and depends upon the right hemisphere, which is more sensitive to emotional features of language.

There are also rare and remarkable circumstances where

impaired interhemispheric communication enables people to simultaneously complete two independent intellectual tasks. The leading character played by actor Dustin Hoffman in the movie *Rain Man* was inspired by such an individual. Kim Peek, characterized as "living encyclopedia," could not only read and digest both facing pages of a book at the same time, but could retain and elaborate driving instructions between any two cities in the world.

Some of the abilities popularly associated with the right side of the brain involve somewhat less defined blocks of information through processing of images, patterns and spatial orientation. These include visual comprehension in recognizing faces, expressing and reading emotions and identifying images and colors.

The left hemisphere is broadly characterized as dealing more with individual steps of a process and piecing together small bits of data into linear and readily articulable thoughts. This is usually described as being better at language expression, calculating with numbers and deductive reasoning.

Nevertheless, as noted by New York Times and Discover magazine science writer Carl Zimmer: "No matter how lateralized the brain can get, the two sides still work together."

Zimmer points out that:

> The pop psychology notion of a left brain and a right brain doesn't capture their intimate working relationship. The left hemisphere specializes in picking out the sounds that form words and working out the syntax of the phrase, for example, but it does not have a monopoly on language processing. The right hemisphere is more sensitive to the emotional features of language, tuning-in to the slow rhythms of speech that carry intonation and stress.

Thinking Whole

Human brains are enormously complex chemical machines containing about 100 billion neurons and 100 trillion synapses, with each hemisphere offering a pretty much universal balance of interactive role features. A two-year study published in the journal Plos One by neuroscientists at the University of Utah scanned the brains of more than 1,000 people ranging in ages from 7 to 29 to determine if they preferred using one side over the other.

Breaking the brains into 7,000 regions to observe patterns indicating dominant right- or left-lateralization, the researchers found little evidence indicating differences. Regardless of self-identifying preferences various subjects expressed, they were more alike than might be imagined. Results showed that while activity was sometimes higher in certain critical regions, both sides of the brain were essentially equal in their activity on average.

As the study's lead author, Jeff Anderson, concluded:

> It's absolutely true that some brain functions occur in
> one or the other side of the brain. Language tends to
> be on the left, attention more on the right. But people
> don't tend to have a stronger left- or right-sided brain
> network. It seems to be determined more by
> connection.

Still, it isn't quite as clear-cut as all that either...the right hemisphere is also involved in processing some aspects of language such as intonation and emphasis. Anderson adds:

> The neuroscience community has never accepted the
> idea of 'left-dominant' or 'right-dominant'
> personality types. Lesion studies don't support it, and
> the truth is that it would be highly inefficient for one
> half of the brain to consistently be more active than

the other. [5]

Nevertheless, as psychological science writer Amy Novotney observes in a 2013 a Guardian article, this vernacular isn't likely to go away any time soon:

> *Human society is built around categories, classifications and generalizations, and there's something seductively simple about labeling yourself and others as either a logical left-brainer or a free-spirited right brainer.*

Unfortunately, while sometimes offering a harmless conversation-starter, the false dichotomy theory can also support self-unfulfilling prophesies, particularly for young people. This can be influenced by performance tests suggesting that someone isn't "good with numbers," or discouraging someone from seeking a dream opportunity calling for creative skills which they believe they lack.

Novotney points out the brain is remarkably malleable, even into late adulthood:

> *It has an amazing ability to reorganize itself by forming new connections between brain cells, allowing us to continually learn new things and modify our behavior. Let's not underestimate our potential by allowing a simplistic myth to obscure the complexity of how our brains really work.*

Are there ways to help our whole brains serve us better in everyday life? Of course there are. An endless variety of popular psychology and self-help books and courses are available to help guide and adjust our thinking habits to recognize "big picture" events and relationships that we are part of, to engage us in ever higher levels of spiritual enlightenment and intellectual thought and to sort out goals most demanding of priority attention and action.

Formally-orchestrated and self-exploratory mental journeys into art, music and literature pursuits extend comprehension and expressions of interconnected yet distinct visual, audible and word-based communication. Studies of mathematics, physics and other sciences form basic language tools, vocabularies and logic structures to make complex theoretical, physical and social systems and our relationships to them less emotionally overwhelming and more naturally intuitive.

Collectively, these teaching resources apply to a wide array of disciplines which inevitably overlap in the learning process. The point is to learn to think holistically, recognizing, above all, that whole-brain thinking is fundamentally a conscious decision. What finally matters most is to avoid subconsciously labeling and limiting yourself as a half-wit.

As Dr. Seuss instructs us:

> *Think left and think right and think low and think*
> *high. Oh, the thinks you can think up if only you try.*

Stimulating Thoughtful Connections

Understanding our enormously complex brain and how it affects each of our individual personalities and proclivities presents a paradox…how can a thought system even begin to comprehend a system vastly more complex than itself?

Nevertheless, natural brain-induced and enabled curiosity and rationality continues to drive humankind to keep trying to understand what makes us collectively and individually "us."

Formalized thinking about how humans think can be dated as far back as 342 BC to observations by the philosopher

Aristotle, who characterized our five senses: sight, sound, touch, taste and smell. Aristotle also hypothesized that there is a direct correlation between brain size and intelligence in animals. If this were true, however, we might have to take thinking lessons from blue whales, whose brains are nearly five times larger than ours, or maybe African elephants, who have brains about three times larger.

Aristotle's era didn't yet know that different parts of the brain have different functions, in turn containing networks of tiny, specialized sensory neuron cells. On closer examination, about 97 percent of the sensory neurons in those elephant brains are located in the cerebellum, which is devoted extensively to sensory motor functions. In comparison, about one-third of those in the human brain are contained in the cerebral cortex, which is broadly characterized as the "thinking" part of the brain.

About 500 years after Aristotle, the Greek physician Galen observed the effects of brain injuries in Roman gladiators and came to the correct conclusion that the brain does control body movements. From a gladiator perspective, that was invariably a deadly way to find this out.

By the 19th century, scientists realized that brains are constructed of specialized cells, and also began to more specifically identify which parts of the brain carried out specific functions. As it turned out, this isn't nearly as clear and simple as might have been imagined, since many of those functions have interdependent connections to other brain regions which must work in concert.

Early in the 20th century, Canadian neurosurgeon Wilder Penfield traced some of these connections and interconnections to feelings and sensations by electrically stimulating different parts of brains in conscious patients.

About that same time, German psychiatrist Hans Berger invented the Electroencephalogram (EEG) to measure electrical activity in the brain. This was followed by an explosion of other devices and methodologies for studying the living brain, including Computerized Tomography (CT), Positron Emission Tomography (PET) and Magnetic Resonance Imaging (MRI), to name but a few.

We now know that the whole, highly interconnected brain is a very active place. Listening to, creating and playing music, for example, involves many parts of the brain. A study carried out by Steven Brown and Lawrence Parsons in Sheffield, England used PET scans to examine brain activity in a group of pianists while performing a concerto by Bach. They reported that the neural activations were so complex and widespread that it was almost easier to list areas of the brain that were not active while playing than to list all those that were.[6]

None of these techniques and discoveries can even begin to describe the true human nature...curiosity, creativity, passions, values and interests that make each of us special and unique individuals. No method or machine yet invented can do this.

Flashing back again to the early 19th century, neuroanatomist Franz Gall thought he could judge someone's personality, character and even their intelligence by simply feeling the shape of their head through a then-popular practice of "phrenology."

In doing so, Gall measured bumps, dips and ridges in the skulls of psychiatric patients, artists and criminals on the theory that those contours matched the shape of the underlying brain...which in turn reflected strengths and weaknesses of an individual's character.

Gall identified and "mapped" 27 fundamental characteristics. A protruding forehead was believed to reflect a benevolent nature, whereas someone with a bump over their ear was thought to have destructive tendencies.

He also assumed that the bigger a particular part of the brain, the stronger that trait would be. That's likely where the expression "getting your head examined" came from.[7]

Although neither of Gall's theories that skull shapes mimic brain shape or that brain contours reflect character traits ultimately proved true, it's now evident that different parts of the brain really do carry out specialized functions. More advanced understanding of links between these physiological and psychological phenomena is vital in seeking ways to prevent and treat brain damage caused by physical injury or disease associated with a variety of psychiatric disorders such as dementia, schizophrenia, Parkinson's disease and autism.

Inspired by the Human Genome Project, the U.S. government launched a "Brain Initiative" in 2013 attempting to work together with many of the largest worldwide research institutions in a coordinated effort to understand and map the human brain. The program is ultimately expected to continue for more than ten years and focus primarily upon developing investigative research technology.

Whole Brain Features and Functions

Recognizing that simplistic characterizations of whole left-right brain "architecture" obviously leave lots of other important "thinking" parts and functions out, let's at least broadly review some prominent elements and what the brain's parts do for us.

The Cerebrum: Located at the top of the brain, this large region is divided into two roughly symmetrical cerebral hemispheres. The right hemisphere controls and processes signals from the right side of the body, and vice versa.

The cerebrum contains the brain's four major lobes, along with several other structures including the hippocampus and basal ganglia.

The brain's prefrontal cortex works closely with the hippocampal formation. It acts like a librarian that organizes retrieval strategies. The hippocampus located under the cerebral cortex plays important roles in the consolidation of information from short-term memory to long-term memory, along with spatial memory that enables navigation.

Toward the middle area lies the limbic system and basal ganglia which strongly influence our memory formation, emotions and sensations of pleasure and pain. These basal ganglia also connect with many other brain structures that play important roles in regulating our movements and thoughts.

The Cerebral Cortex: Looking at the exposed brain, we see a prominent outer part which is deeply folded to optimize its surface area. This can generally be regarded as the primary thinking region, altogether it also manages many of our sensations and perceptions, memories and behaviors.

The cerebral cortex, in turn, divides into four different kinds of lobes:

- Frontal Lobes, which are located on the top front of the brain, have primary roles in speech production, planning of actions, controls of behaviors and empathy. These roles are vital to understanding other people. The frontal lobes are proportionally far larger in humans than in most other animals. They serve as the seat of our intelligence, and as the location of our personalities. They are also the region that develops last in young children when brains are still growing, and they also age fastest at the farther end of lives.

- Parietal lobes, located at the top rear of the brain, integrate sensations and perceptions. Their main functions are to receive and process sensory information from all over the body. For example, they work in concert with the brain's visual cortex to enable special orientations necessary to open a door, comb hair, place lips and tongue in proper positions for speech and navigate through spaces.

- Temporal lobes, located in the bottom front of the brain, play important roles in processing sensory input into derived meanings essential for visual memory, language comprehension and emotional associations. Working with other parts of the brain, they make it possible to sort out meaningful sounds we hear from background noise, understand what other people are saying and recognize individual faces.

- The occipital lobe, located at the rear bottom of the brain above the cerebellum, houses our primary visual functions which process all visual inputs. In doing so, the two halves organize information from the eyes and optic nerves into images which the brain can then recognize and interpret as vision that we only think we "see" directly from eyes.

The Thalamus: This large, dual lobed region is located immediately above the brain stem. It functions somewhat like a multi-media mixing console that connects the cerebral cortex to relay and integrate those sensory perceptions most particularly involving movement. The thalamus also controls sleep and awake states of consciousness, plays important roles in memory formations and emotional expressions and interprets pain perceptions.

The Hypothalamus: This very small part of the brain located just below the thalamus controls the pituitary gland, which, in turn, regulates all hormones. It is also involved in interpreting pain and temperature. The hypothalamus also assures that sugar, oxygen, salt and even temperature are maintained within safe levels. Plus, it regulates important endocrine functions as metabolism, body growth and development.

The Cerebellum: This large cauliflower-shaped part in the back of the brain records and stores all motor learning (ability to walk, ride a bicycle, maintain balance and play piano). It also helps to manage our emotions and our capacity to pay attention through many long-range connections with the frontal lobe at opposite ends of the brain. Damage to this region can lead to various paralyses, such as paraplegic, quadriplegic or partial impairments of specific motor neuron pathways.

BRAIN ANATOMY

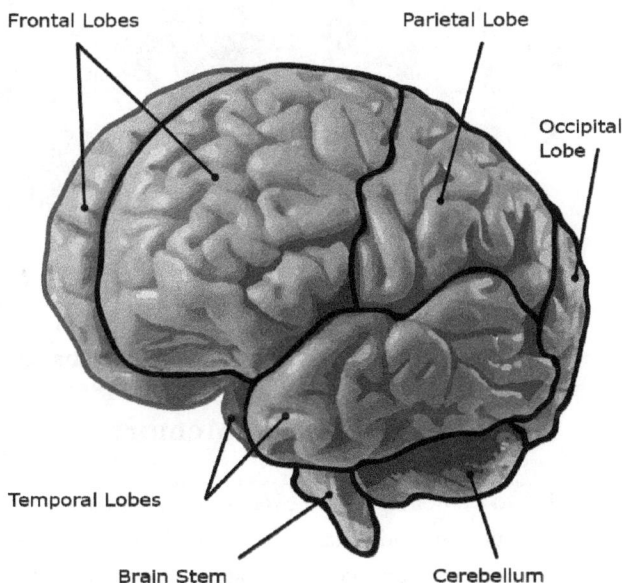

Frontal Lobes

Parietal Lobe

Occipital Lobe

Temporal Lobes

Brain Stem

Cerebellum

LIMBIC SYSTEM

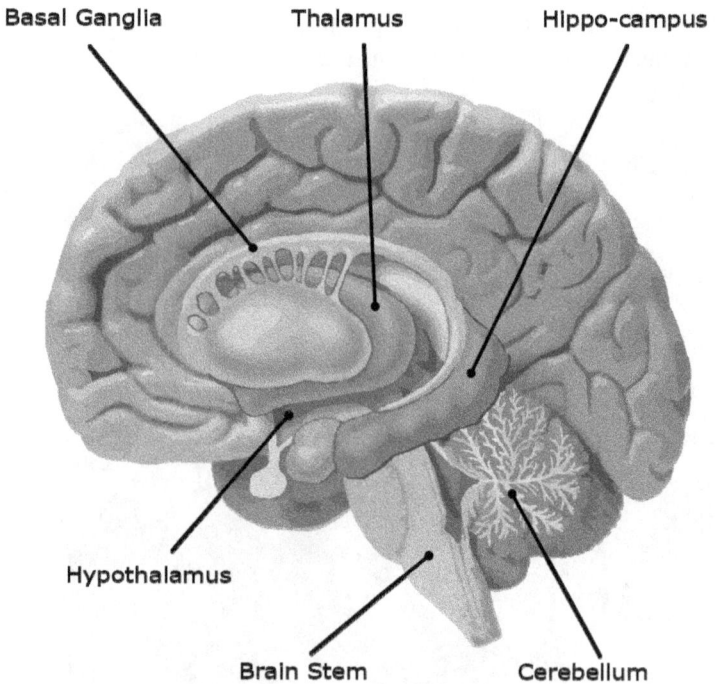

Basal Ganglia   Thalamus   Hippo-campus

Hypothalamus

Brain Stem   Cerebellum

Making and Losing Memories

Our abilities to remember past events and lessons are vital to our safety, function and quality of life. Conscious memory provides a sense of coherence that enables us to connect events in the world to our internal representations. This provides a sense of logic and continuity, serving as a basis for imagining and planning.

Our recorded experiences enable us to create and maintain a sense of identity and engage in social relationships. In doing so, those recollections help us connect our beliefs and feelings about ourselves to people and the world around us.

Some may be surprised to learn that those memory records that seem vividly clear and real aren't actually stored whole in any central brain storage unit. They are not permanently fixed or reliable. Each time we "remember" a moment we construct it from building blocks which represent only rough facsimiles of previous events and conditions. This sort of "episodic memory," which only recalls what we have perceived and understood to have once happened, is seldom 100 percent accurate.

Unlike "semantic memory," which involves concrete knowledge about our world and how we think it works, experiential recollections are not only influenced by our subjective emotional and philosophical viewpoints at the time, but are also colored by subsequent experiences which have modified those outlooks.

The good news is that with regard to episodic memories, accuracy is less significant than consistency. It should also be encouraging to know that the old "use it or lose it" adage applies to the creation of new memory and mental performance capabilities.

Every time we go back over an event in our mind we strengthen and embed memory connections. In 1949, the late Canadian psychologist Donald Hebb published an important observation demonstrating that repeated associations being made between different events created connections between them. He recognized that memory is stored across the cerebral cortex as networks of neurons he called "assemblies," and that the more frequently a synapse was activated, the more easily it could be triggered in the future.[8]

In the mid-1980s my close University of Illinois friend, the late American neuroscientist William "Bill" Greenough, discovered that neural reinforcement through learning is evidenced through high-resolution imaging of synapse connections in rat brains. Bill reared three genetically identical rats in three different environments—impoverished (bare necessities), simple (basic, but not exciting) and enriched (a big space with lots of toys and other rats to interact with). Results showed that the rats reared in the enriched environments had more elaborate branching and significantly more synapses than those in the other two groups.

Now, as people are living longer and longer, more are also inevitably experiencing deleterious effects of aging. Natural losses of brain cells and more abrupt impairments of mental functions through injuries and diseases in aging brains present a growing individual and societal dilemma.

We now know that this brain aging process begins frighteningly early...for many people, even in their 20s. On the other hand, despite losses of cells, brains can also become more efficient over time, adapting to these changes with remarkable plasticity.

Nevertheless, those of us who live long enough to age naturally can also expect to experience having our mental recall and thinking speed for quick decisions slow down. "Executive functions," such as planning ahead, using complex strategies and being flexible will likely diminish. In addition, abilities, at least temporarily, to recall someone's name or find the right word may become more difficult.

The prefrontal cortex and hippocampus are particularly vulnerable to aging. Ironically, the frontal lobes are the last to develop in children, and also first to be effected in oldsters.

Various parts of the brain impacted by natural or traumatic processes have different consequences. Those individuals with damage to their cerebellum, for example, may no longer remember how to ride a bicycle. This can involve losses of what is referred to as "non-declarative" recall experiences including emotional responses that they aren't consciously aware of.

On the other hand, many of these same individuals may have no problem recollecting what they had for breakfast or the name of their favorite band.

Damage to the hippocampus can have a devastating effect on abilities to lay down episodic memories. Studies show this area, sometimes described as the "printing press," is typically more developed in London taxi drivers who constantly exercise route-learning abilities. The hippocampus, along with the cerebellum, are two brain regions capable of growing new neuron cells.

Alzheimer's disease typically results from pathological changes in the hippocampus. People with this and other forms of dementia begin to lose their long-term memories accessible in coded pieces from different parts of their brain as damage spreads across the cerebral cortex. Memories, like words written in the sand, become washed away.

Hopefully, ongoing scientific advancements, perhaps some resulting from the International Brain Initiative, will find ways to prevent such tragedies.

Remembering to Pay Attention

Of course, even "normal" people are different, depending a lot upon what each pays most attention to remembering. Consider the archetypal walking encyclopedia absent-minded professor who forgets where he or she put their car keys. Maybe we can quickly learn a new skill or list of numbers, but can't seem to remember a spouse's birthday.

At a very basic level, there is a difference between what we might be aware of at various times as a "sensation" versus a "perception." For example, whether we smell the presence of a particular flower, or focus our awareness to recognize it.

In other words, sensation can be defined as the detection of external or internal stimuli, whereby perception is the conscious registration and interpretation of that input. At the same time, however, neither experiences need to involve any conscious perception. There are way too many things going on at the same time to process them all. This would be a waste of time and attention for our purposeful minds, which have many other simultaneous tasks to accomplish.

The sensory systems that enable us to be subconsciously or consciously aware of what is going on outside and inside us is truly remarkable and busy. Try to imagine that it has the intriguing capacity to project sensations back to the point of origin. While it might seem that we are seeing with our eyes, tasting with our tongue and touching with our fingers, all of those sensations actually come from neurons inside our brains.

Interesting things happen when those signals somehow get crossed, a condition known as "synaesthesia." About one in 2,000 people experience this blending of two or more senses in which sounds, tastes, smells or words may have a specific color, shape, smell or sound. Contemporary popular musicians Kayne West and Pharrell Williams shared this condition with Duke Ellington, Vincent van Gogh, Wassily Kandinsky, and other accomplished celebrities. Rock legend Jimi Hendrix was so taken by the color purple, as he sensed it every time he played a particular guitar chord, that it inspired his famous song *Purple Haze*.

What we choose to perceive can apparently influence our health and longevity.

American professor Becca Levy carried out a 39-year-long study which evaluated 18- to 48-year-olds regarding long-held influences of psychological outlooks upon physical and mental health. Her team found that those with negative attitudes were significantly more likely to have early heart attacks and strokes. In a separate study, she also found that people who hold negative stereotypes had more memory problems over time.[9]

So maybe that is another good reason to apply some age-old advice. Devote more time and attention to smelling the flowers.

Conscious and Subconscious Awareness

Napoleon Bonaparte advised that the extent of true consciousness is limited only by your ability to love and to embrace with your love the space around you and all it contains. Voltaire advocated a transcendental pathway to achieve this fully enlightened state:

> *Meditation is the dissolution of thoughts in Eternal awareness or pure consciousness without objectification, knowing without thinking, merging finitude in infinity.*

Princeton neurosciences professor Michael Graziano contemplates relationships between our physical brains and transcendental thoughts. In his book *Consciousness and the Social Brain*, he broadly defines consciousness as "the window through which we understand."

Graziano characterizes personal consciousness as:

> *The essence of self-awareness...the spark that makes us us...something lovely that apparently is buried inside us that makes us aware of ourselves and the world.*

Without this awareness, we would have no basis for curiosity or even any realization that a world exists to be curious about. Nor would there be any impetus to seek emotional, artistic, religious or scientific insights.

Origins of Consciousness and Thought

Graziano observes that although neuroscientists know at least in general terms how the human brain's approximately one hundred billion interacting neurons compute information, the big question about how a brain becomes aware of information remains unanswered. What, he asks, comprises basic sentience itself? [10]

Such questions date back in human history to long before the existence of formal science as we know it today. Hippocrates, in the 5th century BC, noticed relationships between brain and mind, observing correlations between damages and losses of mental capabilities. Observing that the mind is created and somehow dies piece-by-piece as the brain does, he elegantly summarized this discovery, writing:

> *Men ought to know that from the brain, and from the brain only, arise our pleasures, joys, laughter and jests, as well as our sorrows, griefs and tears. Through it, in particular, we think, see, hear, and distinguish the ugly from the beautiful, the bad from the good, the pleasant from the unpleasant.*

Alas, not all brain-mind theories have panned out as imagined. In 1642, two thousand years after Hippocrates, Descartes envisioned mind consciousness comprised of an ethereal fluid he called "rescogitans" (mental substance) stored in the brain receptacle. When dissecting brains looking for receptacles he noticed that nearly every structure came in pairs, one similar part on each side. Believing that each individual has but one soul—and being thereby perplexed regarding how it could be divided up and stored in two places—he concluded that the soul must be housed in a small single pineal lump that he discovered at the center of the brain. That pineal body is now recognized as a gland that produces melatonin.

Descartes also arrived at the idea that self-awareness is fundamental to thinking—that thinking requires a thinker. This is summed this up in his famous statement "Cogito ergo sum", *I think, therefore, I am.*

Philosopher David Chalmers framed the challenge of explaining consciousness as two basic problems: an easier one, and a harder one. The easier one is primarily technical...namely to figure out how the brain computes and stores information. The harder one is to explain how we become aware of the essence of awareness itself...something which is presumed to be non-physical, private and scientifically unapproachable requiring a mysterious phenomenon to solve a mystery.[11]

Emanuel Kant referred to this as an unknowable "transcendental apperception of the ego"... seeing the "self" not as something perceived by the senses, but rather as something spiritually eternal which transcends us. In his 1781 book *A Critique of Pure Reason*, he maintained that the mind relies upon "a priori forms," abilities and ideas supplied by divine acts which were always within us, and from which everything else flows.

Co-DNA structure discoverers Francis Crick and Christof Koch advanced a theory in 1990 that this consciousness flows through brain neurons which pass information among each other via oscillating electrical signals. This information is most efficiently linked and maintained between one neuron and another over short periods of time as they oscillate in synchrony at frequencies of 40-70 HZ. This short-term "working memory" consciousness, therefore, might result when the electrical activity of many neurons oscillates together in various parts of the brain.[12]

We trust our senses to inform us of what is "real." Yet

everything we perceive as hard is made up of tiny bits of energetic stuff that has no "solidity" at all. The temperatures we sense are only specific electromagnetic frequencies and wavelengths that are detected by neurons and which are calibrated by our brains to inform us about our surroundings.

Our color perception is an interpretive phenomenon as well. Yellow light, for example, describes transversal electromagnetic wavelengths in the measure in the neighborhood of 590 nanometers.

Those images we "see" in front of us are actually illusory constructs which are assembled behind our eyes in our brains. The sensory impressions of taste and smell depend upon specialized chemical receptors that differentiate between presence of different molecules or ions. Hearing, a mechanical process, relates to how our brains interpret various vibrations within the range of our audio detectors which are caused when something moves air around.

Paying Attention Its Due

Influenced by research addressing ways that sensations of vision, touch and hearing combined in the brain might be used to coordinate movement, Michael Graziano proposes a method referred to as "attention" where the mind focuses upon processing a few items at any given time. Doing so involves a data-handling trick to deeply process some information at the expense of attention to most other information. It does this by constructing simplified schematic models of complex objects and events in the world that can be used to make predictions, to try out simulations and to plan actions.

Graziano theorizes that the brain can also construct models of its own attentional state as well those of others. He writes, for example:

Harry might be focusing his attention on a coffee stain on his shirt. You look at him and understand that Harry is aware of the stain. In the theory, much of the same machinery, the same brain regions and computational processing that are used in the social context to attribute awareness to someone else, are also used on a continuous basis to construct your own awareness and attribute it to yourself.

He therefore concludes that "social perception and awareness share a substrate." [13]

But what gives us the self-conscious ability to wonder about how we wonder at all?

V.S. Ramachandra, author of *The Tell-Tale Brain: A Neuroscientist's Quest for What Makes Us Human*, marvels, as we all should, about what makes higher levels of consciousness possible. He asks:

How can a three-pound mass of jelly that you can hold in your palm imagine angels, contemplate the meaning of infinity, and even question its own place in the cosmos? Especially awe inspiring is the fact that any single brain, including yours, is made up of atoms that were forged in the hearts of countless, far-flung stars billions of years ago. These particles drifted for eons and light-years until gravity and change brought them together here, now. These atoms now form a conglomerate—your brain—that can not only ponder the very stars that gave it birth but can also think about its own ability to think and wonder about its own ability to wonder. With the arrival of humans, it has been said, the universe has suddenly become conscious of itself. This, truly, it the greatest mystery of all. [14]

Charles Fernyhough, a professor in the University of Durham's Department of Psychology, suggests that we don't think hard enough about what we mean by "thinking." By this, he refers to two common usages of the term. He writes:

> One holds that thinking is everything that the conscious mind does. That would include perception, mental arithmetic, remembering a phone number, or conjuring up an image of a pink unicorn.

This first definition simply equates to conscious cognitive processes. And although Fernyhough "thinks" that thinking seems to him to be quintessentially conscious, he suggests that we should also consider "unconscious" cognitive processes which shape the ways we make sense of the world.

Fernyhough asks us to contemplate the experience of thinking "from the inside of Rodin's Thinker's head...what would we see, hear, and feel?" He challenges us to imagine what might be described as the sort of thinking while we're walking to work or soaking in a bathtub, where we have a sense of a flow of inner speech. These constitute personal communications of verbal quality, as though we are talking to ourselves. While it might seem that we have words in our heads, we actually don't. Moreover, we have thoughts that don't sound like words at all.

At the same time, spoken language isn't really necessary for thinking. Fernyhough urges us to move beyond assuming that inner speech is "just one homogeneous kind of thing: a flow of words in the head which appear to us, subjectively, like heard language."

Fernyhough argues that thinking is both conscious and active...a cognitive process that can make new connections and create meaning. He says:

> It is dialogic: it has the quality of an internal

conversation between different perspectives, although the 'give-and-take' quality of external dialogues may not always be immediately obvious. And it is linguistic: verbal for those who use spoken language, visual for those of us who use sign language to communicate with others and with ourselves. [15]

Writings by the late Soviet psychologist Lev Vygotsky suggest that there are two kinds of inner speech, semantic (depth of word understanding), and syntactic (corresponding with traditional parts of speech such as nouns, verbs, prepositions, etc.).

Inner speech often becomes a "note form" version of the external dialogue from which it derives...a condensed form with all of its acoustic properties stripped away, losing qualities of tone, accent, timbre and pitch that distinguish spoken language. Fernyhough refers to this as "condensed inner speech."

At other times, it takes the form of a more complete two-way conversation where, as Fernyhough describes:

[S]ubjectively we do experience a full-blown internal dialogue playing out in our minds.

Here, we...

...have a sense of participating in a true internal conversation, with one point of view answering another, just like a dialogue spoken aloud between two people.

Charles Fernyhough distinguishes between inner speech thinking and consciousness because thoughts often can't be put into words. We can be conscious of things that we can't express verbally "because it has not yet been expanded into full, recognizable language." Vygotsky wrote that this unexpressed kind of thinking could be likened to rain before it falls, where thought is like a "cloud shedding a shower of words."' [16]

Patterns of Recognition and Thought

Our brains do wonderful jobs of sorting out and focusing upon information that we need to know at any given moment by selectively screening out an otherwise overwhelming variety of distractions. As mental organizers, they enable us to see and make sense out of patterns revealing larger and more coherent information pictures.

As Diane Ackerman wrote in a June 2004, New York Times article:

> *The brain is a five-star generalizer. It simplifies and organizes, reducing a deluge of sensory information to a manageable sum. From that small sample, the brain produces an effigy of the world, whose features it monitors. Anything that doesn't fit, or signals trouble, draws a response. As it learns, it compares new phenomena and experiences with old ones.* [17]

But as Ackerman points out:

> *Individuals and events are never identical, only similar in vital ways. The brain doesn't have room to record the everythingness of everything, nor would that be a smart strategy. Exactly remembering a lion only prepares you for the next lion. Instead, the brain files away a sea of clues, alert to the subtlest insinuation of a pattern. Key features of a wren imply those of birds in general. Surviving one cliff is enough to spell danger at other rock forms, even if they're not*

quite the same shape or composition.

Ackerman characterizes the brain as "a pattern-mad supposing machine," which given just a little stimuli, divines the probable.

When information abounds, it recognizes familiar patterns and acts with conviction. If there's not much for the senses to report, the brain imagines the rest.

This remarkable ability of our minds to recognize distinct patterns enables us to consider, sort out, prioritize and act upon complex sets of inputs containing hundreds of features based upon comparisons of lifetimes of recalled lessons. Ackerman points out that just as it keeps us out of trouble, pattern recognition also pleases us, "rewarding minds seduced, yet exhausted by complexity."

As she reminds us,

> *We crave pattern, and find it all around us, in petals, sand dunes, pine cones, contrails. Our buildings, our symphonies, our clothing, our societie—all declare patterns. Even our actions: habits, rules, codes of honor, sports, traditions—we have many names for patterns of conduct. They reassure us that life is orderly.*
>
> *As children, we learn subtle patterns from our parents, including the texture of their senses and their emotional style. Just as we learn the alphabet and that teeth can bite—horse teeth or brother teeth—we learn the configurations of cuddling, the emotional contours of mother's voice, the silhouette of a friend.*
>
> *We rely on patterns, but we also cherish and admire them. Few things are as beautiful as a ripple, a spiral or a rosette. They are visually succulent. The mind savors them. Societies like to invent patterns of action, rules to cushion nature's laws. And word*

patterns: Madam, I'm Adam. Patterns reflect one of the brain's deepest needs—to fill the world with pathways and our lives with a design.

A label for it takes shape in the left temporal lobe. It's not a wolf. It's a woman. The parietal lobe helps you focus on the woman. With the auditory association area, you decipher the sounds—human greeting or vexed grackle? Young or old voice? Happy or worried? Meanwhile, in the brain's dreamy cities and counties, associations wake and endow the vision with meaning.

The limbic system, that expressionist painter, daubs the perception with emotion. It's your mother. You recognize her hair and figure. Memory fills in her name, her upbeat personality, a phone call yesterday, her saying that she had several errands to run. Brain imaging would show activity in many different regions as you weave all the information together and think what feels like a single concept: Mom!

Ackerman warns us to remember, however, that patterns we think we recognize can also be misinterpreted because:

Generalizing, even from concrete details, isn't always accurate. You were wrong. It's not your mother. The woman across the street only bears a resemblance to her. She's not waving to you, but to the person walking behind you.

Recognizing stored patterns from past learning experiences is routinely useful when we apply those lessons to logical conceptualization and problem-solving activities. Our brains do this using a combination of qualitative rules, heuristic processes and more well-defined deterministic assessments to discover and match previous observations to present conditions. An analogy might compare entirely logic-based chess-playing computers in competition with human expert-level players who depend heavily upon patterns catalogued from former winning and losing moves.[18]

Special-case experiences reported by Temple Grandin, an autistic equipment designer for livestock at the Colorado State University Department of Animal Sciences in Fort Collins, Colorado offers some clues about how certain pattern association aspects of the mind work. He writes about this in a Philosophical Transactions of the Royal Society article titled *Does Visual Thinking Work in the Mind of a Person with Autism? A personal Account.*

Grandin reports:

> *My mind is similar to an Internet search engine that searches for photographs. I use language to narrate the photo-realistic pictures that pop up in my imagination. When I design equipment for the cattle industry, I can test run it in my imagination similar to a virtual reality computer program. All my thinking is associative and not linear. To form concepts, I sort pictures into categories similar to computer files.*

Grandin observes that autistic/Asperger cognitive types of specialized thinkers fall into three general categories: visual thinkers who have difficulties with algebra; pattern thinkers who excel at math and music but may have problems with reading or writing composition; and verbal specialists who write and speak well, but lack visual skills.

He writes that in his case:

> *My mind is associative and does not think in a linear*

manner. If you say the word 'butterfly', the first picture I see is butterflies in my childhood backyard. The next image is metal decorative butterflies that people decorate the outside of their houses with and the third image is some butterflies I painted on a piece of plywood when I was in graduate school. Then my mind gets off the subject and I see a butterfly cut of chicken that was served at a fancy restaurant approximately 3 days ago.

Grandin's mind forms concepts from specific photo-realistic pictures stored from memory which are sorted into categories. As a child, he categorized differences between dogs and cats based upon their relative sizes, trying to figure out in the process why a neighbor's small Dachund wasn't a feline. He then had to look for other discriminating visual features such as sound...barking or meowing.

Assuming that other people thought in pictures the same way, he wondered how they could recognize such differences. When he asked them specific questions such as what came to their minds when recalling church steeples, he learned that many saw a generalized shape—sometimes in the form of a stick figure, whereas he saw numerous specific, identifiable photographic-quality images.

Grandin reported that while in his mind's eye he drew many image examples from "a file" in his brain labeled church steeples, an astrophysicist with a mathematical mind he queried described "abstract patterns of motion, people making steeples with their hands. There were no generalized or realistic pictures."

Rather than viewing his special circumstances as a liability, Grandin reflects that his way of seeing the world has distinct advantages:

As a person with autism, I have the typical profile of an area of great skill and an area of difficulty. Algebra was impossible because there was nothing to visualize, but I excelled at art. Thinking in pictures has been a great asset in my business of designing livestock facilities for cattle. I can visualize projects in my mind before they are built. I observed that cattle often refused to walk over shadows, and they were spooked by sparkling reflections or shiny metal on wet floors. These things were obvious to me, but many previous designers had failed to see them. [19, 20]

Human heuristic capabilities currently offer many powerful conceptualization advantages over even highly advanced data processing (or "artificial intelligence") machines in that they discover and draw upon enormously broad and often uniquely personal analogous data sources. While often fallible and imprecise for cognitive reasoning, this "intuitive" pattern recognition approach is sufficient to fulfill most immediate goals through abstracted mental short-cuts and educated trial-and-error guesses.

Big-Picture Systems Thinking

Complex problem-solving typically involves mental attempts to balance holistic "big picture" thinking and reductionist thinking with fullest possible consideration of all known component parts, relevant contributing influences, and linkages between elements that comprise the entire system.

This broad idea is often credited with building upon several influential philosophical and scientific roots. Included are discussions of "holism" advanced by South African statesman Jan Smuts in the 1920s, general systems theory proposed by Ludwig von Betalanffy in the 1940s and cybernetics concepts presented by Ross Ashby in the 1950s along with works by Jay Forrester at MIT in the field of system dynamics.[21, 22, 23, 24]

Broadly described, the general system theory, or "general science of wholeness," recognizes as a truism that "the whole is more than the sum of its parts." It follows, then, that characteristics of a complex "thing" are not explainable from characteristics of isolated parts alone.

As Ludwig von Betalanffy explained, a system is a complex of interacting elements that are open to and interact with their environment and which can acquire qualitatively new properties through emergence. Accordingly, they are generally self-regulating (self-correcting through feed-backs) in a continuing state of evolution.

Thinking holistically encourages us to observe our world, surroundings, issues and connections from larger and more dynamic perspectives before delving into details...a classic lesson of viewing a forest before becoming lost in trees and entangled in underbrush. In doing so, we may avoid recurring problems made even worse by failed attempts to fix the wrong parts. A big picture perspective may also reveal that a "best solution" may be to recognize and exit bad environments that pose undesired risks.

Looking at broader pictures raises and expands abilities to conceive new possibilities. At the same time, it's also important to be able to shift awareness to the smaller component elements. That's a big part of holistic thinking as well.

Much of our mental processing applies "reductionist thinking" which removes outside influences considered as distractions in order to focus attention upon aspects which matter most. Applied to biological and social systems, for example, this often involves removing or amplifying certain outside stimuli to determine which behavioral influences are of greatest and least importance.

The "scientific method" fundamentally employs a

reductionist process, one which has led to pioneering of incredible advances that have made our lives healthier, more comfortable and more productive. The trick is to not only understand which parts of a system to isolate and examine, but also to figure out why they interact together in certain ways and under certain conditions. Attempts to optimize certain of those parts without regard to their overall connections can tamper with the success of the system and the functioning and wellbeing of its surrounding environment.

Consider, for example, the many side effects on warning disclaimers attached to common pharmaceuticals. Pesticides that kill one pesky critter can result in infestations by others which are potentially worse.

Similar methodological problems arise in understanding how the arrangements and interactions of special groups of molecular components which interact as neurons along with hormones and numerous other bodies and systems enable consciousness and logical analyses to better understand how we, altogether—as thinking, moving, changing, self-correcting, procreating systems—"work."

A rather recently emerging goal-results-oriented "integrative thinking" analytical methodology begins by defining a problem to be solved as the difference between a current circumstance and what one wishes to achieve. Its credited originator, Graham Douglas, describes this approach as a process of integrating intuition, reason and imagination in a human mind with a view to developing a holistic continuum of strategy, tactics, action, review and evaluation for addressing a problem in any field as applied.

Originated by Roger Martin, Dean of the Rotman School of Management at the University of Toronto, and colleague Mihnea Moldoveanu, Director of the Desautels Center for Integrative Thinking, the teachable discipline is designed to facilitate associations between known internal and external factors which may have previously not been recognized.

Integrative thinkers are characterized to differ from conventional thinkers in a variety of dimensions. For example, rather than seeking to simplify a problem as much as possible, they instead consider most variables to be salient and focus special attention upon alternative views and contradictory data. In doing so, they embrace a complex understanding of how causality regarding salient features interconnect and interact in multi-directional ways, rather than limiting relationships according to linear, one-way dynamics.

When faced with two opposing solutions forcing trade-off evaluations, integrative thinkers strive for creative resolutions of tension rather than accepting simple choices. The Rotman School of Management website explains this as:

> Generating a creative resolution of the tension in the form of a new model that contains elements of the individual models, but is superior to each.

So what makes a big picture "big," and some ideas larger than others? Although there are, of course, nearly endless circumstances calling for subjective assessments, here are a few considerations.

We might imagine that an idea is big if it helps us sort out ways to make more sense out of confusing conditions, influences and interrelationships in a complex field of events or systems.

It's big if enables us to identify missing parts of a puzzle and recognize how they fit into a coherent picture...to meaningfully connect what previously appeared to be random patterns of fragmentary dots...to provide hierarchical logic structures and guidelines that organize and prioritize information in more useful ways...to hypothesize testable theories that change and illuminate understanding of important principles and issues...an idea is as big as each of us cares to value it.

Natural Aptitudes vs. Nurturing Attitudes

Kevin Kearney had good reasons for observing that his son had a "rage to learn." His son Michael had begun talking at the age of four months, was reading at eight months, had soaked up elementary curriculum by age four, finished high school and entered college by age six, and graduated at age 10.

Psychologist Martha Morelock, who has worked with Michael and other prodigies, agrees with Kevin's observation regarding his son:

> *The kind of intense engagement these children exhibit is a reflection of a brain-based need to learn—a craving for intellectual stimulation matching their cognitive requirements in the same way that the physical body craves food and oxygen.* [25]

Based on numerous interviews with prodigies and their families, David Henry Feldman and Lynn Goldsmith conclude that the prodigy phenomenon relies heavily upon important environmental factors after all…conditions where high intellectual capabilities are nurtured by the convergence of numerous lucky coincidences. We might logically assume that these same beneficial influences apply to almost everyone.

According to Feldman and Goldsmith, prodigies flourish in environments where natural proclivities not only match with an individual's particular domain interest, but also when sufficient motivation exists to put in hours necessary to develop that area of talent.

Important environmental factors include the availability of the domain in the prodigy's geographical location; healthy social/emotional development; family aspects (birth order and gender); education and preparation (both formal and informal);

cultural support; public recognition for achievement; access to training resources; material support from family members; at least one parent completely committed to the prodigy's development; family traditions that favor the prodigy's development; and historical forces, events and trends.

So yes, early bloomers clearly do exist. Whereas Michael Kearney excelled in the academic domain, other young prodigies have dazzled us and previous generations with virtuoso piano performances, amazing mental calculation feats, remarkable artworks and a host of other marvels.

Blaise Pascal, a French mathematician, physicist and philosopher who lived during the 1600s, developed a treatise on vibrating bodies at age nine, wrote his first proof on a wall with a piece of coal at the age of 11, and published his famous *Pascal's theorem* at the age of 16.

During the late 1700s, the German scientist Carl Friedrich Gauss, renowned for major contributions to numbers theory, geometry, astronomy and understanding of electromagnetism, made his first ground-breaking mathematical discoveries while a teenager.

In 1909, William James Sidis became the youngest person to enroll at Harvard College at age nine. One year later, Italian physicist Ettore Majorana was multiplying two three-digit numbers in his head in seconds at the age of four. In 1955, astronomer Truman Henry Safford could square 18-digit numbers at the age of 19.

In 2003, at age 13, Praveen Kumar Gorakavi developed a mathematical formula for perpetual calendar calculations. Two years later he developed a low-cost artificial leg providing knee and ankle movements along with missile technology innovations.

These few "early bloomer" examples of genius raise unresolved questions regarding the relative importance of the roles genes play in creating a genius versus focused goals, nurtured learning and dedicated practice. In the broad answer, mature intellectual development, whether socially sanctified as genius or not, demands a good share of both.

Later bloomers can rise just as tall. Scott Barry Kaufman, a Yale PhD psychologist on the faculty at New York University and author of books and scientific papers about intelligence and creativity represents a good example.[26]

By age three, Scott developed an auditory processing disorder following several ear infections and an operation to drain fluid, and was later sent to a special school for children with learning disabilities. Fortunately, at age 14, a new teacher who recognized his boredom and frustration motivated him to expect more of himself. Scott then began wondering for the very first time what he was actually capable of achieving.

Influenced by the accomplishments of his grandfather, a cellist with the Philadelphia Orchestra, Scott set a goal of playing the instrument in his high school orchestra. Through dedicated immersion in practice, the instrumentation challenges in combination with the structure of classical music began to "gel" in his brain. Achievement of his goal in being selected over other cello orchestra candidates with longer years of experience provided a much-needed confidence boost to pursue other achievements.

Personal experiences prompted Scott Kaufman to question whether talents are unrecognized potentials that must be discovered and developed while young. While recognizing that he's perhaps an outlier experience, he believes that that talent and practice are far more intertwined than commonly imagined. He advises that:

> *Personal characteristics ranging from mathematical to courage aren't determined by gene codes although environment triggers gene expression.*

In many cases those tiny genetic and environmental advantages multiply over the years. For example, a kid who is slightly taller may get picked first for the basketball team, one who can read better gets put into a more advanced reading group and those who are selected for advanced instruction enjoy more rapid progress in broader follow-up academic options. The same conditions can work in reverse, where speech production impediments and other difficulties present special challenges and delays.

Kaufman likens genes to players in his high school orchestra...it required lots of syncing for an overall symphony to sound beautiful. The players also had to be in sync with their section, which, in turn had to coordinate with other sections. If not, not the players would become discouraged from practicing.

According to an "experience-producing drive theory," we tend to seek out learning opportunities that offer recognizable rewards...choices that add up and multiply over the years.

The Makings of Natural Talents

University of California Davis psychologist Dean Keith Simonton argues talent can be viewed as any package of personal characteristics that accelerate the acquisition of expertise, or enhances performance given a certain amount of expertise...to get better faster...or get more "bang for the buck" out of a given amount of expertise.[27, 28]

Scott Kaufman argues that many people have an overly simplistic understanding of this "talent," viewing it as innate—something that is ready to spring forth given the right conditions. But that's not how talent operates. "Talents aren't prepackaged at birth, but take time to develop."

Yes, early bloomers do begin life pursuits with potential long-term advantages. Benefitting from a fast start and focusing like a laser beam rapidly accelerates learning by entering a state of "flow" in tasks found effortless and enjoyable as time recedes in the background.

But that doesn't tell the whole talent story. Take the life-long importance motivation for example. Scott asks,

> *Why do some people who seem to learn particular material quicker than others...others with same amount of deliberate practice perform better?* [29]

As Kaufman points out, motivation is influenced by particular interests, personality traits, values and quirky circumstances which are unique to each of us. As genes pull our attention in certain directions and take us away from processing other information in the environment, we differ in what captures our attention. How we ultimately respond and develop is determined by a lifetime of mutually reinforcing experiences "as nature dances with nurture."

All of this also involves a much wider range of personal characteristics, including levels of desire and drive. Is a special talent absent or simply not apparent because of lack of essential interest and inspiration to put in the necessary effort?

Cognitive research conducted by Florida State University psychologist K. Anders Ericsson and colleagues demonstrates that development of high levels of expertise and performance typically requires at least 10,000 hours of "deliberate" practice. It was acknowledged that this number only represented an average, with substantial individual variation around the mean, and that some people take much longer to become "experts."

Ericsson emphasizes the key importance of motivation—where a motivated individual constantly strives to learn from performance feedbacks supported by knowledgeable mentors who urge them to push beyond previous limits. This applies to a wide range of fields, including medicine, professional writing, music, art, sciences and sports.

As for how much of being an expert is born or made,

psychologist David Hambrick of Michigan State University and Elizabeth Meinz at Southern Illinois University take issue with Ericsson's overly generalized and simplistic "10,000-hour rule." In doing so, they think nature demands at least some fair share of contribution credit too.

While disputing that given a certain level of intelligence and some luck anybody can play a violin duet with YoYo Ma at Carnegie Hall provided that they practice enough, Hambrick comments: "We don't deny the importance of the knowledge and skill that accrue through practice." He adds, "But, we think that for certain types of tasks, basic abilities and capacities— ones that are general, stable across time, and substantially heritable—play an important role in skilled performance." [30]

Hambrick and Meinz tested the sight-reading performances of 57 pianists with widely varying practice experiences ranging from 260 to more than 31,000 hours. Each was asked to play a piece from a score they'd never seen before. While those who had previously practiced more did tend to perform better, this experience only appeared to account for about half of the difference. The researchers concluded that working memory capacity also had a significant impact, likely influencing how many notes a player could look ahead to instantly process.

The authors also challenged another "experts are made" contention that beyond a certain threshold, intelligence is overrated in importance. Based upon results of a Vanderbilt University study of math SAT scores of people with PhDs in science, technology, engineering or math, those with the 99.9[th] percentile at age 13 were found to be 18 times more likely to go on and earn advanced degrees than those who scored better only than 99.1 percent of their age peers.

This survey led Hambrick and Meinz to observe that:

> *Even at the highest end, the higher the intellectual ability—and by extension, the higher the working*

memory capacity——the better.

They conclude that while many limitations can be overcome by practice...

> *No matter how hard you work, it may be what you're*
> *born with or develop very early in life that*
> *distinguishes the best from the rest.*[31]

Research conducted by psychologist Joanne Ruthsatz at Ohio State University's Mansfield campus and violin virtuoso Jourdan Urbach at Yale University disputed a direct correlation between high IQ measurements and achievement of prodigy-level performance. Their study looked at eight prominent child prodigies from various performance domains, most of whom had been featured on national and international television programs by age 10, all with uneven cognitive profiles which typify most prodigies. One was an art prodigy, one was a math prodigy, four were musical prodigies, one had switched from music to gastronomy and another had switched from music to art.[32]

As measured by the Stanford-Binet IQ test, the individual total performance scores ranged dramatically from 108 to 147. In fact, the prodigy with that lowest total score of 108 was measured with a visual score of only 71...which was lower than 97 percent of the general population. Nevertheless, that didn't prevent him from becoming a prestigious award-winning improvisational jazz player who performed at Lincoln Center and Carnegie Hall as a soloist with major orchestras as well as in three movies, all without benefit of any formal composition lessons.

A striking commonality among the eight prodigies was that all scored better than 99 percent of the general population with regard to working memories, with six of them ranking at the

99.9[th] percentile. Working memory was characterized as the ability to retain information over short terms, while at the same time also being able to manipulate and process other incoming information.

This was measured in both verbal and non-verbal domains applying tasks such as processing sentences while having to remember the last word of each sentence, and recalling the location of blocks and numbers in the order they were presented. The ability is closely associated with great musicians such as Mozart, who could memorize musical pieces and manipulate scores in his head.

Overall, the math and music prodigies scored higher than art prodigies in general cultural knowledge, vocabulary, quantitative reasoning, and surprisingly, even in visual spatial skills. The researchers hypothesized that this might be because artistically-talented children tend to actively focus on forms, shapes and detailed surface features of their environments which are "selectively coded." IQ tests, on the other hand, highlight categories, concepts and holistic perceptions at the expense of detail-oriented perception. [33]

Possible Prodigy-Autism Correlations

Researchers are observing interesting family and performance correlations between many people who exhibit high-performance prodigy and autistic savant talents.

Joanne Ruthsatz led the Ohio State University study which reported that based upon an "Autism-Spectrum Quotient" assessment, half of the prodigies they investigated had a family member or a first- or second-degree relative with an autism diagnosis. In addition, both of the first-degree families of individuals with autism and the first-degree families with prodigies displayed three out of five common autism traits: impaired social skills, impaired abilities to switch attention, and a markedly heightened attention to detail.[34]

In a Psychology Today article titled *Will We Ever Find the Next Einstein?* Jonathan Wai, a psychologist at Case Western Reserve University, cites an interesting example of a genetic family prodigy-autism link. Terrence Tao, a professor at UCLA and recipient of the Fields Medal, the equivalent of a Nobel Prize laureate in mathematics, mastered most of the primary school math curriculum while in kindergarten, was discussing Boolean algebra and Albelian groups by age seven, and scored 760 on the math SAT exam by age eight.

Terrance's younger brother, Trevor, was diagnosed with autism at age two. Yet that didn't stop him from winning the Australian Junior Chess Championship at age 14, earning multiple prizes for classic musical compositions, mastering the piano, and receiving a diploma in mathematical sciences.[35, 36]

The Rithsatz team observed that the most striking data revealed in the study identified autistic traits among the individual prodigies compared with the control group. However, this elevation was even smaller than seen in high-functioning autistic people diagnosed with Asperger's syndrome.

Autism, as described by the study, is a developmental disability characterized by problems with communicating and socializing, and a strong resistance to change. Those with Asperger's are more likely than those with autism to have normal intelligence, but still tend to have difficulties with social interaction.

Severe cases of autism involving "prodigious savants" who possess astounding abilities are often paired with challenging language and communication deficits. Psychologist Darold Treffert describes this condition as leaving them with "islands of genius." These individuals often score very low on IQ tests, while demonstrating exceptional brilliance in specific areas such as rapid calculation, and artistic and musical abilities.

Prodigies and savants demonstrate extreme attention to

detail, exceptional memories and operate in high-ability rule-based domains. Rithsatz and Urbach hypothesize that both are possibly born with genetic variants that relate to predetermined tendencies, such as to focus on details which attract them early to domains that deal with systems. This can influence them to develop enhanced abilities to maintain mental representations which apply symbols and build up memory structures which enable them to assimilate and manipulate information faster and faster in their heads.

But as Joanne Rithsatz observes, while autistic savants and prodigies share some striking similarities regarding exceptional talents, savants display many deficits commonly associated with autism that prodigies don't. She suggests that the reason for this might be explained by the presence of some sort of genetic modifier or moderator that prevents the prodigious child from displaying these deficiencies.

Native Intelligence is Tribal Folklore

In 1990, Thomas Bouchard and his colleagues at the University of Minnesota published the results of an identical twin investigation study that attributed about 70 percent of the general population IQ variance to genetics. They observed that identical twins reared apart were eerily similar to identical twins reared together with regard to factors associated with personalities, occupational and leisure-time interests and social attitudes.[37]

Another study conducted by Eric Turkheimer and colleagues studied 320 pairs of seven-year-old twins raised in extreme poverty. The study found that extreme environmental influences upon IQ matter very much indeed. Among the poorest of these twins, the researchers attributed 60 percent of their scorings to shared environments, and very little—approaching zero—to genetics.

Scott Barry Kaufman reminds us to also consider significant social and economic environmental influences across generations which, for example, have been witnessed by a dramatic rise in IQ scores during the 20th century. In doing so, he also warns that IQ sampling and measurement studies tend to lead to overly generalized, often contradictory conclusions where broad understanding of context matters greatly. We humans are collectively and individually very complex creatures who be can't squeezed into neat, universal intelligence and performance categories.[38]

Kaufman notes that "heritability" traits defined for a particular study environment can range from 0.00 to 1.0, depending upon the contributing criteria to be measured. Yet because we also know that genes play some role in the development of any cognitive trait, the precise heritability estimate doesn't really matter in a practical sense. He observes:

> *Our understanding of the factors that contribute to the development of human traits in general—and to IQ in particular—is currently so deficient that we typically do not know if the environmental factors important in development of a particular trait are stable across testing stations, vary somewhat across those situations, or vary wildly across those situations.*

Kaufman acknowledges that genes clearly influence who we are. At the same time, his research, along with his personal achievements, demonstrate that talents spring from what we make of genetic resources we are born with, goals that motivate us, and our disciplined determination to gain ever higher levels of achievements.

We are not born into the world as blank slates, completely at the mercy of the external environment. Instead, Kaufman urges us to recognize that:

The fact that both our genes and our environment contribute to who we are and depend on each other is actually quite a good thing! Give too much control to our environment or our genes, and we lose free will. The way we work gives us a choice.[39]

Kaufman quotes science writer Matt Ridley in recognizing that in attempting to understand the intellectual development of any particular person, nature can never be separated from nurture:

[Genes] are devices for extracting information from the environment. Every minute, every second, the pattern of genes being expressed in your brain changes, often in direct or indirect response to events outside your body. Genes are the mechanisms of experience.

Summarizing this interdependency, Kaufman observes: "talent and practice are complementary, not at odds."

Kaufman emphasizes that parents not only contribute all-important influences to our individual gene pools, but to the environmental pools we swim in as well. Previously mentioned prodigy studies by Feldman and Goldsmith noted that remarkable proclivities most often flourished in nurturing learning environments where families provide healthy social and emotional guidance and support.

Feldman and Goldsmith also linked particular talents to each individual's special domain interests with sufficient motivation necessary to put in the required effort to achieve rewarding and continuing progress.

According to Feldman and Goldsmith, prodigies flourish in environments where natural proclivities not only match with an individual's particular domain interest, but also when sufficient motivation exists to put in hours necessary to develop that area of talent.

Kaufman adds that just as each person's package of characteristics that gives rise to their talents is unique, talents within a single interest domain are highly individual as well.

A person with extremely high levels of perseverance and motivation can offset other less developed characteristics such as memory. He argues that the total package of domain interests and proclivities is much more important than the precise mix.[40]

Scott Kaufman believes that everyone should be encouraged to make contact with as many domains as possible, and to be on the lookout for domains that activate their individual "flow" state. Once entering those personal interest zones, progress can proceed extremely rapidly as challenges and achievements motivate us to excel.

All of us are capable of achieving an extraordinary level of performance in one domain. The key is to find a mode of expression that best allows our unique package to shine. Then, as Dean Keith Simons points out, one talent can transform into another.

For example, a talented artist may become a talented scientist as different personal characteristics "kick in" at different times throughout life-long development.[41]

Kaufman reminds us that that there are always new opportunities for our talents to develop. Life isn't a limited zero-sum gain. Just because someone starts early doesn't mean that others don't burst out later. Having personally demonstrated this reality, he strongly cautions that it is egregious error for any "experts" to suggest limits on what people can ultimately achieve.

Literally Changing Our Minds through Neuroplasticity

Dr. Lara Boyd, a brain research neuroscientist at the University of British Columbia, instructs us to understand that our behaviors can constructively change our minds throughout life. This idea is contrary to the misconception that brains do not change after childhood other than in negative ways. The reality is that every time we learn a new fact or skill we change our brain through "neuroplasticity."

In a December 15, 2015, Ted Talk titled *After Watching This, your Brain will not be the Same,* Dr. Boyd points out that neuroplasticity changes the brain to support learning in three different ways: chemical, structural and functional.

Exercising our capacity to learn new things functions to increase the concentrations and transfers of chemical signals between brain cells (neurons) thus triggering a series of actions and reactions. These changes occur very rapidly to support short-term memory or short-term improvement in the performance of a motor skill.

Physical brain changes which support learning by altering the brain's structure are associated with long-term memory and long-term improvement of a motor skill. These physical brain changes require more time. Boyd offers examples in which we attempt to learn a new motor skill such as playing a piano or learning to juggle. We think that after a practice session we're getting better and better...then returning the next day we experience losses of those improvements. What happened? While in the short-term your brain was able to increase signaling between those appropriate neurons, for some reason those chemical changes were too brief to support your long-term memory.

Boyd explains that structural changes can lead to integrated network changes in brain regions causing them to function together. These changes can even cause certain brain regions that are important for very specific behaviors to change or enlarge.

For example, people who read Braille tend to have larger

hand sensory areas in their brains than those who don't. (Our dominant hand motor region, which is on the left side of our brain if you are right-handed, is typically larger than on the other side).

Dr. Boyd observes that whenever we use a particular brain region, it becomes more excitable and easy to use again, causing it to "shift" with regard to how the networks function together. This neuroplasticity, which is supported by chemical, structural and functional changes, occurs in concert across our whole brain. Altogether, neuroplasticity supports learning, which is occurring all the time.

The exciting news is that we can continue to improve our learning capacities through our nurturing behaviors and practice in our everyday lives. To accomplish this, Boyd encourages each of us to study how and what we learn best, to repeat healthy behaviors and to break those behaviors and habits which are not healthy and to practice until we accomplish our goals.

Boyd urges us to understand that everything we do, everything we encounter, and everything we experience is changing our brains. "And that can be for better, but it can also be for worse." [42]

Avoiding Self-Limiting Stereotypes

Being in a groove doesn't require us to fit into a slot, although hugely prosperous identity typecasting aptitude testing industries attempt to convince us otherwise.

These tests tell us that they can reduce our complex personalities and natural potentials to conform within standardized categories and score our intelligence and capabilities according to definitive statistical measures. We should be smarter than to allow such devices to limit us through diminished expectations.

Squeezing Personality into Standardized Files

First, let's begin with the fallacy that each of us can be defined according to standardized "personality'" tests. In her book *The Cult of Personality Testing*, journalist Annie Murphy Paul points out that there are 2,500 types of these tests, constituting a $400 million per year American industry. The tests variously factor into employment hiring and promotion processes, custody battles and prison parole decisions. Of these, she wrote that "no personality type test has achieved the cult status of the Myers-Briggs Type Indicator" which she regards to have "no scientific basis whatsoever."[43]

Although the "Myers-Briggs Type Indicator" (Typically referred to as MBTI) was purportedly based upon theories postulated in Carl Jung's book *Psychological Type,* not even he would likely endorse it. As Malcolm Gladwell observed in a September 20, 2014 New Yorker article:

> *Jung didn't believe that types were easily identifiable, and he didn't believe that people could be permanently slotted into one category or another. Every individual is an exception to the rule...to stick labels on people at first sight was nothing but a parlor game.*[44]

MBTI tests define key assessment aspects of each respondent's individual personality type in terms of a four-letter code which are tabulated according to forced true/false responses. Categories applied are: extroverted (E) or introverted (I); sensing (S) or intuitive (N); thinking (T) or feeling (F); and judging (J) or perceiving (P). Each individual is then classified in terms of one of 16 possible four-letter codes (such as ESFJ, Carl Jung's ENFP, INPT or ISFJ).

Thinking Whole

Warton University organizational psychologist Adam Grant takes issue with the either/or approach of the system, pointing out, for example, that you can be both a thinker and a feeler. They are not mutually exclusive.

> *When I scored as a thinker one time and a feeler one time. It's because I like both thinking and feeling.*

He said…

> *I should have separate scores for the two.*[45]

An individual's MBTI test results are also likely to change over short periods of time. As philosopher Roman Krznaric observes:

> *If you retake the test after a five-week gap, there's around a 50 percent chance that you will fall into a different personality category compared with the first time you took the test.*[46]

Commenting on brilliant and aggressive MBTI marketing, Cambridge University professor Brian Little observes that the test gives people a chance to discuss their preferences and personality in the workplace—a conversation that otherwise gets crowded out. Equating this to looking into a horoscope, it can give someone the satisfying feeling of "ah-ha! Yes I am an introvert, so please don't bother me."

Little emphasizes that identifying that you're a particular "type" of person such as introvert or extrovert can be fascinating to some. The weakness is that it can also be limiting.

> *If you only see yourself as an extrovert or as one of those four-letter codes on the Myers-Briggs, you will have foreclosed on paths that might open to you if you*

didn't think in terms of types of people.

Brian Little warns that rather than pinning ourselves into categories that limit us:

> *I prefer to not to look at the traits we have but the deeds we do, the projects we pursue, as more of a fruitful inroad into human personality.*[47]

Gregory Boyle at Bond University in Queensland, Australia, agrees that MBTI testing methodologies are overly simplistic:

> *Although this brief characterization may be useful in some applied contexts (such as in predicting an individual's characteristic style of behavior, intellectually and interpersonally), there are evident psychometric limitations of the instrument.*

Boyle concludes:

> *Given the lack of appropriate local norms. It would seem prudent for practitioners to be alert to its possible misuse, and to be cautious in undertaking personality assessments with the instrument.*[48]

David Pittenger, an assistant professor and chair of the Department of Psychology at Marietta College, Ohio, agrees with Boyle and others that many claims offered by MBTI administrators can't be supported because although the test appears to measure something, "many psychologists are not convinced that any conclusions can be based on the test." [49]

Pittenger points out that as a typology, we should expect that MBTI scores would be distributed bimodally rather than normally distributed. He explains this with an analogy:

If you randomly selected 500 people between the ages 18 and 25, measured their heights, and then drew a graph of the results, you would probably have a normal bee-shaped distribution. Most people would have a height close to the mean, say 5'8". Of course, some people will be very short, and others would be very tall, but these extreme scores would be rare. Now, imagine what would happen if you divided your sample by sex. When you redraw the data you should get a bimodal distribution. Women, on average, are shorter than men; but within each sex there will be a normal distribution of heights. The same thing should happen for the MBTI.

Accordingly, as Pittenger observes, we would expect that test scores for those characterized as introverts and extroverts should yield two different curves separately representing each category with no overlap between them. Yet the population data instead shows no evidence of bimodal distribution. Instead, most people score between the two extremes. The test result for a person who scores as an extrovert may be very close to that of another who scores as an introvert.

Standard errors of measurements associated with classifying humans according to rules of rigid dichotomy can lead to very different personality labels because differences between two-letter categories are not nearly as sharp and clear-cut as we might imagine.

Other MBTI measurement validity issues question which test measures truly equate to meaningful assessments of intelligence. As David Pittenger concludes:

Some people are concerned that the tests measure only 'book learning' and do not test 'common sense'. Other people feel that intelligence tests have cultural, racial, and gender biases. Therefore, too conclude that a test is a valid measure of intelligence, it must be shown that the test measures intelligence independent of the testee's education, culture, race, and sex.

Studies comparing individuals labeled in various MBTI categories with logically associated occupation choices have found less correlation than might be expected.

Pittenger illustrates this point by noting that the proportion of extroverted-sensitive-thinking-judging (ESTJs) in the teaching profession is approximately the same found in the general population...about 12 percent.

By the same token, recognizing that certain types of jobs tend to be dominated by men or women, we might expect that this difference might be reflected in MBTI scores as well. Comparing the distribution of those in the nursing profession, which has proportionately more women than those who seek management positions, for example, data suggests that the proportion of MBTI types within each occupation is equivalent to that within a random sample of the population.

Pittenger notes that while many professional organizations, including *The Journal of Psychological Type,* continue to support MBTI, others do not. An Army Research Institute review concluded that available research showed no evidence supporting the utility of the test, and recommended that it not be used for career planning or counseling.[50]

Exceeding Standardized Aptitude, Intelligence and Ability Assessments

A wide variety of standardized tests are used in common practice to obtain information that can be useful in predicting some aspect of a subject's current and predicted levels of performance in numerous fields of endeavor. Included are achievement tests designed to measure an individual's specific motor skills or body of knowledge relative to likelihood of achieving success in a particular work setting, student classroom performance exams, the "Scholastic Assessment Test" (SAT) taken by high school students contemplating college and the "Graduate Records Examination" (GRE) taken by college students wishing to attend graduate schools.

Differences between aptitude, intelligence and ability tests are often ambiguous and typically overlap. Generally speaking, however, aptitude is assumed to represent potential, ability lies in the here and now, and intelligence gets us from where we are to where we might hope to wind up.

Aptitude is often associated with an "Intelligence Quotient" (IQ) measured by various tests applied over more than a century. The "Wechsler Intelligence Scale" and "Stanford-Binet Intelligence Scale," for example, measure verbal comprehension, working memory, perceptual organization, and processing speed abilities rather than results of any specific program instruction. Both are intended to indicate a person's "native ability" to learn from life experiences. Therefore, they are both descriptive in that they measure knowledge and skills, and also predictive in measuring qualities that influence ability to learn new skills and solve novel problems.

Howard Gardner introduced the theory of "Multiple Intelligence," where different parts of the brain have different functions. Logical reasoning is but one of these. Logical reasoning relates to being capable of understanding concepts, analyzing and solving problems, being good at sequential thinking and working with mathematical problems. These characteristics are commonly associated with careers in technical jobs, scientific research, etc. Others forms of intelligence include linguistic, logical, spatial, bodily-kinesthetic, musical, interpersonal, intrapersonal and naturalistic.

Here again, there are numerous variations. Whereas the "Electrical and Electronics Test" and "Personnel Selection and Assessment System" tests measure single aptitudes, the "Armed Services Vocational Battery" (ASVAB) and the "Ball Aptitude Battery" (BAB) measure multiple factors.[51]

Research demonstrates that the ways we, as individuals, develop and use our intelligence to correlate with some brain activity patterns that differ according to individual backgrounds, experiences and life stages.

Adrian Owen and Adam Hampshire at the Medical Research Council in Cambridge conducted cognitive online tests to monitor rehabilitation following brain injuries. In 2010 they applied these methods to devise 12 online tests posted in the Daily Telegraph, Discovery and New Scientist which solicited public participation. Response results from a representative group of approximately 45,000 people determined that at least three separate tests are needed: short-term memory, reasoning abilities and verbal skills. No single IQ factor could explain all variations revealed in the tests.[52]

Owen and Hampshire continued their research at the Brain and Mind Institute in London to investigate what actually happened in the brains of 16 of those who took part. These studies confirmed that the three key factors did indeed correspond to network differences in the various subject's ability to map onto corresponding brain circuits which contribute to that elusive quality broadly referred to as intelligence.

The analyses directed particular attention to such factors as the individual's age, gender and active tendency to play computer games which likely influence intelligence. Observations concluded that while regular brain training games didn't influence performance, those who played other types of computer games did perform significantly better in terms of reasoning and short-term memory.

Short-term memory and logical reasoning was determined

to diminish with age, peaking in late teen years, and rapidly declining thereafter. Verbal intelligence, on the other hand, held up well with the elderly.

Researchers found little correlation between lifestyles and intelligence...physical exercise, weekly alcohol consumption and the number of hours slept each night seemed to have negligible effects on performance. One big exception to this was influence of smoking habits. Forty-per-day puffers had significantly lower short-term memory and verbal scores. Right or left-handedness, numbers of siblings, months of birth and genders were determined to have little impact, although men did tend to perform slightly better than women in terms of spatial short-term memory.

As Scott Barry Kaufman wrote in Psychology Today, confidence has significant influence. When people are put in situations where they expect to fail, there's a high chance that they will...their heads shut down, and their performance mirrors their expectations.

Kaufman notes that we are all probably aware of the stereotype that females are supposed to generally have less aptitude at math and spatial skills than males. Yet when women are asked to imagine themselves as a stereotypical male, they tend to perform better on a mental rotation test then when they aren't given such an instruction.[53]

Women perform worse when asked before taking a mental rotation test to identify themselves as a "private college student." According to the account, having women report their gender prior to taking the tests makes the cultural stereotype more salient to them, causing performance-reducing anxiety.[54]

In another study, the same men and women who completed a mental rotation test were informed that men do better on the task or that women do. Women then performed significantly worse after being told that men do better, whereas those told that women do better performed significantly better.

The same expectation/performance pattern emerged when men were told that women performed either better or worse.[55]

Consistent with other research, males, on average, were more confident and more accurate on mental rotation tests than females. When the confidence factor was taken into account, differences in average scores almost completely evaporated.

In another study, the researchers manipulated participant confidence prior to the experiment by having them complete a difficult line judgment task where there was a nearly equal chance of gender success. After completing the test, the subjects were randomly told that their performance was either above or below average before assigning a second mental rotation test.

Regardless of gender, those who were told their line judgment score was above average performed better, and those who were told their line judgment was below average performed below average on the task. As with other studies, males on average performed better on mental rotation...although there was no performance difference between females in the higher confidence groups and males in the low confidence groups.

Kaufman observes that:

> *Perhaps many of us—male and female alike—when faced with threatening situations, have decreased confidence, which then lowers the working memory resources specific to the task at hand.*

Emphasizing the importance of mindset, Kaufman believes that this applies to just about everyone and in every form of ability—math, writing, artistic, musical, whatever.

Research published in the March/April issue of Child Development by Dario Cvencek, Andrew Meitzoff and Anthony Greenwald at the University of Washington (UW) indicates that gender stereotypes about math develop as early as second grade.

Noting that other studies using self-reported measures show that boys and girls alike make the "math is for boys" linkage, the researchers confirmed that the more strongly respondents associated various academic subjects with either masculine or feminine connotations, the stronger they affirmed that stereotype in testing.

The UW researchers tested this theory by adapting an adult "Implicit Association Test" to children in order to examine three concepts: Gender identity, or the association of "me" with male or female; Math-gender stereotype, or the association of math with male or female; and Math self-concept, or the association of "me" with math or reading.

Boys and girls both exhibited the cultural stereotype associating math with their gender as early as second grade. Accordingly, the report co-authors concluded:

> *Our results show that cultural stereotypes about math are absorbed strikingly early in development, prior to ages at which there are gender differences in math achievement.*[56]

Talents Require Exercise

Broadly stated, the groups of attributes each of us are individually assessed to excel at are referred to as "talents." These are the potentials and capabilities that set us apart from others who test less well in these topics and pursuits. As with multiple categories of intelligence, each of us may self-describe and be described by others as having multiple talents—perhaps some proclivities stronger than others—as well. When recognized, they make us feel good about ourselves, shape our interests and goals and provide benchmarks for seeking improvements.

By the same token, areas where we have performed less

well during early trials can discourage us from trying to improve or excel, imagining that doing so will hopelessly set us up for more failures. Accordingly, we direct our interests to types of pursuits that are more satisfying...winnable. We might readily assume and appreciate that other people are virtually born with different talents, and either graciously or painfully accept this as an apparent fact.

Early experiences with successes and failures, official-seeming standardized testing evaluations very much included, can have big influences on how we visualize ourselves and our future expectations. Those areas where we score well earn a pat on the head, while those not so good may result in a premature dope slap we probably don't deserve.

John Mighton, who barely passed calculus in a freshman-level university course and later earned a PhD in mathematics and advanced the "pioneering knot and graph theory," is an example. Mighton, also an award-winning playwright, attributes his achievements to breaking a task into a series of steps and then practicing repeatedly. He observes:

> *People with expert abilities are generally made, not born and often their abilities arise out of a great deal of repetitive practice and imitation and copying of other peoples' styles and ideas. For instance, chess masters repeatedly play small sets of moves, memorize thousands of positions and obsessively study the games if the masters.*[57]

Daniel Coyle, a strong endorser of cognitive research findings by Anders Ericksson which correlate high levels achievement with many hours of deliberate practice, theorizes how this may happen. Coyle's book *The Talent Code* explains that this focused repetition increases the production of myelin around nerve fibers. This enhances signal strength, accuracy and speed so that sensory responses become more proficient and thoughts more fluent. He observes:

> *The more we fire a particular circuit, the more myelin optimizes the circuit, and the stronger, faster, and more fluent our movements and thoughts become.*[58]

Coyle refers to the talent "sweet spot" as:

> *...that productive, uncomfortable terrain located just beyond our current abilities, where our reach exceeds our grasp. Deep practice is not simply about struggling; it's about seeking a particular struggle, which involves a cycle of distinct actions.*

He describes that deep practice experience as feeling a bit like exploring a dark and unfamiliar room:

> *You start slowly, you bump into furniture, stop, think, and start again. Slowly, and a little painfully, you explore the space over and over, attending to errors, extending your reach into the room a bit farther each time, building a mental map until you can move through it quickly and intuitively.*

Coyle elaborates:

> *Deep practice is built on a paradox: struggling in certain targeted ways—operating at the edges of your ability, where you make mistakes—makes you smarter. Or to put it a slightly different way, experiences where you're forced to slow down, make errors, and correct them—as you would if you were walking up an ice-covered hill, slipping and*

stumbling as you go——end up making you swift and graceful without your realizing it.

Or as Samuel Beckett advised, "Try again. Fall Again, Fall Better."

In his book *Talent is Overrated: What Really Separates World-Class Performers from Everybody Else*, Geoff Colvin reiterates the fundamental importance of practice…the sort of practice that we don't necessarily regard to be unpleasant when we're doing it. With motivation and discipline, we can become much better at anything we do.

Colvin, a senior editor-at-large for Fortune magazine, acknowledges that certain inherited traits influences advantages or disadvantages in some fields. In sports, for example, "a five-footer will never be an NFL lineman, and a seven-footer will never be an Olympic gymnast."

Yet Colvin also points out that we are not generally held hostage to some naturally granted level of talent:

> *We can make ourselves what we will. Strangely, that idea is not popular. People hate abandoning the notion that they would coast to fame and riches if they found their talent. But that view is tragically constraining, because when they hit life's inevitable bumps in the road, they conclude that they just aren't gifted and give up.*

Why don't people shoot for the stars? Colvin answers…

> *Because for most people, work is hard enough without pushing even harder. Those extra steps are so difficult and painful they almost never get done.*

Geoff Colvin recognizes that…

...maybe we can't expect most people to achieve greatness because it's just too demanding. That's the way it must be. If great performance were easy, it wouldn't be rare.

As to why some people are motivated to take those extra steps while most aren't, Colvin leaves this question unanswered. Yet he offers great hope for all who have discovered and acted upon that passion to excel:

...the striking, liberating news is that greatness isn't reserved for a preordained few. It is available to you and to everyone.

He concludes that while...

Talent has little or nothing to do with greatness. You can make yourself into any number of things, and you can even make yourself great.[59, 60]

Yes...but we each might ask, great at what?

Maybe being greater at making our personal lives more satisfying and fulfilling for ourselves and others? Or being greater at doing whatever we're doing for whatever reasons we are choosing to do it...or perhaps making more time for other opportunities and priorities to do even more?

Is it about achieving recognized greatness that propels us to ever higher achievements and rewards? Is it to set greater goals that test our limits...and to maybe challenge whether any such limits actually exist?

Each of our respective priorities for achieving "greatness" are highly personal, most likely including some non-mutually exclusive combination of these ambitions.

Larry Bell

Part Two: The Makings of Genius

USING YOUR WHOLE brain doesn't necessarily qualify you
for modern-day "Renaissance man" (or woman) distinction,
although it may give you a head start. After all, it's a bit
daunting to live up to the romanticized notion of someone who
can do just about everything better than almost everyone else.

The ideal arose during the 1400s, a period of great cultural
change of "enlightenment" which perceived limitless potentials
for human growth. Leonardo da Vinci is broadly recognized as a
noted multi-talented example.

Today, such multi-talented individuals are more frequently
referred to as "polymaths." They are characterized as possessing
a broad spectrum of interests, proficiencies and achievements;
being curious and eager to learn about a variety of topics;
focusing on original and creative problem-solving; and holding
abilities as talented communicators who make complex
principles and ideas accessible to others.

Being a polymath doesn't require genius. It does, however,
challenge us to constantly open and stretch our whole-mind
connections with natural talents developed and applied as
broadly as possible.

In his 1953 essay *The Hedgehog and the Fox,* Oxford
University social and political philosopher Isaiah Berlin presents

a hedgehog who knows a lot about a single, narrow subject, and a fox who knows a little about many subjects. While both of the critter mindsets are deficient, populations that operate with a "hedgehog mindset" appear to be gaining. I have this to be particularly true in academia.[61]

Psychologist Robert Plomin, a professor of behavioral genetics at King's College, London, observes:

> *Nowadays the training is so specialized, But the big advances come from the foxes who know a little bit about a lot of things and can put two and two together, rather than the hedgehogs in the trenches who are burrowing away and trying to find out more and more about less.*[62]

What can we learn about greatness from really smart people...those who are popularly regarded as "geniuses"? After all, what makes them so special? Were they born that way?

Countless well-known examples earned their lofty genius status "the hard way:" through extraordinary effort and perseverance. In doing so, many have exhibited heroic persistence and resilience in repeatedly overcoming daunting obstacles. Some have rallied above poverty and financial setbacks, physical and learning challenges, mental depression, ideological peer resistance and social discrimination and even life-threatening religious and political strife.

We might assume that virtually all have known repeated failures: concepts that didn't pan out as hoped, theorems that couldn't be validated and ideas that were ahead of their time. And while some experienced recognition and rewards during their lifetimes, others who weren't nearly so fortunate bequeathed the richness of their legacies to us.

The selection of following examples was guided by fuller-thinking attributes: broad interests and pursuits, creative

Larry Bell

innovations and influence, analytical and artistic accomplishments, contributions to science and society and most important of all, passionate dedication to high ideals and purposes.

Altogether, they can inspire and challenge us to set goals and expectations that reach farther, aim higher and think better.

1. **Aristotle**
   (Open source image)
2. **Leonardo da Vinci**
   (Open source image)
3. **Thomas Jefferson**
   (Source: Library of Congress)
4. **Benjamin Franklin**
   (Source: Library of Congress)
5. **Albert Einstein**
   (Open source stock photo)

6. Nikola Tesla
   (Open source stock photo)

7. Thomas Edison
   (Source: Bachrach Studios)

8. Marie Currie
   (Open source stock photo)

9. Winston Churchill
   (Source: Library of Congress)

10. Stephen Hawking
    (Source: NASA)

Aristotle: Bringing Discipline to Logic

MUCH OF OUR current day thinking, including attempts to think about thinking, can be traced back to Athens, Greece between the 3rd and 4th centuries BC. Broadly considered then to be the center of the academic universe, Athens was the home of the most renowned philosophers, none more historically celebrated than Socrates and his student Plato, who in turn influenced a brilliant scholar named Aristotle.

Aristotle's record of achievements is stupendous. Credited by many as being the world's first genuine scientist, his surviving works contain expansive, yet detailed studies of natural phenomena which reflect clear distinctions between theories and direct observations essential to understanding the modern-day "scientific method."

He identified relationships between various scientific disciplines and established what might be characterized as the first true research institute and library. The research institute and library served as a place for scholars to learn and join in collaborative inquiry and take advantage of a systematic organization of reference materials. The diversity of Aristotle's own surviving works reveals virtually boundless interests—topics including biology and zoology, meteorology, philosophy and logic, politics and government, rhetoric and linguistics and aesthetics and poetry.

Recognizing the Importance of Historical Context

There can be no doubt that Aristotle's prolific contributions to scientific and logical discourse profoundly influenced intellectual rhetoric and creative enlightenment. At the same time, it should also be recognized that taken within the context of his life and times, concepts of science and precepts of moral governance which framed his theoretical perspectives differed in many fundamental aspects from those we now take for granted.

For example, in Aristotle's time, various brain functions had not yet been discovered to be connected with processes associated with thinking, memory or control over behaviors and body functions.

Memory, according to Aristotle, was he defined as "De Anima," involved repetitive "imprinting" of an appearance of a past experience upon a semi-fluid bodily organ that repeatedly undergoes several changes. He reasoned that memory then occurs when the stimuli are too complex for the semi-fluid bodily organ to receive all of the impressions at once. Such changes were believed to be the same as those involved in the operations of sensation, common sense and thinking.[63]

Aristotle reasoned that "slow-witted people" have good memories because fluids in their memory organ used to imprint experiences don't tend to wash away as readily…at least not unless they are so slow and the surface of the organ is so hardened that it cannot receive new imprints.

Very young and older people were thought to have imprinting problems as well. Children were believed to have greater difficulties imprinting memories because their organs undergo rapid changes, while imprinting by older people becomes stunted by organ decay.[64, 65]

Quick-witted people were believed to suffer from the same memory problems as the young because rapid changes in the imprinting organ made it more difficult to fix new images. (I would much prefer to apply this explanation rather than the aging alternative to myself.)

As for meteorology and planetary sciences, Aristotle adopted a pre-Socratic view of the planet being comprised of different combinations of the four fundamental elements: earth, water, air and fire. Each of these, in turn, was to be characterized by their possession of a unique pair of elementary qualities: heat, cold, wetness and dryness.

In Aristotle's categorical world of thinking, earth was by definition cold and dry, water was cold and wet, air was hot and wet, and fire was hot and dry. Each of these elements had a natural place in an ordered Cosmos, with a natural tendency to move toward this natural place. Therefore, earthly solids naturally fall, while fire, unless prevented, rises ever higher.

Aristotle, like other scholars of his time, accepted that the Earth is in the center of the Universe, with the Moon, Sun and other planets revolving about it in a succession of concentric crystalline spheres. Those heavenly bodies weren't believed to be comprised of the same four terrestrial elements, but rather, made up of supernatural intellects which guided their travels.

That Earth-centric view of the Universe and Solar System persisted for nine more centuries until the Italian astronomer, mathematician and philosopher Galileo Galilei and his telescope proved otherwise. Such heresy got him in real trouble with the church establishment, which charged him with heresy twice, nearly got him executed, and banned his books.

Charged with "impropriety" for not going along with the prevailing establishment and being too closely aligned with a previous one nearly caused Aristotle to lose his life. Socrates, who was previously convicted and executed for the same charges, was far less fortunate.

A Background of Privilege, Accomplishments and Consequences

Aristotle was born in 384 BC into an environment of courtly privilege and consideration. His father, Nicomachus, was a personal physician to the Macedonian King Amyntas II, and Aristotle remained close to the royal family after his father died. His mother, Phaestis, died when he was young.[66]

Around the age of 17, Aristotle left his birthplace in the small town of Stagira on the northern coast of Greece to enroll in Plato's Academy, founded in 387 BC in Athens. He maintained a scholarly relationship with Plato, a student of Socrates. Although both were considered to be gifted scholars, Aristotle disagreed with some of Plato's philosophical treatises.[67]

Following Plato's death in 348 BC, his friend Hermias, King of Atarneus in Mysia, invited Aristotle to his court where he remained for three years. While there, he met and married the king's niece Pythias, his first wife, who bore him a daughter named after the mother.

Seven years later, King Phillip of Macedonia handsomely compensated Aristotle to tutor his son, the then 13-year-old Alexander the Great. The teacher and student became close friends. Aristotle's view toward Eastern conquest and his attitude towards Persia was anything but humanitarianly compassionate. He counseled Alexander to be:

> *A leader to the Greeks and a despot to the barbarians,*
> *to look after the former as after friends and relatives,*
> *and to deal with the latter as with beasts or plants.*[68]

Aristotle's appointment to head the Royal Academy of Macedonia also involved giving lessons to two other future kings, Ptolemy and Cassander.

Aristotle returned to Athens in 335 BC after Alexander, who succeeded his father King Phillip, conquered the city. Since Plato's Academy was then being headed by Xenocrates, with Alexander's blessings, Aristotle created his own school called the "Lyceum." There, he was believed to be the first teacher to organize his lectures into courses and to assign them a place in a syllabus.

Lyceum Science and Philosophy

Aristotle divided sciences into three general categories: productive, practical and theoretical. The productive sciences not only included engineering and architecture, which yield tangible products such as bridges and houses, but also disciplines such as strategy and rhetoric, where a product is something less concrete, such as victory on the battlefield or in the courts.

Practical sciences, most notably ethics and politics, were those associated with guiding behaviors. Theoretical science involved those that have no product and no practical goal, but in which information and understanding are sought for their own sake. He divided these into three groups: physics (the study of nature), mathematics and theology.

As a scientist, Aristotle recognized and accounted for the roles played by human interpretations and personal associations which influence our understanding of the world and its objects. In doing so, his inquiries, although not always leading to accurate conclusions, were always conducted in a genuinely objective spirit where he was ready and willing to confess ignorance when evidence was lacking. He emphasized that theories that conflict with observed phenomena should never be trusted.

Aristotle's science and philosophical thinking applied a disciplined and systematic concept of logic aimed at providing a universal process of reasoning that would allow humans to learn every conceivable thing about reality. He characterized deduction as arising from a reasonable argument in which:

> [W]hen certain things are laid down, something else
> follows out of necessity in virtue of their being so.

This precept became the basis for what philosophers now refer to as a "syllogism," where a logical conclusion is inferred from two or more other premises of very particular forms. This view was at odds with Plato's teachings, which noted deduction simply follows from premises, which lead to seemingly logical conclusions.[69]

Aristotle defined main components of reasoning in terms of inclusive and exclusive relationships. In doing so, however, he prescribed a moral code of conduct for "good living" wherein some restrictive laws of logic can be subordinated to personal conflicting values. In such instances, it is up to the individual to reason cautiously while developing his or her own judgment. He observed that "man is a political animal," and that humanity's defining character, among others in the animal kingdom, is rationality.[70]

Topics addressed both at Aristotle's Lyceum and through his personal work were enormously broad in scope, while in many cases, also remarkably specific. Earth sciences, for example, were stated to include "all the affectations we may call common to air and water, and the kinds and parts of the earth and the affectations of its parts." In his treatise *Meteorology*, Aristotle discussed topics ranging from natural disasters to astrological events.

His varied and precisely detailed studies of zoology and marine biology were without precedent at a time more than 20 centuries before the microscope was invented. Much of this work involved classifying mammals, reptiles, fish and insects into myriad categories with copious information regarding their various anatomies, diets, habitats, modes of copulation and reproductive systems.

Perhaps he can be forgiven for sometimes not getting everything entirely right…he imperfectly attempted to classify animals too broadly based upon certain features, such as species with red blood being vertebrates versus those without labeled cephalopods. After all, his mistakes gave many centuries of scientists who followed him something more to do.

Later Years and Legacy

After his wife Pythias died, Aristotle embarked upon a romance with, and later married, a woman named Herpyllis. Herpyllis was rumored to have been given to Aristotle as a slave by the Macedonian court of King Phillip and his son. The couple had a son who was named Nicomachus, after Aristotle's father.[71]

Aristotle's relationship with that court had cooled as Alexander's behavior became more and more megalomaniac, with the king proclaiming himself divine and demanding that Greeks prostrate themselves before him in adoration. Aristotle's nephew Callisthenes, who had been appointed upon his recommendation as historian of Alexander's Asiatic expedition, was falsely charged and executed for opposing the king.

Aristotle was charged with impropriety for his previous relationship with Alexander's government following the sudden death of Alexander the Great and overthrow of his reign of power in 323 BC. Aristotle fled to Chalcis in 321 BC to escape prosecution and execution and died a year later by drinking a poisonous hemlock beverage. He'd been charged with the same offenses that ended the life of Socrates in 399 BC.[72]

In death, Aristotle left behind an estimated one million words of his surviving works recorded on papyrus scrolls. These scrolls are estimated to represent around one-fifth of his total output. Although his writings generally fell out of use soon afterwards, their retrieval more than seven centuries later has significantly influenced Western thought on humanities and social sciences.[73]

Whereas Plato and Aristotle are both ranked by many historians as being the greatest philosophers who have ever lived, it is Aristotle who might better be credited for his contributions to intellectual empiricism, as his work inspired other great thinkers and artists during the Renaissance.[74]

One such thinker and artist was named Leonardo da Vinci.

Leonardo da Vinci: An Original Renaissance Man

LEONARDO DA VINCI epitomizes the Renaissance ideal of a "Universal Genius." Still widely recognized as one of the greatest artists of all time, he also engaged and excelled in an amazing variety of engineering and scientific endeavors ranging from machines for military defense and warfare, architecture and cartographical mapping, innovative concepts for flight and detailed studies of botany and human anatomy.

The era of Renaissance humanism which influenced Leonardo's remarkable diversity recognized none of today's prevalent boundaries and mutually-exclusive polarities between science and art. His successes in both types of endeavors drew upon broad curiosity about the natural world combined with his highly developed observational skills and dedicated attention to detail.

In addition to such masterpiece works as the *Mona Lisa, The Last Supper,* and his iconic drawing of the *Vitruvian Man,* the more than 13,000 pages of recorded drawings, notes and scientific thoughts on nature he produced throughout his life fuse art with natural philosophy: the forerunner of modern science.

Leonardo da Vinci left a legacy of insights into his personal life and thoughts which he constantly recorded. Those topics range from mundane lists of groceries; names of people who owed him money; designs for wings for flying and shoes for walking on water; sketches and details of subjects and compositions for paintings and sculptures; architectural planning and design concepts; nature observations regarding plants, rock formations, and whirlpools; and other nearly endless subjects.

His inventive mind remains truly remarkable despite the fact that relatively few of his designs were actually realized during his lifetime. Many of his concepts weren't technically feasible due to lack of scientific information. Others were so ahead of his time that they required modern metallurgy and engineering advancements which only occurred centuries later.

Examples of both include a fundamentally unfeasible flapping "ornithopter" flying machine, and another with a helical rotor. His concept for armored double-hull ships used for military and commercial applications was successfully adopted long after his death.

Some of da Vinci's numerous inventions were not only implemented, but were highly beneficial in his day. His designs for an automated bobbin winder, and a machine for testing the tensile strength of wire, proved revolutionary even then.[75]

Unlike Michelangelo, Raphael and most other religious artists of his time, Leonardo saw the world as logical rather than mysterious. He was also a fundamentally different kind of scientist than Galileo, Newton and others who followed him. Although Leonardo's observational approach to science attempted to understand a phenomenon by describing and depicting it in utmost detail, it did not emphasize experiments or theoretical explanations.

Early Life

Leonardo da Vinci was born out of wedlock in 1452 in the Vinci region of the Medici-ruled Republic of Florence. His father, Piero da Vinci, was a notary, and his mother, Caterina, was a peasant woman.

All of Piero's six legal heirs were born out of the third of his three formal marriages, that to Lucrezia Cortigiani. His second marriage, when Leonardo was age 16, was to 21-year-old Francesca Lanfredini, who died without children. Piero's first marriage was to a sixteen-year-old, Albiera Amadori, who also died young without children.[76]

At age 14, Leonardo was first introduced to informal studies of Latin, geometry, mathematics and many other subjects as an apprentice in the studio of renowned artist Andrea del Verrocchio. There, he along with other interns, was exposed to drafting, chemistry, metallurgy, metal working, plaster casting, leather working and carpentry, as well as drawing, painting, sculpting and modeling. By 1472, at age 20, Leonardo was considered a master in the Guild of Saint Luke, a respected organization of artists and doctors of medicine.[77]

Verrocchio demanded that his students develop a deep knowledge of anatomy through studies and drawings of muscles, tendons and other visible anatomical features. Leonardo pursued such studies with great interest and diligence. He received permission to dissect human corpses at the hospital of Santa Maria Nuova in Florence, and later, at hospitals in Milan and Rome. His surviving notebooks contain hundreds of anatomical sketches, detailed drawings and written descriptions, including those of the mechanical functions of skeletons, and even a fetus in utero.[78]

Leonardo's morgue studies carefully recorded physiological effects of age and human emotions, rage in particular. Many of his drawings illustrate figures with significant facial deformities and signs of illness...expressions which later factored into his paintings.

Young Leonardo also dissected and studied anatomies of

various animals including horses, cows, monkeys, bears, birds and frogs. Comparing their anatomies with humans, he concluded that the heart is central to the circulatory system in all beings. He demonstrated how the heart functions by creating wax models of the cerebral ventricles and a glass aorta using grass seeds in water to observe blood circulation through the aortic valve.

Since Leonardo lacked a formal education in Latin and mathematics, many contemporary scholars have tended to fully credit him as a scientist. He nevertheless taught himself Latin in the 1490s, later studying mathematics under the tutelage of Luca Pacioli. He prepared a series of drawings for Pacioli's 1509 book *De Divina Proportione*.

Creative Life and Environment

Florence, during Leonardo da Vinci's lifetime, was home to great artists and philosophers. Luminary figures included painters Piero della Francesca and Filippo Lippi, sculptor Luca della Robbia and writer and architect Leon Battista Alberti. Such influential leaders were followed by Leonardo's teachers Verrocchio, Antonio del Pollaiuolo and painter-sculptor Mino da Fiesole. Leonardo was a contemporary of Botticelli, Domenico Ghirlandaio and Perugino, and of course, Michelangelo and Raphael.

While all three of these High Renaissance giants were contemporaries of one another, they were not actually of the same generation. Leonardo was 23 years old when Michelangelo was born, and was 31 when Raphael was born. Raphael died at age 37 in 1520, the year after Leonardo died. Michelangelo then lived on for another 45 years.[79]

Historian Anonimo Gaddiano has written that in 1480 Leonardo was living with the Medici and working in the Gardens of the Piazza San Although Marco in Florence. The site was a

Neo-Platonic academy the Medici had established for elite artists, poets and philosophers. Between 1482 and 1499 he worked in the service of Ludovico il Moro in Milan to paint the *Virgin of the Rocks* for the Confraternity of the Immaculate Conception, and *The Last Supper* for the monastery of Santa Maria delle Grazie.

Other commissions during that period were impressively diverse. They included floats and pageants for special occasions, a dome for the Milan Cathedral and a clay model for a huge equestrian monument to Francesco Sforza which, though never constructed, would have required 70 tons of bronze. Michelangelo insulted Leonardo by implying that the 1492 monument design was never constructed because he was unable to cast it. In 1509, the bronze that had been set aside for this purpose was used for a cannon to defend the city from the invasion of Charles VIII. To add insult to injury, invading French troops used Leonardo's life-size clay monument model for target practice after Ludovico Sforza was overthrown during the Second Italian War of 1499.

In 1500, Leonardo, along with his assistant and a mathematician friend, fled Milan for Venice as guests of monks in the Monastery of Santissima Annuziata and St John the Baptist. In 1502, he traveled throughout Italy in the service of Cesare Borgia, the son of Pope Alexander VI, as his chief military architect and engineer. In this role he created a strategic map which described defensive methods to protect Cesare Borgia's stronghold town Imola from naval attacks. Leonardo produced another defense map for the Chiana Valley which included a proposed sea dam to supply Florence with water throughout all seasons.

In 1503, Leonardo returned to the Guild of Saint Luke in Florence where he spent two years designing and painting a fresco mural of *The Battle of Anghiari* for the main room in the Palazzo della Signoria, today known as the Pallazzo Vecchio.

Michelangelo, his competitor, designed a companion piece, *The Battle of Cascina.*

The following year he settled an old score. Leonardo joined an effort to relocate Michelangelo's statue of *David* over his rival's objections.[80]

Leonardo went to Florence in 1507 to sort out some estate problems with his brothers following the death of their father, then moved back to Milan in 1508. Between 1513 and 1516, he spent extended periods in the Vatican in Rome under Pope Leo X. Raphael and Michelangelo were also very active there.

By this time, Leonardo had cultivated important royal and religious mentors. King Francis I of France recaptured Milan in 1515, and Leonardo was known to be present at a meeting of Francis and Pope Leo X in Bologna. Francis commissioned da Vinci to create a mechanical lion that could walk forward and then open its chest to reveal a cluster of lilies. In reward for his services, Francis awarded Leonardo a comfortable pension and prestigious manor house, now a public museum, near the king's residence at the royal Château d' Ambroise.

Leonardo's Living Legacy

Leonardo da Vinci lived out his final years in France at the home awarded to him by his close friend Francis I. He died in 1519 at age 67 of what is believed to be a stroke. Although Leonardo was initially buried at the Chapel of Saint-Hubert in the Château d' Amboise, his remains were relocated to an unknown location after the chapel's destruction in 1802.

The noted Italian painter, architect and historian Giorgio Vasari wrote a fitting tribute to Leonardo's genius in his 1568 book *Lives of Artists:*

> *In the normal course of events, many men and women are born with remarkable talents; but occasionally, in*

a way that transcends nature, a single person is marvelously endowed by Heaven with beauty, grace and talent in such abundance that he leaves other men far behind, all his actions seem inspired and indeed everything he does clearly comes from God rather than from human skill. Everyone acknowledged that this was true of Leonardo da Vinci, an artist of outstanding physical beauty, who displayed infinite grace in everything he did and who cultivated so brilliantly all problems he studied he solved with ease.

Historian Liana Bortolon wrote in 1967:

Because of the multiplicity of interests that spurred him to pursue every field of knowledge...Leonardo da Vinci can be considered quite rightly, to have been the universal genius par excellence, and with all disquieting overtones inherent in that term. Man is uncomfortable today, faced with a genius, as he was in the 16th Century, five centuries have passed, yet we still view Leonardo with awe.[81]

Larry Bell

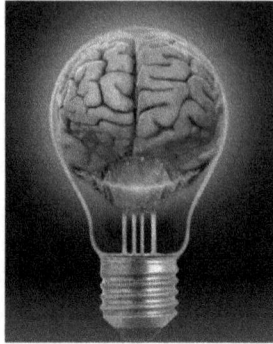

Thomas Jefferson's Heroic Wisdom

TWO CENTURIES AFTER Leonardo, history spawned another awesome thinker with a multiplicity of interests.

There can be no doubt that Thomas Jefferson used all parts of his brain. In addition to being regarded as one of the most influential figures of the democratic republic in America's first half-century, his interests and talents evidence remarkable diversity and depth.

Jefferson began his early career as both a land surveyor and lawyer. He played the violin for satisfaction and was a voracious reader, amassing a vast personal library throughout his life.

An accomplished linguist, Jefferson spoke several languages. This interest extended to studies of Native American Indian vocabularies. He was an avid student of science, horticulture in particular, and was also a competent mathematician.

Jefferson was an amateur inventor of small practical mechanical devices. Included in his repertoire of inventions were: a revolving book stand, a "great clock" powered by gravitational pull of cannonballs, a polygraph device to duplicate writing; a moldboard plow used in his fields; and even the swivel chair he sat in while composing much of America's most historic document, the *Declaration of Independence*, at age 33.

As a self- taught architect, Jefferson designed the campus plan for the University of Virginia which he founded and served as the first rector of. He was particularly influenced by Andrea Palladio's *The Four Books of Architecture* which outlined principles of classical design.

Passionately committed to education, he also established the National Academy at West Point, and served as president of the American Philosophical Society.

Although not regarded as a great orator, he was most certainly a prolific, gifted and legendary writer. One of his many important and lasting legislative authorship contributions was a *Bill for Establishing Religious Freedom.* Another established the *Land Ordinance of 1784,* whereby Virginia ceded to the national government vast areas it claimed northwest of the Ohio River for division into sections which became additional states.

Jefferson's range and substance of accomplishments are legendary. He served as Governor of Virginia during the Revolutionary War and with John Adams in the Continental Congress, who he later succeeded as America's third president from 1801 to 1809.

Both were originally close friends, until a 1790s Federalist/Republican political rift divided them. Active correspondence between the two resumed in 1812 with an exchange of 158 letters over the next 14 years.

Jefferson had previously served as vice president under Adams. Before that, as President George Washington's Secretary of State, he strongly opposed a national debt and national bank advocated by Alexander Hamilton, believing that states should be responsible to retire their own debts.

Although Jefferson admired Washington's leadership skills, he believed that Washington's Federalist Party was leading the country in the wrong direction.

Background and Philosophy

Thomas Jefferson was born in 1743 in the Colony of Virginia as the third of ten children. His father Peter Jefferson, a planter and surveyor, died when he was fourteen years old.

Jefferson's formal education began at a local school run by a Scottish Presbyterian minister. At the age of nine he began studying the natural world and three languages: Latin, Greek and French. Six years later he boarded with the family of Reverend James Maury near Gordonsville, Virginia where he was introduced to history, sciences and the classics.[82]

Thomas entered the College of William & Mary at the age of 16 where he studied mathematics, metaphysics and philosophy. There he became particularly enamored with the ideas of John Locke, Francis Bacon and Isaac Newton, who he ultimately considered the three greatest men who ever lived.[83]

All three had a profound influence upon his political philosophy and values.

Locke (1632-1704) defended the idea that all men are by nature free and equal, rather than subjects of monarchs, with rights to life, liberty and property. Locke also defended the principle of majority rule, the separation of legislative and executive powers and the rights to stage revolutions against coercive powers, including churches.

Bacon, an English philosopher in the late 1500s and early 1600s, bravely challenged Aristotelian ideas that placed the Earth in the center of the Universe or that scientific truth can be reached entirely by way of authoritative arguments. He instead argued that truth requires evidence from the real world.

Newton's late 1600s and early 1700s scientific discoveries are so numerous and varied that many consider him to be the father of modern sciences. He helped to define laws of gravity and planetary motion, explained the properties of light and color and co-founded the field of calculus.

Jefferson was also inspired by the writings of Charles Montesquieu, a French philosopher of the early 1700s who is famous for articulating the theory of separation of powers.

Drawing important lessons from all three of these towering intellects, Jefferson believed that citizens have "certain inalienable rights," and that "rightful liberty is unobstructed action according to our will, within limits drawn around us by the equal rights of others." He also championed trial by jury "as the only anchor yet imagined by man, by which a government can be held to the principles of its Constitution."

Whereas Jefferson tended to shun organized religion, he was nevertheless influenced by both Christianity and Deism. He had been baptized in youth, and he even became a governing member of his local Episcopal Church in Charlottesville, which he later attended with his daughters. Although Federalists attacked him as an atheist during the 1800 presidential election, he donated money to the American Bible Society, observing that the Four Evangelists delivered a "pure and sublime system of morality" to humanity.[84]

Jefferson abandoned "orthodox" Christianity during his college years. He declared in 1803 after reviewing "New Testament" teachings: "I am a Christian in the only sense in which [Jesus] wishes anyone to be." [85]

His strong interest in religious lessons is evidenced in biblical teachings he recorded titled *The Life and Morals of Jesus of Nazareth*. The document, which omitted miraculous supernatural references, is also known as the *Jefferson Bible*.

Jefferson's proposed constitutional bill to establish religious freedom forbade state support of religious institutions or enforcement of religious doctrine. Although his attempt at passage failed, it was later successfully revived by James Madison.[86,87]

As a life-long champion of religious choice, Jefferson's

Virginia Statute for Religious Freedom, which was ratified in 1786, declared that men "shall be free to profess...their opinions in matters of religion."

Troubled Life and Legacy

Thomas Jefferson encountered personal, political and cultural demons of his era that continue to haunt his legacy.

Upon the death of his father and together with his marriage to his third cousin Martha Wayles Skelton (a 23-year-old widow), Jefferson inherited 135 slaves, 11,000 acres and large estate debts which took many years to reconcile. Whereas financial problems plagued Jefferson throughout his life, his slave ownership, his policies regarding American Indian re-settlements and his strong advocacy for limitations on executive powers continue to fuel public controversy today.

Jefferson was widely criticized by both political parties during the late 19th century. Conservatives blamed his democratic philosophy for influencing the era's populist movement, while Progressives sought an even more activist federal government.

Liberal politics has vacillated back and forth since then. In the 1930s, Franklin D. Roosevelt and New Deal Democrats celebrated Jefferson's struggles for "the common man." Many even reclaimed him as their party's founder. This perspective took an abrupt and opposite shift following the Civil Rights Movement of the 1950s and 1960s. His background as a slaveholder precipitated particularly hostile scrutiny when DNA testing supported allegations of a sexual relationship with his slave Sally Hemings.[88]

Jefferson's marriage to Martha, a skilled pianist whom he accompanied on the violin, was reportedly devoted, but also difficult and short. Tragically, only two of the six children born to their union survived. Martha, who suffered from diabetes and other health problems, died at the age of 33, just a few months after the birth of their last child.

Thomas pledged to Martha never to marry again, so that the children would never have another mother. He kept that promise.[89]

Some historians argue that Jefferson was an opponent of slavery his whole life, doing all he could within a limited range of available legislative options to end it. Others criticize him as a racist for acting contrary to his words as a slaveholder. Each individual must decide which—or perhaps whether both—of these positions are most valid.

Those holding the more benevolent view may recognize that while most of Jefferson's approximately 600 slaves were born on his plantations, he is known to have purchased some for purposes of reuniting families.

He said "My first wish is that labourers may be well treated." Accordingly, he provided them with financial or other incentives, while also allowing them to grow gardens and raise their own chickens.[90]

Jefferson believed that slavery was harmful to both slave and master, but had reservations about releasing unprepared slaves into freedom and advocated gradual emancipation. In keeping with this philosophy, he proposed a gradual voluntary training and resettlement program to the Virginia legislature. A section of his bill—one which was stricken by other Southern delegates—bravely criticized King George III's role in promoting slavery in the colonies.[91, 92, 93, 94]

During Jefferson's brief practice of law, seven of his cases defended slaves. His defenses invoked "Natural Law" to argue:

> *Everyone comes into the world with a right to his own person and using it at his own will...This is called personal liberty, and is given him by the author of nature, because it is necessary for his own*

sustenance. [95, 96, 97]

Jefferson later incorporated this sentiment into his preamble of human rights in the *Declaration of Independence*, declaring that "all men are created equal" …one of the best-known sentences the English language. [98]

As president, in plotting borders for nine new states in their initial stages, Jefferson wrote an ordinance banning slavery in all territories. Extensive congressional revisions to his proposal were made, including a rejection of the ban on slavery. His provisions banning slavery, later known as the *Jefferson Proviso,* were modified and implemented three years later in the Northwest Ordinance of 1787, which became law for the entire Northwest. [99, 100]

Although President Jefferson stressed "equal and exact justice to all men," minority rights and freedom of speech, he truly was mostly silent on the issues of slavery and emancipation. This reticence might be considered somewhat understandable, given that a very dangerous rift existed among north-south states on the subject.

As Jefferson wrote in an 1805 letter to William Burwell: "I have long since given up the expectation of any provision for the extinguishment of slavery among us." That same year, he wrote to George Logan, saying "I have carefully avoided every public act or manifestation on that subject." [101]

Thomas Jefferson strongly argued that citizens have "certain inalienable rights" and that "rightful liberty is unobstructed action according to our will, within limits drawn around us by the equal rights of others." This being the case, his presidency has also come to be criticized for "civilization program" policies which turned out badly at the time for many of America's original citizens, its Native Indians.

Some historians will argue that Jefferson's policies did little to promote assimilation, and were primarily a pretext to seize lands.[102]

The Jefferson administration aggressively pursued peaceful Indian treaty alliances which encouraged adaptation and assimilation to "civilized" agrarian culture. Some, including Shawnees led by Black Hoof, the Creek and the Cherokees, accepted. Others did not, including a tribal group that broke off from Black Hoof which was led by Tecumseh.[103]

Jefferson should not be unfairly regarded as someone who was bigoted towards Indians or other races. He refuted the prevalent notion of his time which viewed Indians as inferior people, maintaining that they were equal in body and mind to those of European descent.

Jefferson's interest in American Indian cultures was evident in efforts to study and understand several different tribal vocabularies. As president, he instructed Lewis and Clark to collect and record different languages revealed through encounters during their historic expedition.

Following his presidency, Jefferson packed 50 of those Native American vocabulary lists in a chest intended for river boat transfer, along with other prized possessions, to Monticello. Unfortunately, only a few fragments were recovered from a muddy James River bank after a thief discarded the documents as worthless.[104]

Although Jefferson never achieved his goal of realizing equal rights for all citizens, his principles and actions left an indelible legacy that forever changed America and the world. His recognition of a need for a national military university, for example, led to establishment of the United States Military Academy at West Point in 1802.[105]

Recognizing the important role of education to engender a stable society, Jefferson also advocated for the establishment of publicly-funded schools accessible to students from all social strata and based entirely on ability. In 1819, at age 76, he founded the University of Virginia, became its principle architect, planned the curriculum and served as the first rector upon its opening in 1926. The most controversial feature of Jefferson's plan for the university was a library—rather than a church—placed at the campus center.

While Thomas Jefferson left great gifts to our nation, he died deeply in debt at the age of 83 with little or nothing to leave to heirs. His death occurred just hours before that of John Adams, his longtime friend and rival. Attendants found a gold locket around his neck where it had been for more than 40 years containing a small faded blue ribbon which tied a strand of his wife Martha's brown hair.

His remains were buried at Monticello under a self-written epitaph:

> *HERE WAS BURIED THOMAS JEFFERSON, AUTHOR OF THE DECLARATION OF AMERICAN INDEPENDENCE, OF THE STATUTE OF VIRGINIA FOR RELIGIOUS FREEDOM, AND FATHER OF THE UNIVERSITY OF VIRGINIA.*

The interior of the Jefferson Memorial in Washington contains a 19-foot statue likeness. Engraved passages inscribed near the roof include one that reads:

> *I have sworn upon the altar of God eternal hostility against every form of tyranny over the mind of man.*

Thomas Jefferson was true to that oath.

Benjamin Franklin's Inventive Diplomacy

THOMAS JEFFERSON'S "BELOVED and venerable" friend Benjamin Franklin recognized him as a remarkable and unique American patriot and colleague. Upon being asked about an appointment to serve as Ambassador to France, a position previously held by Franklin: "Is it you, Sir, who [will] replace Doctor Franklin?", Jefferson responded, "No one can replace him, Sir; I am only his successor."

Jefferson and Franklin first met at a revolutionary assembly of the Second Continental Congress, where Jefferson was among the delegates representing Virginia, and Franklin among those representing Pennsylvania. The two strongly supported active resistance against Great Britain, and they worked together along with John Adams, Roger Sherman and Robert Livingston in drafting the Declaration of Independence.

Franklin's path to that Continental Congress and beyond is also marked with numerous other major landmark achievements, both personal and public, of remarkable diversity. His legendary roles as philosophical writer, civic leader and activist, scientist and inventor and international diplomat have appreciably impacted America and the Western World.

Larry Bell

Early Life

Benjamin Franklin was born in Boston on January 17, 1706 to the second wife of Josiah Franklin, a maker of soap and candles. His mother, Abiah, was born in Nantucket, Massachusetts to Peter Folger, a miller, and his schoolteacher wife, Mary Morrill, a former indentured servant.

Altogether, Josiah had fathered seventeen children. His first wife, Ann Child, died after their seventh was born, and together with Abiah, the couple produced ten more. Benjamin was their eighth.[106]

Unlike Jefferson, young Ben had a very limited formal education. While Josiah and Abiah, both devout Puritans, had wished for their son to study with the clergy, the family could only financially manage to enroll him for two years, plus enable him to take additional classes at a Boston Latin School.

Benjamin ended school attendance at age twelve to become apprenticed to his brother James, a printer. It was a trade he soon mastered as a foundation for wealth, recognition and influence. He learned to read early under the tutelage of a private teacher, a life-long passion he pursued tirelessly, and also taught himself writing skills.

Franklin was inspired by essays written by Joseph Addison and Sir Richard Steel which had been featured in The Spectator, a periodical first published in 1711. Recognizing the importance and rarity of competent prose writing, he read them repeatedly. He later recalled this experience in his autobiography as being "of great use to me in the course of my life" and "a principal means of my advancement."[107]

In 1722, 16-year-old Benjamin began writing a series of essays of his own which appeared in a weekly newspaper founded by James. The New-England Courant invited readers to contribute, and Benjamin, unbeknownst to either his brother James or those outside readers, did so under the pseudonym authorship of "Silence Dogood."

With characteristic wit, Benjamin's fictionalized articles rudely lampooned topics and characters from funeral eulogies to students from Harvard University. Matters got out of hand when authorities jailed James for three weeks following an unflattering essay by "Silence Dogood" about the Provincial Governor.[108]

Young Franklin, the real culprit, took over the newspaper and then had "Mrs. Dogood" (quoting "Cato's Letters") proclaim:

> *Without Freedom of Thought and there can be no such Thing as Wisdom; and no such Thing as public Liberty without Freedom of Speech.*[109]

He also wrote in *Silence Dogood no. 8, 1722*:

> *In those wretched countries where a man cannot call his tongue his own, he can scarce call anything his own. Whosoever would overthrow the liberty of a nation must begin by subduing the freeness of speech.*[110]

Some months later, after a bitter quarrel, Benjamin secretly left home hoping that brother James wouldn't "go to law" and reveal his responsibility for the subterfuge.

Path to Affluence and Influence

At age 17, Benjamin set off for New York to seek work as a printer. Unsuccessful in finding desired opportunities, he soon went on in 1724 to Quaker-dominated Philadelphia, which was more open and religiously tolerant to those of his Puritan background.

One of Franklin's new printing contacts, Pennsylvania

Larry Bell

Governor Sir William Keith, encouraged him to set up business for himself, and even offered to arrange for his passage to England, to lend him money and to recommend him to stationers and booksellers. Those turned out to be empty gestures. Not until his ship was out at sea did he realize that Keith had not delivered the letters of credit and introductions as promised.[111]

Franklin secured work as a printer in London, returning to Philadelphia in 1728 at age 20 to set up a printing shop with a partner on borrowed money. Business prospered, initially producing a contract to print Pennsylvania's paper currency. The company later became a public printer for New Jersey, Delaware, Maryland and other projects.

Benjamin soon began publishing his own *Pennsylvania Gazette,* which was ranked among the best colonial newspapers. Between 1732 and 1758 he added a *Poor Richard's Almanac,* authored under the pseudonym "Richard Sanders," which became a huge public success, selling thousands of copies annually. He ended The Almanac with a 12-page preface titled *Father Abraham's Speech* which later became famously known as *The Way to Wealth,* citing proverbs concerning hard work, thrift and financial prudence.[112]

Although the Gazette gave Benjamin Franklin a large readership forum, like other newspapers of the period, it was often poorly printed with little news content that would qualify as professional journalism. Nevertheless, it made a broader contribution to the unique culture that distinguished Philadelphia from her neighbors prior to the upcoming Revolution.[113]

Franklin's public recognition extended to Europe. Upon visiting London between 1724 and 1726, he was warmly greeted by such other famous people as explorer James Cook, theologian-scientist Joseph Priestley, and philosopher David Hume. Many years later, in 1759, he spent three weeks at

Hume's home in Edinburgh, which he described as "the densest happiness of my life." [114]

He also financially prospered. By age 42 Franklin become wealthy enough to retire from active business, having already achieved a distinctive gentleman status. He became a profitable silent partner in the printing firm of Franklin and Hall, moved to a spacious new home in "a more quiet part of town," bought several slaves, and even acquired a coat of arms.

By the late 1740s Benjamin Franklin became one of wealthiest colonists in the northern part of the North American Continent.

Civic and Cultural Leader

Benjamin Franklin instituted a variety of civic, cultural and educational initiatives long before retiring from profitable business pursuits. One was a *Juno of Leather Apron Club* he organized in 1727. Juno was modeled after English coffeehouses as an informal venue to debate questions of morals, politics and natural philosophy. [115,116]

Since books were rare and expensive, Juno members donated their own shared library. As Franklin wrote:

> *A proposition was made by me that since our books were often referr'd to in our disquisitions upon inquiries, it might be convenient for us to have them altogether where we met, that upon occasion they might be consulted, and by clubbing our books in a common library, we should, while we lik'd to keep them together, have each of us the advantage of using the books of all the other members, which be nearly as beneficial as if each owned the whole.* [117]

Juno's organization led to the creation of the Library Company of Philadelphia. An intercolonial version of Juno framed the formation of the American Philosophical Society, of which Jefferson subsequently served as president.

Known to have "that hard-to-be-govern'd passion of youth" with a reputation for dalliances with *low Women,* Franklin apparently desired a more stable civic life, taking Deborah Read as his common law wife in 1730. He also brought a son William into that marriage, born of a woman who has never been identified. Deborah died in 1774, following their son Franky who died at age four. Sarah, their daughter, survived both of them.

In 1743, Franklin successfully proposed a paid police force and organized a volunteer fire company. Six years later he published educational plans which led to the Academy of Philadelphia, which in turn led to his founding of the University of Pennsylvania.[118]

Benjamin Franklin was also active in organizing a militia for the defense of the colony against a possible invasion by the French and Spaniards, whose privateers were operating in the Delaware River. In addition, he was appointed Clerk of the Pennsylvania legislature in 1736, Postmaster of Philadelphia in 1737, member of Philadelphia City Council in 1738, Justice of the Peace in 1749 and City Alderman and member of the Pennsylvania Assembly in 1751.

In 1759 Franklin, a middle school drop-out, finally got some academic recognition as well. "Dr. Franklin" received an honorary degree from University of Saint Andrews in Scotland, followed in 1762 by another from the University of Oxford.

Scientist and Inventor

Although Franklin never regarded science to be as important as public service, he still managed to make the necessary time and effort to become a major figure in this field through inventions, discoveries and innovations related to electrical phenomena in particular.

Benjamin Franklin's numerous contributions are legendary. He created the distinction between insulators and conductors and invented a battery for storing electrical charges. He coined new English words for sources of electricity: conductor, charge, condense, armature and electrify. He showed that electricity was a single "fluid" with a positive and negative or plus and minus charges—not, as traditionally thought, two kinds of fluids. He demonstrated that plus and minus charges, or states of electrification of bodies, had to occur in equal amounts—a critical scientific principle known today as the "Law of Conservation of Charge."[119]

Franklin first became interested in exploring the phenomenon of electricity in 1746 after seeing some of his London friend Archibald Spencer's lectures using static electricity for illustrations. Two years later, in 1748, Franklin constructed a multiple-plate capacitor that he called an "electrical battery" by placing panes of glass between lead plates, suspended with silk cords and connected by wires.

Franklin received an "electric machine" sent to his Library Company by an English correspondent in London, Peter Collinson. Franklin had previously sent piecemeal reports of ideas and experiments to Collinson. These were published in 1752 in an 86-page book titled *Experiments and Observations on Electricity*. The publication went through five English editions, three in French, and one each in Italian and German.[120]

Benjamin Franklin's thunderstorm kite experiment is legendary. It led to an invention which has since saved countless lives. At the same time, it might very well have cost him his own.

He later reported:

When rain has wet the kite twine so that it can

> conduct the electric fire freely, you will find it streams out plentifully from the key at the approach of your knuckle, and with this key a phial, or Leyden jar, may be discharged; and from electric fire thus obtained spirits to be kindled, and all other electric experiments [may be] performed which are usually done by the help of a rubber glass globe or tube; and therefore the sameness of the electrical matter with that of lightening completely demonstrated. [121]

Having (fortunately for us all) survived the experiment, he then proposed:

> ... attaching "upright rods of iron, made sharp as a needle and gilt to prevent rusting, and from the foot of those rods a wire down the outside of the building into the ground...Would not these pointed rods probably draw the Electrical Fire silently out of the cloud before it came nigh enough to strike, and thereby secure us from that most sudden and terrible mischief! [122]

Franklin's innovation didn't end with the lightning rod. He can also be credited for his wood-burning stove, which warmed American homes for more than 200 years, along with bifocal eyeglasses, the odometer and a now forgotten glass harmonica, the "armonica." Other Franklin ideas included observations about the Gulf Stream and proposals for matching grants and Daylight Saving Time.

Perhaps greatest of all, he invented himself.

Disputed Diplomat

By 1753, Franklin had become a royal officeholder of the British government, appointed as the deputy postmaster general in charge of mail in all northern colonies. Attempting to leverage this official position, he proposed a "Plan for the Union" in 1754 to organize a common defense against the French. The plan was adopted by the Albany Congress, but failed to win necessary support in colonial legislatures and was resisted by the king's advisors.

Despite this diplomatic setback, the experience enabled Franklin to become acquainted with important imperial officials and gain visibility and respect as a colonial leader.

In 1757, Franklin was delegated to go to England as an agent of the Pennsylvania Assembly with the purported purpose of persuading the family of William Penn, as the proprietor of Pennsylvania, to allow the Colonial Legislature to tax its ungranted lands. The mission's real aim, however, was to oust the family from power, and to make the colony a royal province.[123]

Franklin spent the next 18 years in London, along with his son William, then 27 years old, and two of his slaves.

Yes, Franklin, as with Jefferson, was a slaveholder. In the context of the times, slavery was common and virtually unchallenged throughout the British colonies. In the 1750s, an estimated half of all Philadelphia property owners had slaves.[124]

By the late 1750s Franklin began to argue against slavery from an economic perspective, becoming a prominent, but "cautious," abolitionist. He freed all of his slaves by 1770.

It is true, however, that while he came to openly oppose the system of slavery and the international slave trade commerce, like Jefferson, he refused to publicly debate the issue at the 1787 Constitutional Convention. In fact, also like Jefferson, he tended not to participate in verbal debates there at all.[125]

Franklin's ongoing engagements with fellow colonists and British sovereigns raised suspicions of disloyalties to many on both camps. His public persona as a "royalist" became reinforced through privileged political connections with Lord Bute. These connections enabled him to have his son William, then age 31, appointed Royal Governor of New Jersey.

He also encountered other political challenges on the home front. Upon returning to Pennsylvania in 1762, he had to deal with a heated dispute involving Scotch-Irish settlers in the Paxton region of Western Pennsylvania who were angered with the Quaker-dominated Pennsylvania Assembly over the body's unwillingness to finance military protection from local Susquehannock Indians. This occurred in the aftermath of the French and Indian War and Pontiac's Rebellion, which led a vigilante group to attack and murder settlers in the town of Conestoga who they believed to be Indian sympathizers.

About 250 of the "Paxtony boys" who marched to Philadelphia in 1764 to present their grievances to the legislature agreed to disperse on a promise by Franklin that their issues would be considered.

Franklin shared the outrage of felt by many others regarding the Conestoga murders. His *Narrative of the Late Massacres* concluded that the Conestoga would have been safe among any other people on earth, no matter how primitive, except for the "white savages from Pekstang and Donegall!"

In any case, following a failed election bid to the Pennsylvania Assembly, Franklin returned again to London.

Benjamin Franklin soon faced new problems arising from the English Parliament's Stamp Act of 1765, which created a firestorm of opposition in the colonies. Although Franklin also opposed the legislation, he arranged for a firm owned by his friend John Hughes to become the official stamp agency for Pennsylvania, believing the legislation to be inevitable. The deal nearly ended Franklin's political position in American public life, and produced violent threats against Hughes's mortal life as well.[126]

Franklin had badly misjudged the situation when he advised

Hughes:

> *A firm loyalty to the Crown and faithful adherence to the government of this nation will always be the wisest course for you and I to take, whatever may be the madness of the populace or their blind leaders.*

Angry mobs prevailed in preventing enforcement of the Stamp Act everywhere in North America.

Franklin succeeded in restoring a measure of colonial respect by publicly denouncing the Stamp Act before the British Parliament. He later reported that the entire experience shook his confidence in the wisdom of British officials and caused him to appreciate his "Americanness" as never before.

Over the next several years, Franklin sought to bridge a growing gulf between the colonies and British government. Between 1765 and 1775 he wrote 126 newspaper pieces intended to rationally explain positions of each side to the other.[127]

Many on both sides, however, also had reservations about Franklin...the English thought him too American, and Americans saw him as being too English.

Any aspirations Franklin may have had to gain imperial influence sufficient to heal a growing colonial rift were destroyed by a plan that went seriously wrong. In 1772 he recovered and exposed a batch of letters written in the 1760s by Thomas Hutchinson, then lieutenant governor of Massachusetts, which revealed indiscreet remarks about a need to abridge American liberties.

Franklin likely assumed that the letters would somehow blame the imperial crisis on native officials such as Hutchinson to absolve the ministry in London of responsibility...thus allowing his friends in the ministry such as Lord Dartmouth to settle the differences.

Larry Bell

The idea backfired. In January 1774, Franklin was viscously criticized by the British solicitor-general before the Privy Council and court. He was fired as deputy postmaster two days later, and sailed back to America.[128]

Revolutionary

Although many colonists continued to be wary of Franklin's true loyalties—some even suspicious that he might be a British spy—upon returning to Philadelphia Franklin was immediately elected to the Second Continental Congress.

In 1776, he was dispatched to France as a premier agent in a congressional commission seeking that country's military and diplomatic recognition. Franklin played superbly upon the French aristocracy's liberal sympathies for oppressed Americans whom they viewed as impoverished residents of primitive, undeveloped land full of forests and savages...scarcely capable of producing enlightened thinkers.

Franklin played to such sentiments with the well-cultivated image of a democratic folk genius from that forsaken American wilderness. In violation of all diplomatic protocol, he appeared before the Court of Versailles...the most formal and elaborate court in all Europe, with a simple brown-and-white linen suit, a fur cap, and with no customary wig or sword.

His presence and pleadings were enormously successful in securing military and diplomatic alliances with France in 1778. These agreements later proved crucial in obtaining shipments of munitions vital in support of an upcoming American Revolution.

Franklin is also credited with having played another important role in bringing about a final peace treaty with Britain in 1783. In violation of their original instructions and the French alliance, American peace commissioners signed a separate peace with Britain. Franklin later apologized for this transgression in an eloquent letter to Charles Gravier, the compte de Vergennes,

Louis XVI's chief minister.[129]

American Legend

Following eight years in France, Benjamin Franklin returned to America in 1784. His return was not entirely welcoming. Congress ignored his request for some land in the American West, and another for a diplomatic appointment for his grandson.

In 1790, just a month before his death, Franklin signed a memorial requesting that Congress abolish slavery. After his death, the Senate refused to go along with the House in declaring a month of mourning.

Benjamin Franklin, like most of us—geniuses or not—lived an imperfect life. Although many of his diplomatic efforts may have proven to be misguided failures, it can also be plausibly argued that he was among America's greatest, most effective diplomats.

Franklin continues to be revered as a great symbol of American enterprise spirit and work ethic identity...one who above all articulated the lasting principles and values of the emerging American nation...the importance of hard work, education, community spirit, self-governing institutions and opposition to authoritarianism, with both political and religious tolerance.

Benjamin also exemplifies American commitment to free enterprise, objective science and the pursuit of creative innovations to solve practical needs. Here, perhaps above all, his integrated left-right brain vision reveals limitless and ageless human potentials.

Few, if any other people continue to be as popularly quoted as Franklin. The wisdom of thirteen virtues he recorded at age twenty offer lessons which still warrant contemplation:

1. "Temperance. Eat not to dullness; drink not to elevation."
2. "Silence. Speak not but what may benefit others or yourself; avoid trifling conversations."
3. "Order. Let all your things have their places; let each part of your business have its time."
4. "Resolution. Resolve to perform what you ought; perform without fail what you resolve."
5. "Frugality. Make no expense but to do good to others or yourself, i.e., waste nothing."
6. "Industry. Lose no time; be always employ'd in something useful; cut off all unnecessary actions."
7. "Sincerity. Use no hurtful deceit; think innocently and justly, and, if you speak, speak accordingly."
8. "Justice. Wrong none by doing injuries, or omitting the benefits that are your duty."
9. "Moderation. Avoid extremes; forbear resenting injuries so much as you think they deserve."
10. "Cleanliness. Tolerate no uncleanliness in body, clothes, or habitation."
11. "Tranquility. Be not disturbed at trifles, or at accidents common or unavoidable."
12. "Chastity. Rarely use venery but for health or offspring, never to dullness, weakness, or the injury of your own or another's peace or reputation."
13. "Humility. Imitate Jesus and Socrates."

While he obviously and admittedly didn't live up to all of them, he wrote in his autobiography:

> I hope, therefore, that some of my descendants may follow the example and reap the benefit.[130]

American writer and journalist Walter Isaacson ranks Franklin as:

> *The most accomplished American of his age and the most influential in inventing the type of society America would become.* [131]

There is some evidence to support that acclaim. More than two centuries after his death, Benjamin Franklin's ongoing likeness on the $100 bill, along with many warships, towns and counties, educational institutions and corporations named in his honor, remind us of his impact upon us all.

Larry Bell

Albert Einstein: A Visual Visionary

IT'S DIFFICULT TO imagine anyone who exemplifies a greater genius in the popular minds of most people than Albert Einstein. Not many people realize, however, that his revolutionary accomplishments can be traced to surprisingly late-blooming beginnings and very inauspicious academic performance history. This story is richly chronicled in a comprehensive book *Einstein, His Life and Universe: the Basis for Genius.* [132]

Einstein was truly a whole brain thinker—a creative force whose fertile mind visually conceived thought experiments, developed and expressed complex thoughts in the disciplined language of mathematics, and was fueled and lubricated by a passion for music.

The products of his thinking delivered far more than he originally advertised in writing to his friend Conrad Habricht in 1905. While working as a low-level patent examiner, Einstein wrote:

> *I promise you four papers. The first deals with radiation and the energy properties of light and is very revolutionary, as you will see if you send me your work first.*

That paper postulated that light could be regarded both as a wave as well as a stream of tiny particle packages called "quanta."

He went on:

> *The second paper is a determination of the true sizes of atoms...The third proves that bodies on the order of magnitude 1/1000 mm, suspended in liquids, must already perform an observable random motion that is produced by thermal motion. Such movement of suspended bodies has actually been observed by physiologists who call it Brownian motion.*

Using statistical analysis of random collisions, that third paper established the true existence of atoms and molecules.

Einstein continued that:

> *The fourth paper is only a rough draft at this point, and is an electrodynamics of moving bodies which employs a modification of the theory of space and time.*

This later became famously known as the "Special Theory of Relativity."

That same year, he was also working on a short addendum to that fourth paper which drew a relationship between energy and mass. The addition envisioned bending of light beams and warping of space. That relationship is briefly and most famously of all summarized as $E=mc^2$. His predictions of how much gravity actually bends light were later validated during a 1919 solar eclipse.

In addition to revolutionary scientific impacts of Einstein's visionary concepts, his work also led to many important technological advancements by others. Included are photoelectric cells, lasers, fiber optics, semiconductors and nuclear power. Regarding the latter, he theorized and actively warned against development of the atomic bomb.

Benefits of a Long Childhood

As a child, Einstein was slow in learning how to talk. He exhibited evidence of a condition known as "echolalia," and possibly a mild form of autism or Asperger's syndrome. Whenever he had something to say, he would first softly whisper it to himself two or three times until it sounded good enough to pronounce out loud. That quirk prompted his family maid to refer to him as "der Depperts" (the dopey one). Some relatives described him as "almost backwards." [133]

Einstein believed that his slow verbal development later served as an advantage, allowing him to observe with wonder the everyday phenomena others took for granted. He later reflected:

> When I ask myself how it happened that I in particular discovered the relativity theory, it seemed to lie in the following circumstance. The ordinary adult never bothers his head about the problems of space and time. These are things he has thought as a child. But I developed so slowly that I began to wonder about space and time only when I was already grown up. Consequently, I probed more deeply into the problem than an ordinary child would have. [134, 135]

Einstein retained the curiosity and awe of a child throughout his life. He wrote to a friend:

> People like you and me never grow old. We never cease to be like curious children before the great

mystery into which we were born.[136]

Young Einstein, however, was far more than an ordinary child. He recalled his father's gift to him of a magnetic compass at the age of four or five as such a profound *"great awakening experience"* that he trembled and grew cold. He marveled that the needle behaved as if influenced by mysterious powers of some hidden force, manifesting a sense of wonder that motivated him throughout his life.

As he later reminisced,

> *I can still remember——or at least I believe I can remember——that this experience made a deep impression on me. Something deeply hidden had to be behind things.*[137]

Walter Isaacson reminds his readers that the magnetic compass experience may be correlated with Einstein's life-long interest in field theories to describe nature. In a gravitational or electromagnetic field there are forces that can act on a particle at any point, and equations of field theory describe how these change as one moves through the region. His Theory of General Relativity is based upon equations that describe a gravitational field. Throughout his life he fervently pursued hope that such field equations would form a basis for a "Theory of Everything."

Young Einstein exhibited abundant imagination, confidence and tenacity that persisted throughout his life. Above all, he believed "Imagination is more important than knowledge."

Albert Einstein was perpetually drawn to contemplate and seek simpler solutions to complex puzzles, and was willing to challenge orthodox assumptions that others took for granted. His sister, Maja, remembered that he persistently succeeded in building houses of cards up to 14 levels tall.

He reported in a 1935 interview:

As a boy of 12, I was thrilled to see what is possible to find out truth by reasoning alone, without the help of any outside experience. I became more and more convinced that nature could be understood as a relatively simple mathematical structure.[138]

That early insight paid big dividends. In 1895, 16-year-old Einstein imagined what it would be like to ride alongside a light beam. A decade later, this boyhood musing provided the conceptual foundation for two great advances of 20th century physics: relativity and quantum theory. Then in 1915, only one more decade after that, he followed that light beam of imagination to produce his everlasting crowning scientific accomplishment…the General Theory of Relativity.

It is not true, as often reported, that Einstein failed math as a student. His sister Maja recalled that by the age of 12 he could solve complicated problems in applied arithmetic. Young Albert mastered differential and integral calculus before the age of 15, learned geometry and algebra on his own through textbooks and tackled new theories by attempting to prove them through basic logic.

Regarding the Pythagorean Theorem, for example, he later recalled:

After much effort I succeeded in 'proving' this theorem on the basis of the similarity of triangles…It seemed to me 'evident' that the relations of the sides of the right-angled triangles have to be completely determined by one of the acute angles.

(He was referring here to a relationship where the square of the lengths of the legs of a right angle add up to the square of the length of the hypotenuse.)[139]

Thinking in Pictures

Albert Einstein did not respond well to mechanical learning of languages such as Latin and Greek, and more generally admitted to having a bad memory for words and texts. Nevertheless, he more than made up for any such deficiencies with a rich visual imagination. As he once told a psychologist:

> *I rarely think in words at all. A thought comes, and I may try to express it in words afterwards.*[140]

Many of those imaginings were accompanied with his passionate love of music, Mozart's sonatas in particular. As he once said: "Mozart's music is so pure and beautiful that I see it as a reflection of the inner beauty of the Universe itself." He told a friend: "Like all great beauty, his music was pure simplicity."

His son, Hans Albert said:

> *Whenever he felt he had come to the end of the road or faced a difficult challenge in his work, he would take refuge in music that would solve all his difficulties.*

It seems that his father could hold two thoughts together in his mind simultaneously. Hans observed that while wrestling with General Relativity:

> *He would often play his violin in the kitchen late at night, improvising melodies while he pondered complicated problems. Then suddenly in the middle of playing, he would announce excitedly, 'I've got it!' As if by inspiration, the answer to the problem would have come to him in the middle of music.*[141]

Larry Bell

Albert Einstein also had the ability to visualize concepts in terms of mathematical logic structures, whereby equations can describe theoretical and observable realities. This language system, for example, enabled him to imagine how the electromagnetic field equations discovered by James Clerk Maxwell would manifest themselves to a boy riding alongside that hypothetical light beam.[142]

Those "thought experiments" revealed mysterious worlds of possibility and reality that previously seemed unimaginable even to the most advanced theorists of his era. One, for example, visualized that the experience riding in an accelerating elevator in space would be indistinguishable from feeling the sensation of gravity.

Another thought experiment conceptualized how "space time" is warped by an interplay between matter, motion and energy. He likened this circumstance to rolling a bowling ball onto the two-dimensional surface of a trampoline. Then when some billiard balls are added, they move toward the bowling ball not because it exerts some mysterious attraction, but rather, because of the way it curves the trampoline fabric.

Einstein's visual thinking was encouraged by important early influences. One was a popular 21 volume illustrated series of *People's Books on Natural Science* written by Aaron Bernstein. The book was given to him at age 10 by Max Talmud, a medical student who was frequently invited to dine with Einstein's family.

Bernstein asked readers in one book dealing with light to imagine being on a speeding bullet that was shot through the window of a train. He noted that it would incorrectly seem that the bullet entered at an angle. This is because the train would have moved between the time the bullet entered one window and exited on the other side. Similarly, due to the speed of Earth through space, the same misconception must be true of light passing through a telescope.

The book series was inspirational. Bernstein declared:

> *Since each kind of light proves to be exactly the same*
> *speed, the law of the speed of light can well be called*
> *the most general of nature's laws.*

He exclaimed:

> *Praised be this science! Praised be the men who did it!*
> *And praised be the human mind, which sees more*
> *sharply than does the human eye.*[143, 144]

Max Talmud also introduced the young Einstein to other life-
long interests. Together they studied the philosophical works of
Immanuel Kant, David Hume and Ernst Mach regarding what
can be known about reality. Perhaps most important of all,
Talmud gifted Einstein with a textbook of geometry two years
before he was scheduled to learn the subject in school.

Einstein was thrilled by revelations brought to light in that
"scared little geometry book." He recalled:

> *Here were assertions, as for example the intersections*
> *of three altitudes of a triangle in one part, which—*
> *though by no means evident—could nevertheless be*
> *proved with such certainty that any doubt appeared to*
> *be out of the question. This lucidity and certainty*
> *made an indescribable impression on me.*

Einstein later noted at an Oxford lecture: "If Euclid failed to
kindle your youthful enthusiasm, then you were not born to be a
scientific thinker." [145]

Visual thinking was again encouraged when, as a student of
age 16, Einstein attended classes in the Swiss village of Aarau.
These classes were based upon the philosophy of a Swiss

educational reformer of the early nineteenth century, John Heinrich Pestalozzi. The program emphasized that "visual understanding is the essential and only true means of teaching how to judge things correctly."

The Aarau curriculum stressed the importance of nurturing individuality, inner dignity and hands-on observations that proceeded to intuitions and individualized conceptual thinking. This was the opposite of what Einstein characterized as the German militaristic authoritarianism which he eternally rebelled against.

Einstein recalled:

> *In Aarau, I made my first rather childish experiments in thinking that had a direct bearing on the Special Theory. If a person could run after a light wave with the same speed as light, you would have to have a wave arrangement which could be completely independent of time. Of course, such a thing is impossible.*[146]

His year at Aarau was spent in preparation for an attempt to be accepted for admission at Zurich Polytechnic, a school with a solid reputation in engineering and science "for specialized teachers in mathematics and science."

Although he greatly enjoyed Aarau, Einstein was a less than a stellar student, whose mediocre grades were mixed with good ones. He was required to do remedial work in chemistry, and reportedly had "great gaps" in knowledge of French, the subject in which he performed worst of all. He did manage well enough at Aaru, however, to gain admittance to Zurich Polytechnic at age 17.

Prior to attending Zurich Polytechnic, and with the purpose of becoming admitted, Einstein wrote his first essay on theoretical physics at age 16 which he titled *On the Investigation of the State of Ether in a Magnetic Field.* The 14-page handwritten paper was based upon an accepted theory at that time which conceived of light as a wave that rippled and propagated throughout the Universe by some unseen and unknown substance (ether) much as water does. Subscribing to this this idea, he wrote: "An electric current sets the surrounding ether in a kind of momentary motion."

Einstein's later works demolished that theory.

The Rebellious Nonconformist

As Banesh Hoffman, Einstein's collaborator in later years, observed:

> His early suspicion of authority, which never wholly left him, was to prove of decisive importance. Without it he would not have been able to develop the powerful independence of mind that gave him the courage to challenge established scientific beliefs and thereby revolutionize physics. [147]

Einstein had a better intuition for physics than for math. He later reflected:

> It was not clear to me as a student that a more profound knowledge of the basic principles of physics was tied up with the most intricate mathematical methods. [148]

Near the end of his life, he lamented:

> At a very early age, I made an assumption that a successful physicist only needs to know elementary mathematics. I realized that this assumption of mine

was completely wrong.

At Zurich, Einstein persisted in challenging teaching of popular physics theory orthodoxy. His professor in a course titled *Physical Experiments for Beginners* gave him the lowest possible grade...flunking him. His habit of seldom showing up for the course resulted in a March 1899 written request by that professor that Albert receive an official "director's reprimand due to lack of diligence in physics practicum." [149]

When he did attend the laboratory, his independence still got him in trouble. His friend and early biographer Carl Seelig reported that one day, when given an instruction sheet for a particular experiment, Einstein naturally flung the paper into the waste paper basket and proceeded to pursue the experiment in his own way.

The professor asked an assistant, "What do you make of Einstein? He always does something different from what I have ordered."

The assistant replied: "He does indeed, Herr Professor, but his solutions are right and the methods he uses are of great interest." [150]

Another of those laboratory experiments turned out very badly. An explosion in 1899 severely damaged Einstein's right hand and required stitches. The injury made it difficult to write for two weeks, and forced him to give up his beloved fiddle playing for even longer.

Einstein's insolent attitude and obvious disdain for authority prompted one of his early teachers to proclaim him unwelcome in his class. When he insisted that he had committed no offense, the teacher replied: "Yes, that is true, but you sit there in the back row and smile, and your presence here spoils the respect of the class for me."

Einstein later recalled that the same teacher had gone on to "express the wish that I leave the school."

When asked why he didn't instead enter a field like medicine, or even law, Einstein replied, "Because I have even less talent for those subjects. Why shouldn't I at least try my luck with physics?" [151]

Believing that many Zurich Polytechnic lectures were out of date, Einstein and some friends read the most recent theories on their own. Included were papers by Gustav Kirchhoff on radiation, Herman von Helmholtz on thermodynamics, Heinrich Hertz on electromagnetism, Ludwig Boltzmann on statistical mechanics, and a lesser-known theorist, August Foppl, who wrote a popular text titled *Introduction to Maxwell's Theory on Electricity* that called into question the concept of "absolute motion."

Foppl considered a question regarding the induction of an electric current by a magnetic field. He wondered:

> *If it is all the same whether a magnet moves in the vicinity of a resting electric current or whether it is the latter that moves while the magnet is at rest.*

Einstein began his 1905 Special Relativity paper considering the same issue. [152]

In 1898, Einstein finished first in his class with an average score of 5.7 out of a possible 6 in his intermediate exams. His next major graduation hurdle required the acceptance and completion of a research thesis topic.

Einstein's first proposed to do an experiment to measure how fast Earth was moving through ether based upon then-accepted wisdom which he would famously destroy with his Special Theory of Relativity. His idea was to reflect light from a single source which was reflected in two different directions. That proposal was rejected.

His next proposal, also rejected, was to explore a link between the ability of different materials to conduct electricity as suggested by electron theory. He finally settled on doing a research paper on heat conductivity. Doing so to accommodate his professor's particular interest, he later dismissed the topic as being of no interest to him. Nevertheless, it caused him to graduate at nearly the bottom of his class with a score of 4.9, barely enough to earn a diploma.[153]

Einstein was at this point a low-ranked graduate of a teaching college without a paying job, research accomplishments or academic advocacy. This was four years before a 1905 "miracle year" when he upended traditional physics, and was nine years before he finally succeeded in getting a doctoral dissertation accepted.

Fortunately, a low-level patent office opportunity came through for him in 1902. The Swiss Council officially elected him "provisionally as a Technical Expert Class 3 of the Federal Office for Intellectual Property."

He enjoyed the work.

> I was able to do a full day's work in only two or three hours. The remaining part of the day I would work out my ideas.

The patent examiner job reinforced one of Einstein's important talents...his ability to conduct thought experiments in which he could visualize how a theory would play out in practice. On the other hand, he said:

> An academic career in which a person is forced to produce scientific writings in great amounts creates a danger of intellectual superficiality.[154]

Philosophical Independence

Einstein's strong spirit of independence fiercely rejected

regimentation and ritualistic thinking, including traditional mechanical school learning: "The teachers at the elementary school seemed to me like drill sergeants."

Later in life, this came to include subscription to any religious identity and orthodoxy.

As his friend, Philipp Frank, noted:

> There arose in Einstein an aversion to the orthodox practice of the Jewish or any traditional religion, as well as to attendance at religious services, and this he never lost.

As Walter Isaacson notes, however:

> He did retain from earlier childhood and religious phase a profound reverence for the harmony and beauty of what he called the mind of God as it was expressed in the creation of the Universe and its laws. [155]

Einstein formally renounced Judaism in 1986, stating:

> There is nothing in me that can be described as a 'Jewish faith.' However I am happy to be a member of the Jewish people.

He later said:

> The Jew who abandons his faith is in a similar position to a snail that abandons its shell. He is still a snail. [156, 157]

Albert's religious outlook became closely aligned with the deterministic view of Baruch Spinoza, Jewish philosopher from

Amsterdam (1632-1677). Like Spinoza, Einstein believed that laws of nature, once we could fathom them, decreed immutable causes and effects. This accorded with his frequently quoted statement that "God did not play with dice" by allowing any events to be random or undetermined.

As Spinoza taught: "All things are determined by the necessity of divine nature."

Einstein's words and examples stressed the importance of independent thinking. He once said: "It is important to foster individuality, for only the individual can produce good ideas."

Near the end of his life, he was asked by the New York State Education Department what schools should emphasize. He replied:

> In teaching history there should be extensive discussion of personalities who benefitted mankind through independence of character and judgment.

Skepticism and resistance to "received wisdom" became his hallmark. He wrote to a friend in 1901, "A foolish faith in authority is the worst enemy of truth." [158]

Ironically, Einstein himself apparently acknowledged the futility of combating that enemy. He conceded: "To punish me for my contempt for authority, fate made me an authority myself." [159]

Einstein's Earth-Shaking Legacy

A February 2016 announcement which the Royal Swedish Academy accurately described as "a discovery that shook the world" affirmed that Einstein had been proven right. Just as his 1916 General Theory of Relativity had predicted, sensitive Earth-based instruments recorded that gravity waves emanating from the collision of two black holes a billion light years away jiggled space-time with invisible cataclysms which reached us.

That faint "chirp" signal which was received at separate facilities in different states lasting only a fifth of a second was greeted by thousands of scientists as a loud opening bell for a whole new era of astronomical revelations.

The amazing discovery earned the award of a 2017 Nobel Prize in Physics to Rainer Weiss at MIT, along with Kip Thorne and Barry Barish of the California Institute of Technology. Together with legions of other dedicated scientists and technicians at the Laser Interferometer Gravitational-wave Observatory (LIGO) and its sister organization, the LIGO Scientific Collaboration, they innovated and demonstrated a marvel of dedicated achievement which was more than 40 years in the making.

The LIGO program constructed two L-shaped antennas, one in Hanford, Washington, and the other in Livingston, Louisiana. There, laser lights bounce along 2.5-mile-long arms in the world's biggest vacuum tunnels and monitor the shape of space.

Weiss and Thorn hatched the idea in an all-night 1975 hotel brainstorming session. Following the work of others, they calculated that a typical gravity wave would change the laser-measured distance between two detection mirrors by an almost imperceptible distance of one part in a billion trillion...less than the diameter of a proton.

Weiss reported that it took the team two months after receiving the signal before they were convinced that it was what they hoped. Since then, in conjunction with a new European detector (Virgo), at least four more black hole collisions have been documented.

LIGO instruments detected ripples in the space-time grid produced by a different type of event on August 17, 2017, which recorded the collision of two neutron stars. In addition to gravity waves, the spectacle released visible light which was observed by Earth-based telescopes. Initially appearing as a bright explosion of blue, the color soon faded to a deep red.

The discovery confirmed, as expected, that collisions of neutron stars produce enormous gamma-ray bursts, along with about half of all heavy elements which are dispersed in gases that eventually settle down and condense to form new stars and planets.

Einstein's rich visual thinking has revealed a dynamic Universe no one had previously imagined...one in which what we call "gravity" results when matter and energy warp the geometry of space-time in much the same way that a heavy sleeper sags a mattress.

He imagined space-time as a condition so elastic that it can expand, tear and collapse into black holes which are so dense that even light can't escape them.

He envisioned that those gravity waves from motions of black holes and other dense remnants of dead stars would stretch and compress space in orthogonal directions as they pass an observer, just as sound waves compress air.

He correctly theorized that those waves would travel at the speed of light.

Perhaps most important of all, Albert Einstein thought us that we should never abandon our natural childlike curiosity and sense of wonderment.

Thinking Whole

Nikola Tesla's Spark of Genius

AS CLEAR EVIDENCE that great geniuses don't necessarily agree with one another, Einstein's brilliant contemporary, Nikola Tesla, didn't regard him to be all that much of an expert. The prolific inventor of more than 700 patents who is famously credited for developing alternating current didn't subscribe to what he termed *Einstein physics* at all.

Regarding Einstein's general relativity theory, Tesla wrote:

> I hold that space cannot be curved, for the simple reason that it can have no properties. It might as well be said that God has properties. He has not, but only attributes and these are our own making. Of properties we can only speak when dealing with matter filling the space. To say that in the presence of large bodies space becomes curved is equivalent to stating that something can act upon nothing. I, for one, refuse to subscribe to such a view.

At age 81, Tesla even claimed to have developed his own scientific principle regarding matter and energy. He wrote in a 1937 letter that his "dynamic theory of gravity" would "put an end to idle speculations and false conceptions, as that of curved space." That theory was never publicly disclosed.[160]

Although Nikola Tesla had a strong engineering and scientific background in classical physics, his views exhibited prevailing 19th century assumptions. He disagreed with an emerging theory that atoms are composed of smaller subatomic particles, asserting that there was no such thing as an electron creating an electric charge. Instead, he believed that atoms were immutable…that they could not change or be split in any way.

Tesla reasoned that if electrons existed at all, they did so as some sort of "fourth state" of matter—or "sub atom"—that could only exist in an experimental vacuum and had nothing to do with electricity. He also accepted the prevailing orthodoxy that electrical charges were transmitted within an all-pervasive "ether."

A Remarkably Talented Eccentric

Nikola Tesla was a remarkably creative intellect and unconventional personality whose innovative achievements were momentous. In addition to conceptualizing tremendous benefits of Alternating Current (AC), he also contributed major advancements in many technologies, including wireless communications, lasers, x-rays, radar, lighting, and robotics to name but a few.

Tesla valued practical innovation above all other intellectual virtues. He begins his autobiography titled *My Inventions,* stating:

> *The progressive development of man is vitally dependent in invention. It is the most important product of his creative brain. Its ultimate purpose is the complete mastery of mind over the material world, the harnessing of the forces of nature to human*

needs.[161]

Unlike Einstein's theoretical cosmic perspective, Tesla placed a high value on inventing things that would improve peoples' everyday lives. He wrote:

> *An inventor's endeavor is essentially lifesaving. Whether he harnesses forces, improves devices, or provides new comforts and conveniences, he is adding to the safety of our existence. He is also better qualified than the average individual to protect himself in peril, for he is observant and resourceful.*[162]

Similar to Einstein, Tesla was a visual thinker. He reportedly seldom made drawings before working from what has been described as a nearly photographic memory to execute the construction stage of his engineering concepts.

He wrote that he observed to his delight that he could "visualize with great facility" needing no models, drawings or experiments.

> *I could picture them as real in my mind. Thus I have been led to consider a new method of materializing inventive concepts and ideas, which is radically opposite to the purely experimental and is in my opinion ever so much more expeditious and efficient.*

He went on to explain that becoming engrossed with details and defects of an apparatus diminishes concentration on an original concept. Therefore, his method was different:

> *I do not rush into actual work. When I get an idea I start at once building it up in my imagination. I change the construction, make improvements and*

> *operate the device in my mind. It is absolutely*
> *immaterial to me whether I run my turbine in thought*
> *or test it in my shop. I even note if it is out of*
> *balance. There is no difference whatsoever, the results*
> *are the same.*

Also like Einstein, at an early age Tesla was passionately fond of mathematical studies with a facility to visualize figures and perform operations in his head. He recalled:

> *Up to a certain degree of complexity it was absolutely*
> *the same whether I wrote symbols on the board or*
> *conjured them before my mental vision. But freehand*
> *drawing, to which many hours of the course were*
> *devoted, was an annoyance I could not endure.*
> *Perhaps my aversion was simply due to a predilection*
> *I found in undisturbed thought.*[163]

Tesla's behavioral manifestations and personal autobiographical accounts evidence of mental disturbances which include Obsessive Compulsive Disorder (OCD), hallucinations and a likely touch of autism. For example, he loathed jewelry and round objects, wouldn't touch human hair, was obsessed with the number "three," and compulsively polished every dining implement using exactly 18 napkins.

As he recalled:

> *I had violent aversion against earrings of women but*
> *other ornaments, as bracelets, pleased me more or less*
> *according to design. The sight of a pearl would*
> *almost give me a fit but I was fascinated with the*
> *glitter of crystals or objects with sharp edges and*
> *plane surfaces. I would not touch the hair of other*
> *people except, perhaps at the point of a revolver.*[164]

As with Einstein, Tesla referred to having a "late awakening" of his talents. In contemplating a reason for this, he recounted:

> *In my boyhood I suffered from a particular affliction due to appearances of images, often accompanied by strong flashes of light, which marred the sight of real objects and interfered with my thought and action. They were pictures of things and scenes which I had already seen, never of those imagined. When a word was spoken to me the image of the object it designated would present itself vividly to my vision and sometimes I was quite unable to distinguish whether what I saw was tangible or not. This caused me discomfort and anxiety.*

As an example of distress, he recalled witnessing a funeral or other nerve-racking spectacle where the image would persist despite all efforts to banish it. To overcome this anxiety, he repeatedly performed mental operations to imagine other scenes, pushing the uncomfortable images farther and farther back in his mind. He constantly did this until he was 17 years old when, as he reported, his "thoughts turned to serious invention."

Persistent light flash sensations disturbed his sleep. He reported that on one occasion upon returning from a shooting expedition with a prominent French manufacturer:

> *I felt a positive sensation that my brain had caught fire. I saw a light as though a small sun was located in it and I passed the whole night applying cold compressions to my tortured head. Finally the flashes diminished in frequency and force, but it took more than three weeks before they wholly subsided. When a second invitation was extended to me, my answer was NO!*

Those luminous phenomena and images continued to manifest themselves from time to time when a new idea opened up possibilities. He reflected:

> *Every time, before falling asleep, images of persons or objects flit before my view. When I see them I know that I am about to lose consciousness. If they are absent and refuse to come out it means a sleepless night.*[165]

He was a tirelessly disciplined worker who claimed to require only two hours of sleep per night...except for dozing from time to time to recharge his batteries. He made it a habit to walk between eight and ten miles per day, plus ritually curled his toes one hundred times for each foot every night to stimulate his brain cells.

Tesla emphasized the importance of nurturing youthful imagination. He wrote in his autobiography:

> *Our first endeavors are purely instinctive, promptings of an imagination vivid and undisciplined. As we grow older, reason asserts itself and we become more and more systematic and designing. But those early impulses, although not immediately productive, are the greatest moment and may shape our very destinies. Indeed, I feel now that had I understood and instead cultivated instead of suppressing them, I would have added substantial value to my bequest to the world. But not until I had attained manhood did I realize that I was an inventor.*[166]

Regarding the importance of diligence and discipline, he wrote:

> *I am credited with being one of the hardest workers*

and perhaps I am, if thought is the equivalent of labor, for I have devoted to it almost all of my waking hours. But if work is interpreted to be a definite performance in a specified time according to a rigid rule, then I may be the worst of idlers. Every effort under compulsion demands a sacrifice of life energy. I have never paid such a price. On the contrary, I have thrived on my thoughts.[167]

Prior to his death in 1943, Tesla's habit was to walk to the park every day to feed pigeons. He recalled:

I have been feeding pigeons, thousands of them for years. But there was one, a beautiful bird, pure white with light grey tips on its wings; that one was different. It was female. I had only to wish and call her and she would come flying to me. I loved that pigeon as a man loves a woman, and she loved me. As long as I had her, there was a purpose to my life.

Although there were times when he made considerable sums of money, he died penniless.[168]

A Challenging and Influential Life

Nikola Tesla's life began in 1856 in Serbia within the Austrian Empire's Croatian military frontier. His interest in engineering and physics might be traced to influences of both of his parents. His father was an Eastern Orthodox priest with a talent for making home craft tools and mechanical appliances.

He credited his mother as also being "an inventor of the first order." She constructed tools and devices, created the finest apparel and furnishings from thread which she spun and at 60 years old possessed fingers "still nimble enough to tie three

139

knots in an eyelash." [169]

His mother's father was also an Eastern Orthodox priest. Still, regarding his family's religious background, Tesla later didn't consider himself to be a "believer in the orthodox sense." He said:

> To me, the Universe is simply a great machine which never came into being and will never end...

And...

> ...what we call 'spirit' is nothing more than the sum of the functionings of the body. When this functioning ceases, the 'soul' or the 'spirit' ceases likewise. [170]

Reminiscent of Einstein's philosophy, Tesla wrote in his autobiography:

> Religious dogmas are no longer accepted in their orthodox meaning, but every individual clings to faith in a supreme power of some kind.

He believed:

> We all must have an ideal to govern our conduct and insure contentment, but it is immaterial whether it be one of creed, art, science or something else, so long as it fulfills the function of a dematerializing force. It is essential to the peaceful existence of humanity as a whole that one common conception should prevail. [171]

Young Tesla studied German, arithmetic and religion in primary school, later attending high school at the Higher Real

Gymnasium in Carlstadt, Croatia. His ability to perform integral calculus in his head reportedly prompted teachers to suspect that he was cheating.

He enrolled at Austrian Polytechnic in Graz, Syria on a scholarship in 1873, initially never missed a lecture, and earned highest grades possible. When that scholarship ended after his second year, he became addicted to gambling, a costly obsession he later conquered.

Tesla never received a university diploma. Unprepared for graduation examinations, he asked for and was denied a time extension. As he recounted:

> *After finishing the studies at the Polytechnic Institute and University I had a complete nervous breakdown and while the malady lasted I observed many phenomena strange and unbelievable.*[172]

He then moved to Maribor where he worked as a low-wage draftsman. The brilliant college drop-out then moved to Budapest, Hungary in 1881 to work as a draftsman at the Central Telegraph Office and was soon promoted to a chief electrician position.

Nikola moved to America in 1884 to take a job working on the planning of large city utility projects at Edison's Machine Works on Manhattan's Lower East Side. One of those assignments was to develop a high voltage arc lamp-based lighting system, a technology that was incompatible with Edison's low voltage incandescent market.

He later reported that his first and perhaps only meeting with Edison was a memorable event in his life:

> *I was amazed at this wonderful man who, without early advantages and scientific training had accomplished so much. I had studied a dozen*

*languages, delved into literature and art, and had
spent my best years in libraries reading all sorts of
stuff that fell into my hands, from Newton's
'Principia' to the novels of Paul de Kock, and felt
that most of my life had been squandered. But it did
not take long before I recognized that it was the best
thing I could have done.*[173]

Tesla's later revolutionary alternating current design proposals
were never implemented, and he quit his position after only six
months.

Soon after leaving Edison's company in 1885, Tesla and
some investors founded their own company, Tesla Electric Light
& Manufacturing, which proceeded to patent his new arc
lighting concept along with new types of AC motors and
electrical transmission equipment. The enterprise later folded,
and Tesla lost control of the patents, leaving him broke.

In 1887, together with two new investors, Tesla then
formed the Tesla Electric Company. The new company
developed an AC induction motor...a concept affording large
advantages for long-distance, high-voltage transmission.
Engineers at Westinghouse Electric & Manufacturing recognized
the importance of the design, and the company negotiated a
licensing deal. A Westinghouse-General Electric merger
arrangement later purchased the patent from Tesla's company.

Tesla's achievements following that period were
transformative. He accomplished the first successful wireless
energy transfer to power electronic devices in 1891, conducted
the earliest demonstration of fluorescent lighting, and influenced
the development of modern electrical generators and turbine
designs.

In 1893 the Westinghouse Electric Company implemented
Tesla's AC system to light the World Columbian Exposition in
Chicago. The demonstration proved to be more efficient than

the direct current (DC) system marketed by Edison, and rapidly became the basis for most modern electric power distribution systems.

In 1895, Tesla and Westinghouse developed the world's first hydroelectric power plant at Niagara Falls.

Unfortunately, financial success proved fleeting. At the turn of the century Tesla set up a laboratory in Shoreham, Long Island featuring a "Wardenclyffe Tower" project intended to provide intercontinental wireless communications which was financed by J.P. Morgan and acclaimed architect Stanford White.

The tower was intended to function as a more powerful transmitter in competition with a Marconi radio-based system which Tesla regarded as a copy of his design. Nevertheless, Marconi's system beat him in December 1901 by successfully transmitting the letter "S" from England to Newfoundland, prompting investors put their money on that system. As a result, Tesla's building and tower were never completed. He ran out of money, and along with his previous Colorado Springs, Colorado laboratory, was foreclosed on for debt.

Tesla unsuccessfully attempted to sue Marconi for infringement on his wireless patents in 1915. His finances never recovered.

Nikola Tesla never married. Believing women to be superior, he regarded himself to be unworthy. At the same time, he expressed indignation towards the "new woman" of the era who was losing femininity in trying to be in power.

As reported in an August 1934 *Galveston Daily News* interview, he said:

> *In place of the soft-voiced gentle woman of my reverent worship, has come the woman who thinks that her chief success in life lies in making herself as much as possible like man—in dress, voice and*

actions, in sports and achievements of every kind...The tendency of women to push aside man, supplanting the old spirit of cooperation with him in all the affairs of life, is very disappointing to me.

During his both illustrious and troubled career, Nikola Tesla had many famous and successful friends including Mark Twain and French actress Sarah Bernhardt.

Sadly, he died broke, alone and undiscovered for two days in a New York hotel room. His true genius was only recognized and appreciated many years later.

Thomas Edison: The Wizard of Menlo Park

THOMAS ALVA EDISON (1847-1931), Tesla's earlier rival
in the "electric current war," began life with fewer financial and
educational advantages, but ended with much greater lifetime
business rewards and public acclaim. Despite a lack of formal
schooling or academic degree, he is recognized as America's
most prolific inventor of more than one thousand patents related
to such innovations as incandescent electric lights, the
microphone, telephone receiver, stock ticker, phonograph,
movies, and office copiers.

Edison's legacy of achievement is also commemorated by
numerous companies that bear his name. Included are: Edison
General Electric (which merged with the Thomson-Houston
electric company to form General Electric); Commonwealth
Edison (now part of Ecelon); Consolidated Edison; Edison
International; Detroit Edison (a unit of DTE Energy); the Edison
Electric Institute (a trade association); the Edison Ore-mining
Company; the Edison Portland Cement Company; Ohio Edison
(which merged with Centerior in 1997 to form First Energy);
and Southern California Edison.

A major Edison innovation was the creation of the first

modern industrial research laboratory in Menlo Park in
Middlesex County, New Jersey, which is also named in his
honor. The facility, which covers an area of two city blocks, was
established for the specific purpose of producing constant
technological innovations and improvements.

Philosophy and Religion

As with Einstein and Tesla, Edison took a dim view of
institutionalized orthodox religion. He wrote: "I do not believe
in the God of the theologians, but that there is a Supreme
Intelligence I do not doubt." [174]

Edison stated in an October 2, 1910 *New York Times*
magazine interview:

> *Nature is what we know. We do not know the gods of
> religion. And nature is not kind, or merciful, or
> loving. If God made me—the fabled God of the three
> qualities of which I spoke: mercy, kindness, love—He
> also made the fish I catch and eat. And where do His
> mercy, kindness, and love for that fish come in? No,
> nature made us—nature did it all—not the gods of
> the religions.* [175]

That quotation drew considerable criticism from those who
branded him as an atheist, prompting Edison to further clarify
his position in a letter:

> *You have misunderstood the whole article, because
> you jumped to the conclusion that it denies the
> existence of God. There is no such denial, what you
> call god I call Nature, the Supreme intelligence that
> rules matter. All the article states is that it is doubtful
> in my opinion if our intelligence or soul or whatever*

> *one may call it lives hereafter as an entity or disperses*
> *back again from whence it came, scattered amongst*
> *the cells of which we are made.*[176]

Edison was an advocate for a free-thinking rational inquiry "scientific deism" philosophy espoused by political philosopher and activist Thomas Paine's *The Age of Reason; Being an Investigation of Time and Fabulous Theology.* As he later reflected, "I can still remember the flash of enlightenment that shone from its pages."[177]

Paine challenged the legitimacy of institutionalized religion in general, and was most particularly critical of what he saw as corruption and political ambition within the Christian Church.

Deist philosophy held that all things in the Universe, even God, must obey laws of nature, and accordingly, rejected the concept that such a God suspends these laws to intervene in human affairs. Accordingly, many deists rejected the beliefs of any one religious "true faith," and were skeptical of miracles and rituals advanced by what was referred to as "priest craft."

Edison defended Thomas Paine and his anti-theological outlook. He wrote:

> *He [Paine] has been called an atheist, but atheist he*
> *is not. Paine believed in a supreme intelligence as*
> *representing the idea which other men often express by*
> *the name of 'deity.'*[178]

Early Background and Education

Born as the seventh and last child of Samuel and Nancy Edison in Milan, Ohio, Thomas grew up in the small and economically declining community of Port Huron, Michigan. In comparison with Einstein's and Tesla's families, the Edison's were far less prosperous, a circumstance that significantly influenced his exemplary and inherited learning and work values.

He attended formal schooling only for a few months, and gained his true education through home tutoring by his mother, insatiable reading interests and self-initiated science experiments.[179]

Angered by rigid and oppressive teaching policies, Edison's mother withdrew her seven-year-old son from the Port Huron, Michigan elementary school after three months of attendance. As reported by Edison biographer Matthew Josephson, she fiercely objected to forcing and prodding practices, and was dedicated to allowing him flexibility to experiment with various ways of nurturing his love of learning. Nancy Edison introduced eager young Thomas to vast worlds of science, philosophy and literature. He later recalled that "the first book in science I read when a boy" was R.G. Parker's *School of Natural Philosophy,* which explained how to perform chemistry experiments at home. He performed every experiment in the book.

His mother also bought Thomas *The Dictionary of Science* which further spurred his passion for the subject. The book prompted him to spend all of his spare money purchasing pharmacy chemicals and collecting bottles, wires and other items for experiments he conducted in the basement of his family's home.

Edison's biographer Josephson noted:

> *His mother had accomplished that which all truly great teachers do for their pupils, she brought him to the stage of learning things for himself, learning that which most amused and interested him, and she encouraged him to go on it in that path. It was the very best thing she could have done for this singular boy.*

Those interests were expansive. By the age of 12, Edison had read great works by Shakespeare and Dickens, Edward Gibbons' *Decline and Fall of the Roman Empire,* David Hume's *History of England, The Cooper Union for Advancements of Science and Art,* Victor Hugo's epic, *Les Misérables,* and much more.

Above all, Thomas was particularly interested in subjects related to science and inventions, including steam engines, electricity, battery power, electromagnetism and especially the telegraph.[180, 181]

Thomas was fascinated by demonstrations of the cross-country telegraph by Samuel F.B. Morse in the late 1830s. This led him to build his own the telegraph set, to practice the Morse code, and to focus more attention to other wonders of electricity. He also pursued self-motivated studies of mechanics, chemical analyses, manufacturing technologies and Newtonian physics which emphasized practical applications.

About a year after securing a job in 1859 as Grand Trunk railroad newsboy for a day-long run between Port Huron and Detroit, Edison got permission to put his five-hour layover in Detroit to good use by installing experimental laboratory equipment in a baggage car. This arrangement turned out badly in 1862 when a train lurch caused some chemicals to spill and set his small laboratory on fire.

Edison later variously attributed the train incident to a significant hearing loss which motivated his devotion to learning even more. As he reflected, "Deafness probably drove me to reading." At 15 years old, he became one of the first people to use the Detroit Free Library with card number 33.

One self-described explanation of the train incident attributed his hearing impairment to being struck on his ears by a conductor when the box car fire caused him to be thrown off the train along with his apparatus and chemicals in Smiths Creek, Michigan. A later, more charitable account, modified this story to say that the injury was caused when the conductor took hold of his ears to help lift him back onto the moving train.[182, 183]

Larry Bell

At age 20, Edison secured work in Cincinnati, Louisville, Indianapolis, Memphis and Boston as an itinerant Western Union telegraph operator. The job suited his interest in learning more and more about telegraphy, including how to improve the equipment. His private experiments filled his rented lodgings with chemicals and junk metal. As an associate at that time observed, "He spent money buying apparatus and books, and wouldn't buy clothing. That winter he went without an overcoat and nearly froze." [184]

Persistent Breakthroughs

By 1969, Edison's entrepreneurship as an inventor began to really take off. His patent applications included a telegraphic stock ticker which became standard office equipment in America and Europe, and a printing telegraph for gold bullion and foreign exchange dealers. He also figured out how a central telegraph office could control the performance of equipment from remote locations, and developed a method to transmit as many as four messages over a single wire.[185]

On July 18, 1877 as Edison tested an automatic telegraph which had a stylus to read coded indentations on strips of paper, the friction revealed an unexpected hum that attracted his attention. As Douglas Tarr at the Edison National Historical Site in West Orange, New Jersey reported:

> Edison seemed to reason that if a stylus going through indentations could produce a sound unintentionally, then it could produce a sound intentionally, in which case he should be able to reproduce the human voice...A talking machine! [186]

Edison worked on and off over more than two decades to advance that concept to do much more than just talk. His innovation ultimately produced sound quality that brought high fidelity music to homes of world audiences.

In 1879, Edison's Menlo Park laboratory demonstrated the first high-resistance incandescent light which passed electricity through a thin platinum filament in a glass vacuum bulb to delay melting. After the original model worked only for an hour or two, Edison went on to try carbonized filaments made of almost every imaginable plant material, including some specially ordered fibers from the tropics.

He later recalled: "Before I got through, I tested no fewer than 6,000 vegetable growths, and ransacked the world for the most suitable filament material." The best performer proved to be carbonized filaments of common cotton.[187]

Many more innovations followed during the late 1880s and early 1890s. In the area of photographic optics, for example, Edison demonstrated the potential of using tough, flexible celluloid motion picture film, worked out mechanical problems of advancing the film steadily across a photographic projection lens without tearing and linked a new motion picture camera with an improved phonograph featuring synchronized sound, producing the "Kinetoscope" that projected "talking" images on screens.

Edison built a West Orange, New Jersey laboratory complex in 1887 which was ten times larger than his famous Menlo Park facility. Its 60,000 square foot main building contained a library with a great three-story hall and two galleries where Edison's desk sat in the center surrounded by 10,000 books. That elegant library became Edison's final resting place upon his death on October 18, 1931. As Russian-born Martin Andre Rosanoff, a chemist hired by "the Old Man" commented:

> *Had Edison been formally schooled, he might not have had the audacity to create such impossible things.*

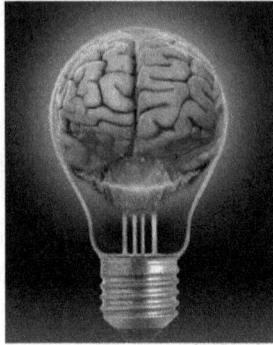

Marie Curie's Radiant Life and Works

MARIE CURRIE, ALSO a contemporary of Einstein, Tesla and Edison, illuminated the field of physics and chemistry in many ways. Against huge odds, she smashed through huge barriers imposed by gender discrimination, nationalistic political prejudice and economic hardship to accomplish great historic scientific discoveries, doing so with strong ethical conviction and an enormously generous spirit of social compassion.

Her discoveries have become everyday terms in both public and scientific lexicons. She coined the word "radioactivity," named the element "polonium" after her beloved native country Poland and defined the international standard for radioactive emissions eventually named for her and her husband Pierre...the "curie."

Dr. Curie's contributions to science are legendary. She was the first person to win the Nobel Prize twice, and the only one to win it in two different fields of science—physics and chemistry.

Together with husband Pierre Curie, and her former professor Henri Becquerel, she was first awarded the 1903 Nobel Prize in Physics...

   ...in recognition of the extraordinary services they

have rendered by their joint researches on the ionizing radiation phenomena discovered by Professor Henri Becquerel.

Just eight years later, Marie Curie received the Nobel Prize in Chemistry…

…in recognition of her services to the advancement of chemistry by the discovery of the elements radium and polonium, by the isolation of radium and the study of the nature and compounds of this remarkable element. [188]

Marie Curie became the first woman ever appointed to teach at Sorbonne University in Paris, where she filled a post formerly held by her deceased husband Pierre, and later founded the Curie Institutes in Paris and Warsaw. She also set a fine example for others in her family who followed her passions and commitments. Her eldest daughter, Irene Joliot-Curie, won the Nobel Prize in Chemistry in 1935.

Still, Marie Curie exhibited a demeanor of hallmark humility throughout her life. Albert Einstein, who knew her well and respected her character, reportedly remarked that she was probably the only person who could not be corrupted by fame. [189]

Strong Philosophical and Professional Principles

Marie subscribed to a personal and scientific outlook of "positivism" introduced by French philosopher August Comte, which stressed empirical rather than theoretical approaches to problem-solving and humanitarian services. This philosophical foundation was evidenced in her strong belief in equal rights for women and non-violent imperatives to achieve constructive social changes.

Her positivist orientation motivated her to seek understanding of mysteries in the world from a scientific than more traditional "God's will" religious perspective. Originally raised in Catholicism, she later became agnostic. This change was likely influenced by the tragic deaths of a sister of typhus fever, followed by her mother of tuberculosis four years later when she was ten years old.

A passage she wrote at age 16 after her cousin's child was stillborn reveals her disdain for false piety:

> *Let everybody keep his own faith so long as it is sincere. Only hypocrisy irritates me—and it is as widespread as true faith is rare...I hate hypocrisy.*[190]

Marie put her true moral convictions into practice. Despite a life of financial hardships, she gave much of her Nobel Prize award money to friends, family, students and research associates, and insisted that other monetary gifts and awards be given to scientific institutions she was affiliated with rather than to herself. She also refrained from patenting the radium-isolation process because she wanted to make it freely available for public good.

Nobel laureate Curie's primary attention later turned to the World War I effort. In 1914, she and her 17-year-old daughter Irene went to battlefront to use their mobile radiography units referred to as "Little Curies" to diagnose injuries of wounded soldiers suffering broken bones and bullet wounds. By the height of the conflict she also raised money that financed auto mechanic shops to construct 20 vehicles to carry the units.

She wrote in a 1915 letter:

*I am resolved to put all my strength at the service of
my adopted country since I cannot do anything for my
unfortunate native country just now.*[191]

Humble and Challenging Beginnings

Maria Sklodowska, (then nicknamed "Manya" and later
becoming Marie Curie), began her life in Warsaw, Poland under
control of the Russian Empire. Her family's economic
conditions were difficult. Manya's once-prosperous paternal and
maternal relatives had lost their properties and fortunes through
patriotic involvements in Polish national uprisings aimed at
restoring independence.

Manya's father was a well-respected mathematics and
physics teacher. He also directed two Warsaw gymnasia schools
for boys which were later shut down by Russian authorities. Her
mother had founded a private boarding school for girls.

Manya was a precocious learner who began reading at age
four. She began attending a boarding school for girls at age ten,
graduating at the top of her class at age 15.

Nevertheless, due to her gender and Russian anti-Polish
policies at the time, she wasn't allowed admission to any
regional university. As an alternative, Manya and her sister
Bronia studied and tutored through an underground Warsaw
educational project known as the "Flying University."

The two sisters remained close and devoted to one another
throughout their lives. Each made an agreement to financially
help the other to advance studies. Manya began by supporting
Bronia's studies in France by first becoming a tutor, and later
working as a governess for a wealthy farming family in a remote
area of Poland.[192]

Bronia returned the bargain by helping her sister move to
Paris at age 24. Manya then became known as "Marie," her
name's French equivalent. Upon arrival, Marie attended high

school at the College Sevigne, and also studied physics and mathematics at the University of Paris.

Marie barely subsisted in Paris on very meager resources. Her clothing was inadequate for cold winter conditions, and she reportedly fainted occasionally from hunger.[193]

Her intelligence and dedication to studies met the challenges of rapidly learning a new language and prevailing over financial hardships. Marie graduated first in her undergraduate classes, and received a master's degree a year later at the Sorbonne. She then went on to receive a doctorate degree in 1903 from City of Paris Industrial Physics and Chemistry Higher Education Institute, becoming the first woman in France ever to complete a doctorate.[194]

Major Scientific Breakthroughs

Marie's experiences at the Sorbonne proved transformative in her life and career. There, she met and married an instructor, Pierre Curie, who shared her passion for science. Together they studied radioactive materials and made important discoveries.

Marie and Pierre Curie initially directed particular attention to uranium products known as pitchblende and torbenite (also called "chalcolite"), both of which had the curious property of being even more radioactive than the uranium extracted from them. Their investigations caused them to deduce that the ore must therefore contain some other unknown radioactive component.

By the end of 1898, they discovered that the ore actually contained not just one, but two previously unknown chemical elements. Marie named one "polonium" after her beloved native Poland. The other was named "radium" after the Latin terms "radius" or "ray." [195]

Scientific interest in the topic of radiation had earlier roots in Wilhelm Roentgen's 1895 discovery of the existence of x-rays, although the mechanism behind their production was not yet understood.

The following year, Henri Becquerel discovered that uranium salts emitted rays that resembled x-rays in penetrating power and that this radiation, unlike phosphorescence, didn't depend upon an external source of energy. Instead, it seemed to arise from the uranium itself. This observation prompted Marie to investigate the strange phenomena as a doctoral thesis under Becquerel's supervision.

Marie, together with her husband, correctly figured out that the radiation emanating from the uranium salts expressed a fundamental property of the atoms of these substances and not only a phenomenon occurring around those atoms. Their studies also revealed that each radioactive element gave off enough of its own energy to disintegrate and reduce the mass of the original substance. These observations contributed advancements to scientific understanding of the structure of atoms.[196]

Entirely appropriate recognition of Henri Becquerel's and Pierre Curie's shared Nobel Prize for these discoveries should not, however, diminish Marie's special distinction in the award.

As reported in the book *Marie Curie* by Robert William Reid:

> *The research idea was her own; no one helped her formulate it, and although she took it to her husband for his opinion she clearly established her ownership of it. She later recorded the fact twice in her biography of her husband to ensure there was no chance of ambiguity. It [is] likely that already at this early stage of her career [she] realized that...many scientists would find it difficult to believe that a woman could be capable of the original work in which she was involved.[197]*

Surviving Personal Tragedy and Public Ridicule

Tragedy intervened in Marie's personal and professional life when her husband and intellectual companion was run over and killed by a horse-drawn carriage. Following Pierre's death, she became scientifically—and later romantically—involved with physicist colleague Paul Langevin who was estranged from his wife at the time.

Media tabloids ruthlessly exploited Marie Curie's high scientific profile to great advantage, accusing her of breaking up his marriage. She was a convenient target. In addition to gender bias towards professional women, she was a foreigner from Poland, a country unfavorably associated with a Russian Tsar.

Marie ended her relationship with Paul Langevin after it became obvious that it would damage her spirit and career. Public attitudes in France towards scandal at that time, particularly towards women "home breakers," tended towards xenophobia.

Later, by strange coincidence, Marie's granddaughter, Helene Langevin-Joliot, married Langevin's grandson, Michael.

Competitors for the coveted Nobel Prize in Chemistry actively attempted to turn bad publicity over the scandal to their own advantages. To his great credit, her former professor and fellow Nobel laureate Henri Bacquerel strongly and successfully supported her for that honor over opposition of those who expressed prejudice against her and women in general.

Still, stresses over the matter seemed to take a toll on Marie's health. After accepting the prize she was hospitalized with depression and kidney problems.

Marie Curie died at age 66 in 1934, and was buried in the same cemetery as her husband Pierre. The cause of her death is generally attributed to either aplastic anemia or leukemia resulting from massive exposures to radiation, which were not generally understood at that time. She was known to carry test tubes full of radioactive isotopes in her pocket, stored samples in her desk drawer, and was exposed to unshielded equipment while serving as a radiologist in field hospitals during the war.

Dr. Curie was even known to remark about the pretty blue-green light that the radioactive metals emitted in the dark.

She literally died for her science. Due to high levels of radioactive contamination, her papers—even her cookbooks—from the 1890s are still considered too dangerous to handle. All remain in lead-lined boxes, and those who wish to access them must wear protective clothing.

Winston Churchill's Bulldog/Black Dog Legacy

SIR WINSTON CHURCHILL, the "British bulldog" who inspired his countrymen to resist German invasions under World War siege by Adolph Hitler, also fought a personal war black dog war against periodic sieges of depression.

Churchill's bulldog and black dog battles occurred at an extremely complex and challenging time when the future of Europe and the United States were at stake. The results would forever be determined by which of three competing ideologies: Fascism, Nazism or Stalinism, our side would choose as vital wartime partners.

Some might also argue that both of those dogs played important roles in contributing to his undisputed legacy as a great world leader at a critical time.

Churchill's Life and Times

Winston Churchill's lasting legacy as a British politician and statesman, military officer and tactician, popular author, accomplished painter and inspirational speaker reveals an impressive whole-brain thinking capacity. All the more remarkably, his oratorical skills overcame speech impediments that few listeners ever became aware of.

Winston was born in 1874 to a life of special privilege in his family's home, Blenheim Palace in Oxfordshire, as a direct descendent of the Dukes of Marlborough among highest ranks of British aristocracy. His paternal grandfather, John Spencer-Churchill, 7th Duke of Marlborough, had been a Member of Parliament (MP) for ten years. His father, Lord Randolph Churchill, had also been an MP.

Although Churchill's mother, Jennie Churchill, was a socialite who came from a wealthy American background, his family tended to live beyond their means and were frequently in debt. His parents were estranged from one another from the time Winston was very young, and he didn't spend much time with either of them.

His father was a remote figure in his life, and he said of his mother, "I loved her dearly, but at a distance." [198]

Young Winston was first introduced to basic reading, writing and arithmetic by his governess, who became a close friend, confident, nurse and mother substitute throughout his life. He was later educated in three independent schools where he was generally known as a stocky boy with red hair who typically earned mediocre grades and talked with a stutter lisp.

Winston's lateral lisp continued throughout his life. He wore specially-designed dentures to aid his diction, and ensured that his public speeches were carefully prepared not only to inspire, but also to avoid impediment hesitations.

Winston Churchill never excelled as a student scholar. While he did well in history and English language courses, he avoided classical studies required for natural advancement to upper school. He finally succeeded in gaining admittance to the Royal Military College in Sandhurst after previously failing the entrance exam three times.

Larry Bell

A Meteoric Political Rise

Winston Churchill's rapid rise to high positions of statesmanship was truly remarkable. Using his mother's influence in high society to arrange military postings in active campaigns, he first came to public prominence as a war correspondent upon serving in the British army during the Anglo-Sudan War and the Second Boer War in South Africa.

By 1904, he abandoned his former conservative political position to become affiliated with the Liberal Party, yet remained staunchly anti-Socialist and suspicious of trade unions. By 1911, he became First Lord of the Admiralty. Churchill served the party between 1914 and 1918 both as President of the Board of Trade and Home Secretary during the First World War.

Churchill was removed from his First Lord of the Admiralty position following a failed 1915 Dardanelles Campaign. Britain had suffered several setbacks during the first months of the war. On September 22, 1914, the German navy sunk a number of British ships at Dogger Bank (60 miles off the east coast of England in the North Sea), killing 1,459 sailors. On the 16th of December, German ships penetrated close enough to British shores to attack Scarborough, Hartlepool and Whitby, causing 137 fatalities.

Altogether, the Dardanelles Campaign, which was intended to knock Turkey out of the war, instead resulted in thousands of Allied casualties with no military gain. Churchill took the brunt of the blame and the public's anger.

There is evidence that Churchill actually enjoyed the war. In July 1914, as Britain prepared for a looming catastrophe, he wrote to his wife: "I am interested, geared up and happy. Is it not horrible to be built like that?"

Churchill admitted in a 1916 letter to David Lloyd George's daughter:

I think a curse should rest on me—because I love this
war. I know it's smashing and shattering the lives of
thousands every moment, and yet, I can't help it, I
enjoy every second of it.[199]

While remaining in the Parliament, Churchill briefly resumed active army service to rehabilitate his reputation on the Western Front as commander of the 6th battalion of the Royal Scott Fusiliers. He also returned to government service as Minister of Munitions, Secretary of State for War and Secretary of State for Air.

By 1930, he was once again a Conservative Party politician who had been a member of British Parliament for three decades. He had also risen to the position of Stanley Baldwin's Chancellor of the Exchequer six years earlier, but was removed from office after proving to be ineffective during a period of peace and prosperity of the 1920s. Churchill was replaced by former Birmingham Mayor Neville Chamberlain, who managed the treasury much better.

Conservative Prime Minister Stanley Baldwin selected Churchill to succeed him when he retired in 1937, a time when storm clouds of war were once again forming overhead.

By 1940, Hitler had torn up a 1938 Munich Agreement signed by Neville Chamberlain, allowing Nazi Germany to annex portions of Czechoslovakia and create a new territory called Sudetenland. Churchill had objected to that pact, charging before the Commons chamber: "You were given the choice between war and dishonor; you chose dishonor and will have war."

Churchill had been warning about threats posed by Nazi Germany, and had campaigned for British rearmament. Those positions were proven right after Hitler's invasion of Poland.

Upon replacing Chamberlain as PM, the social manner of each starkly contrasted with one another. Whereas

Chamberlain's demeanor was sober, polite and friendly, Churchill was brash and often arrogant. He also drank excessively, reportedly quipping: "I have taken more out of alcohol than it has taken out of me." [200]

Churchill's speeches as Prime Minister inspired British courage and resistance as the Commonwealth and Empire stood nearly alone against an impending German invasion during the terribly difficult days of 1940-41. He told the House of Commons on June 4, 1940:

> We shall defend our island, whatever the cost may be, we shall fight on the beaches, we shall fight on the landing grounds, we shall fight in the fields and in the streets, we shall fight in the hills, we shall never surrender. [201]

Later that same month, he told members of Parliament:

> Let us therefore brace ourselves to our duties, and bear ourselves that, if the British Empire and Commonwealth last for a thousand years, men will say, 'This was their finest hour.' [202]

After America entered the war in 1942, the crisis was over. Churchill told the House of Commons: "Now this is not the end. It is not even the beginning of the end. But it is, perhaps, the end of the beginning."

Churchill became Leader of Opposition to the Labour Government following his conservative Party's 1945 defeat. He immediately recognized and warned about yet another emerging threat of an "Iron Curtain" of growing Soviet influence in Europe. These concerns were not new. Addressing the House of Commons in 1937 he had said: "I will not pretend that, if I had to choose between communism and Nazism, I would choose communism." [203]

Winston Churchill's European leadership continued for nearly two decades following Nazi surrender. He was reelected Prime Minister in 1955, while also remaining an MP until 1964.

Black Dog Periods

Throughout his life, Churchill experienced episodes of deep depression which he himself referred to as "black dog" periods. Others today characterize these conditions as likely evidence of manic depression or "bipolar disorder."

As for possible causes, some speculate that such episodes may have been influenced by traumatic external events such as his dismissal from the Admiralty after the Dardanelles disaster in WWI. Another theory might attribute the condition to a physical brain injury which occurred at age 18 when he fell 29 feet from a bridge. He was unconscious for three days, and lay bedridden for three months.

Throughout his life, Churchill occasionally became so paralyzed by despair that he spent extended times in bed, had little energy, few interests, lost appetite, couldn't concentrate and was minimally functional for months. This was known to have happened at least twice during the 1930s, and was also reported in earlier decades.

These dark periods alternated with times of high energy levels when he stayed up dictating dozens of books until two or three in the morning, awakened early and talked incessantly about whirling thoughts. President Franklin D. Roosevelt once remarked: "He has a thousand ideas a day, four of which are good."

Churchill admitted to occasional suicidal impulses. He once recounted:

I don't like standing near the edge of a platform when

Larry Bell

> *an express train is passing through. I like to stand back and, if possible, get a pillar between me and the train. I don't like to stand by the side of a ship and look down into the water. A second's action would end everything. A few drops of desperation.*

He also expressed concerns about his own condition. In a 1911 letter to his wife, Clementine, upon hearing that a friend's wife had received help for depression from a German doctor, he wrote:

> *I think this man might be useful to me—if my black dog returns. It seems quite away from me know—it is such a relief. All colours come back into the picture.*[204]

During his later years, after 1940, Churchill's trusted physician Lord Moran prescribed amphetamines and a barbiturate to help him sleep.

Churchill developed strong interest and considerable skill as a painter of hundreds of landscapes, interior scenes and portraits. This activity appeared to help him overcome periods of depression, particularly following his 1915 forced resignation as First Lord of the Admiralty. His teacher and artist friend Paul Maxe became a lifelong painting companion.[205, 206]

Other satisfying leisure interests included building structures as an amateur bricklayer. One such place was on his residential property, where he bred butterflies.

Some have hypothesized that Winston Churchill's many achievements may have actually resulted from his bipolar condition rather than in spite of it. An essay in psychiatrist historian Anthony Storr's book *Black Dog, Kafka's Mice, and Other Phenomena of the Human Min"* observes:

> *Had he been a stable and equable man, he could*

never have inspired the nation. In 1940, when the odds were against Britain, a leader of sober judgment might well have concluded that we were finished.[207]

As Churchill, who joined Chamberlain's pallbearers, said of his former nemesis in a generous eulogy:

In one phase men seem to have been right, in another they seem to have been wrong. Then again, a few years later, when the perspective of time has lengthened, all stands in a different setting.[208]

He later ended his last speech before the House of Commons in 1955, saying:

The day may dawn when fair play, love for one's fellow men, respect for justice and freedom, will enable tormented generations to march forth triumphant from the hideous epoch in which we have to dwell. Meanwhile, never flinch, never weary, never despair.

Sir Winston Churchill honored his own counsel.

Larry Bell

Stephen Hawking's Cosmic Mindfulness

BRINGING US INTO the present era, it is difficult to imagine a more famously iconic whole brain thinker than Stephen Hawking. His advanced and innovative contributions to theoretical physics and quantum mechanics continue to influence the ways scientists envision the Universe...and perhaps, even a multi-Universe.

Hawking's visionary thinking also demonstrates inspirational personal lessons which each of us can apply to our immediate world. Just as he has visualized a Universe with no time-space boundaries demarking a "Big Bang" beginning or ending, his visionary mind and spirit refuses to be bounded or silenced by physical infirmities.

Background of a Reluctant Genius

Young Stephen Hawking didn't begin his remarkable life as a promising academic scholar. That evidence emerged much later.

Born on January 8, 1943, in Oxford, England, to Frank and Isobel Hawking, he had three siblings: two younger sisters, and an adopted brother. Although his parents weren't wealthy, both had earned degrees from Oxford University College.

The couple originally met shortly after the beginning of the Second World War at a medical clinic in London where Frank was conducting research and Isobel was employed as a secretary. Frank later headed the division of parasitology at Briton's National Institute for Medical Research.

Stephen's parents placed a high value on providing good educations for their children. His own began with a slow start at the Byron House School in Highgate, London, where his reading progress lagged behind expectations.[209, 210]

Nevertheless, Stephen exhibited the outward appearance of a very normal, if not exceptionally brilliant, child. At age eight he attended Saint Albans High School for Girls which admitted boys at one of their houses.[211, 212]

His family's original plan was for Stephen to transfer to a more highly-regarded Westminster School by age 13. This would require him to earn a scholarship because the tuition rates were beyond their economic means.

Having experienced a temporary illness on the critical scholarship examination day, Stephen continued his studies at Saint Albans.

Although not particularly successful academically, Stephen demonstrated an aptitude for scientific subjects. He enjoyed building model airplanes and ships, developed an interest in extrasensory perception, and constructed a simple computer out of clock parts, an old telephone switchboard and other recycled components.[213, 214]

Stephen also began to take a special interest in mathematics, and even considered a pursuit of college study in that field. His father discouraged that idea, preferring instead that his son prepare for a medical career which would afford better employment opportunities. He also wished for Stephen to attend Oxford University College, his and his wife's alma mater.

His father got his second wish...but not his first. At age 17, Stephen's grades were good enough to land him a scholarship at

Oxford, but instead of medicine, he decided to study physics and chemistry. Nevertheless, his scholastic performance continued to be undistinguished…or worse.

He reported being bored and lonely during his first 18 Oxford months, describing the academic work "ridiculously easy." He recognized that his professors regarded him to be a lazy and difficult student. Poor study habits made final exams a difficult challenge, and he focused attention upon answering theoretical physics questions, rather than those requiring factual knowledge.[215, 216]

Those academically unremarkable Oxford years introduced Stephen to other interests and satisfactions, including classical music and science fiction. He also coxed the college rowing team, where his daredevil spirit in steering his team on risky courses damaged some boats.[217, 218]

Stephen's Oxford grades were barely good enough to qualify him for admittance to graduate study at Cambridge University. This would prove to begin a time of legendary personal and intellectual challenges and achievements.

Hawking's Unbounded Universe

Although Stephen was accepted at Cambridge University, his training in mathematics was deemed inadequate to pursue that field of choice. As an alternative, he fortuitously opted to pursue studies in cosmology, and was assigned to work under the supervision of Dennis William Sciama, who was reputed to be a leading expert.[219]

While at Cambridge, Stephen was diagnosed with a rare, early-onset, slow-progressing motor neuron disease referred to as amyotrophic lateral sclerosis (ALS), which has gradually paralyzed him over the decades. This original prognosis, however, was wrong in predicting that he had only two years to live. Stephen led a brilliant and productive life until his death at the age of 76 in 2018.

Despite initially falling into a deep depression after his diagnosis, he returned to his research studies and developed a reputation for both brilliance and brashness, both of which were made manifestly evident when he publicly challenged the work of noted astronomer Fred Hoyle and his student Jayant Narlikar at a June 1964 lecture.[220, 221]

As portrayed in the popular movie, *The Theory of Everything,* Stephen married his first wife Jane Wild whom he met shortly before his diagnosis with ALS...a relationship which he later said gave him something to live for. Their son Robert was born in 1967, daughter Lucy in 1970, and their third child Timothy in 1979.

Stephen's Cambridge doctoral thesis expanded a theorem of a space-time singularity in the center of black holes which had previously been proposed by Roger Penrose for application to the entire Universe. In 1966, Hawking received a PhD in applied mathematics and theoretical physics, specializing in general relativity and cosmology.

During the 1960s, Stephen had been influenced by the works of Branden Carter, Werner Israel and David C. Robinson. There studies had concluded that, as John Wheeler predicted, all black holes can be described by properties of mass, electrical charge and rotation.

In 1970, Hawking postulated what has become known as the *Second Law of Black Hole Dynamics.* It was one of four laws of black hole mechanics he proposed with James M. Bardeen and Branden Carter which drew an analogy to principles of thermodynamics.

His first book, coauthored with George Ellis, was published in 1973: *The Large Scale Structure of Space-Time.* [222, 223]

Discussions with Yakov Borisovich Zeldovich and Alexi Starobinsky during a 1973 trip to Moscow spurred Stephen's interest in the study of quantum gravity and quantum mechanics.

Larry Bell

Their work showed that according to the "Uncertainty Principle," rotating holes emit particles.[224, 225]

Stephen collaborated with Roger Penrose to study and apply gravitational singularity theorems in the framework of General Relativity, leading to a theoretical prediction that black holes emit radiation subsequently referred to as "Hawking radiation." Together, they published a proof that if the Universe obeys the General Theory of Relativity and fits any of the models of physical cosmology, then it must have begun as a singularity.

According to Hawking's theory, black holes can exhaust their energy until they evaporate. This later became accepted as a significant theoretical physics breakthrough. In 1974, soon after publishing that research, he became one of the youngest scientists to be elected as a Fellow of the Royal Society.

Like other advanced theoretical thinkers, Stephen Hawking's concepts haven't always panned out. While serving in 1970 as a visiting professor at the California Institute of Technology (Caltech), he engaged his colleague and friend, Kip Thorne, in a wager that the dark star Cygnus X-1 was a black hole. Some scientists at the time disputed whether black holes even existed. Stephen acknowledged in 1990 that he lost the bet...which was to become the first of several of such losses.

Stephen's 1981 proposal that "information" in a black hole is irretrievably lost when it evaporates violated a growing consensus among physicists. He joined in agreeing with them in January 2014, referring to his previously alleged loss of information in black holes as his "biggest blunder." [226]

Hawking went on to investigate a new line of quantum theory research which might explain how the Universe began. A 1983 model he published with Jim Hartle, now known as the Hartle-Hawking state, proposes that the Universe had no boundary in space-time before the Big Bang.

This proposal replaced the classical Big Bang models by

representing a condition analogous to a model of Earth's globe where one cannot travel north of the North Pole. There is no boundary there either...it is simply where all north-running lines meet. Similarly, any notion regarding the beginning of the Universe also becomes meaningless.[227, 228, 229]

Hawking theorized in 1985 that if his no-boundary proposition is correct, when the Universe stops expanding and eventually collapses, time would then run backwards. A paper by Don Page, along with independent calculations by Raymond Laflamme, led him to withdraw this concept.[230]

Since 2006, along with Thomas Hertog and Jim Hartle, Hawking has developed a "top-down cosmology" which proposes that from a "many worlds" quantum mechanics perspective, the Universe's current configuration cannot be predicted from any one particular initial state. Instead, the Universe had not only one unique initial state, but many.[231, 232, 233]

A Visual Visionary

As ALS gradually robbed Stephen of his ability to write, Hawking developed compensatory visual methods which included seeing equations in terms of geometry. Physicist Werner Israel later compared this with achievements of Mozart composing an entire symphony in his head.[234, 235]

During the 1970s, Stephen transitioned to becoming more intuitive and speculative in his research approach. Rather than always insisting upon mathematical proofs, he told his Caltech friend Kip Thorne, "I would rather be right than rigorous."

By the late 1970s, his speech had also deteriorated to the point where he could only be understood by family and closest friends. He initially communicated by raising his eyebrows to choose letters on a spelling card.

In 1986, an audible device called the "Equalizer" enabled

him to select phrases, words or letters from a program of about 2,500-3,000 menu options which were made accessible through a small computer attachment to his wheelchair. He commented: "I can communicate better now than before I lost my voice."

Stephen's verbally-dictated publishing activity continued. In 1993, he co-edited a book on Euclidean quantum gravity with Gary Gibbons, along with a collected edition of his own articles on black holes and the Big Bang.

In 2005, after losing control of his hands, he began to control a new speech-generating device through movements of cheek muscles. Although British, he stuck with his original American accent version, even after other choices later became available.

As characterized by Jane, his first wife, Stephen was fiercely independent of making concessions for his disability. As she described him, he preferred to be regarded as "a scientist first, popular science writer second, and in all ways that matter, a normal human being with the same desires, drives and dreams as the next person." [236]

She also noted: "Some people would call it determination, some obstinacy. I've called it both at one time or another." He resisted use of a wheelchair until the end of the 1960s, and then ultimately returned to his spirited Oxford racing boat days to become notorious for wild wheelchair driving. [237]

Later pressures on that marriage resulting from the impacts of his celebrity status, intrusions into their family lives by nurses and assistants and contrasting views with his wife regarding her religious faith, reportedly influenced a divorce. Whereas Jane was a devout Christian, Stephen has stated that he is "not religious in the normal sense," and believes that "the Universe is governed by the laws of science." [238]

During a 2011 American *Discovery Channel* interview, he reflected:

We are each free to believe what we want, and it is my view that the simplest explanation is that there is no God. No one created the Universe and no one directs our fate. This leads me to a profound realization. There is probably no heaven, and there is no afterlife either. We have one life to appreciate the grand design of the Universe, and for that, I am extremely grateful.

He commented in another interview with El Mundo:

Before we understand science, it is natural to believe that God created the Universe. But now science offers a more convincing explanation. What I meant by 'we know the mind of God' is we would know everything that God would know, if there was a God, which there isn't. I'm an atheist.[239]

But perhaps, as I observed in my previous book *Cosmic Musings: Life Beyond Self,* answers to God questions aren't really nearly that simple after all.

And as discussed in the very next section of this book, connections between emerging sciences of quantum mechanics and metaphysical theories take on tantalizingly religious implications as well.

Larry Bell

Part Three: Extreme Thinking

SCIENTIFIC ADVANCEMENTS HAVE led us to thresholds of strange new worlds of contemplation beyond familiar references of human experience. Quantum theory, for example, has uprooted traditional Newtonian views of a Universe where time is linear, gravity "pulls," space has measurable dimensions, or even that a singular "reality" exists outside the influence of our individual thoughts.

Transformational innovations of this new era are applying observed, yet poorly understood, principles to create thinking machines with seemingly limitless capacities. Such inventions are already extending—even redefining—the meaning of "artificial intelligence."

If humans can invent machines which are increasingly smarter than we are, where does this lead? Are we in a sense "playing God" in a way that will render human reasoning obsolete? Can we integrate technological "thinking parts" into our biological anatomy to repair and replace failed sensory and motor response systems...just as we presently do with other organ and limb prosthetic devices?

Can we successfully compete with smart and tireless autonomous systems in commercial work settings? Are we ultimately destined to become extensions, as well as extenders,

176

of our innovations? And as Christof Koch asks...

> ...*will the products of our discovery and innovation influence us to reinvent ourselves with the "bigger brains" which will be needed to keep pace with our inventions?*

Throughout history, wonderfully resourceful minds have enabled humans to anticipate, adapt to and survive extreme circumstances. Those same powers of imagination and intellect which have transported members of our species to the Moon and back, now lift us forward to explore new worlds of challenge and opportunity.

In doing so, our greatest discoveries may reveal marvelous human potentials we have never fully appreciated.

Larry Bell

Alternate Realities of Quantum Mechanics

WHATEVER SKEPTICAL VIEWS Stephen Hawking and Albert Einstein may have expressed about God and religion, both have delved deeply into mysterious workings of nature at a subatomic level which, to our conventional senses, take on extrasensory, supernatural manifestations.

The "new science" of quantum mechanics goes so far as to suggest a "preposterous" possibility that everything in the physical Universe exists only as illusory inventions of our individual minds. Whereas this concept presents a radical departure from traditional Western thought, it doesn't seem nearly so alien to much older Eastern philosophies.

Generally speaking, whereas Western philosophies tend to emphasize learning new things about what reality is, ancient Hindu and Buddhist literature speaks of removing veils of ignorance that stand between us and what we really are. And where Western religions tend to envision a Universe divided into separate material and spiritual aspects, Eastern teachings make no dichotomous distinctions between material and spiritual manifestations.

Quantum mechanics challenges any notion of material

Thinking Whole

reality altogether, making no distinction between mass (quanta) and their energetic and mysteriously unpredictable relationships with individual observers. In doing so, it has yielded replicable evidence that powers of mind over matter, and realities much stranger than presumed fictions, can no longer be casually dismissed merely as quack clichés.

New Worlds of Science and Thought

As Gary Zukav observes in his illuminating book *The Dancing Wu Li Masters: An Overview of the New Physics,* the "new physics" shakes foundations of the "old" physics. The "old physics" has assumed that there is an external world "out there" which exists apart from the "I" which is "in here." This "I" within each of us can observe and measure the world without changing it.[240]

Zukav urges us to reconsider the old, traditional way of thinking which emphasizes that an "absolute truth" exists "out there" which we become closer to understanding each time our scientific approximations become closer to explaining it. Such explanations don't necessarily reflect the way things (or phenomenon) really are...or as Einstein put it, "We still will not be able to open the watch."

While Einstein made major contributions to the development of quantum mechanics theory, he spent much of his career arguing against it. He nevertheless acknowledged its advantages in explaining subatomic phenomena. Most importantly, it worked.

Niels Bohr, a Danish physicist who earned a Nobel Prize in 1922 for his contributions to quantum mechanics, argued famously with Einstein on the subject. Einstein lamented, "Alas, our theory is too poor for experience." Whereas Bohr replied, "No, no! Experience is too rich for our theory."[241]

Perhaps the most astonishing evidence of quantum mechanics weirdness relates to experiments where a single

Larry Bell

photon of light is projected from a precise position towards two slits on shielding wall in front of a photographic plate that records which one the photon passes through. Whichever mark was randomly checked first by any observer invariably correlated with the recorded placement of the hit, whereas the other slit option was always blank.

The astounding question is how light knows which slit to pass through at the precise moment it is being observed? There is presently still no way to predict this.

American mathematical physicist and quantum mechanics theorist Henry Stapp wrote:

> The central mystery of quantum theory is, how does information get around so quick? How does the particle know there are two slits? How does the information about what is happening elsewhere else get collected to determine what is likely to happen here? [242]

Some noted scientists, Stephen Hawking included, argue that quantum theory supports a simultaneous "many worlds" state of reality. One interpretation of this possibility is illustrated by "Schrödinger's Cat," a thought experiment proposed by Viennese physicist Erwin Schrödinger.

Imagine that a cat is insidiously placed inside a sealed box with a device which can release poisonous gas to kill it. There is a 50 percent chance that the random decay of a particular atom in the killing device will trigger the gas to be released within a specified period of time before the box is to be opened. As with Einstein's unopenable watch, we can't witness what happens from outside the box...and we won't know if the poor cat is alive or dead until we open it.

We logically assume that there is either good news or bad for the cat even before we open the box...both conditions can't possibly be true. Strangely, a quantum theory interpretation suggests otherwise, whereby the cat is in a kind of limbo...both alive *and* dead at the same time.

At the instant someone looks into the box, that observer's "wave function" splits the world into two branches, each with a different edition of the cat. One reality branch has the cat being alive, and the other has the cat exhausting at least one of its nine lives. It follows then, that just as there are different simultaneous editions of the cat in different worlds, there are uncountable editions of us...all of which are equally "real."

There are many other interpretations of quantum mechanics...all of which seem unbelievably strange.

As Werner Heisenberg, one of the key quantum mechanics founders, wrote:

> *I remember discussions with Bohr [in 1927] which went through many hours till very late at night and ended almost in despair; and when at the end of the discussion I went alone for a walk in the neighborhood park I repeated to myself again and again the question: Can nature possibly be as absurd as it seemed to us in those experiments?* [243]

Heisenberg is credited with validating a fundamental "uncertainty principle" where, unlike Newtonian physics which works well in the visible world, in the subatomic realm it is impossible to know both the exact position and momentum of a particle at the same time. The more we know about one condition, the less we know about the other. We are then left to choose which of these two properties we wish to determine.

Not knowing exactly where a particle is and where it is headed makes it impossible to calculate what will happen next. The only option is to assign a certain probability that a particular group of such particles will likely behave in a certain way...a "tendency" for something to happen.

As Heisenberg described this uncertain tendency:

> It was a quantitative version of the old concept of 'potential' in Aristotelian philosophy. It introduced something standing in the middle between the idea of an event and the actual event, a strange kind of physical reality just in the middle between possibility and reality.[244]

Whereas Newton's laws depict events which are quite easy to understand and picture, probabilities of phenomena addressed by quantum mechanics defy conceptualization, and are impossible to visualize. They also defy logic as we understand it.

Heisenberg wrote:

> The mathematically-formulated laws of quantum theory show clearly that our ordinary intuitive concepts cannot be unambiguously applied to the smallest particles. All the words or concepts we use to describe ordinary physical objects, such as position, velocity, color, size, and so on, become indefinite and problematic if we try to use them of elementary particles.[245]

Traditional science works to construct theories such that for every evidence of "absolute truth," there is a corresponding element in the theories. This is not the case with quantum theory.

Newton, for example, applied his investigations to calculate movements of the Moon and planets around the Sun using his own mathematics. His findings matched observations of astronomers, establishing a rational celestial mechanics which viewed the Universe as a "Great Machine." Without Newtonian physics, human space programs would never have occurred.

Nevertheless, even Newton couldn't explain how gravitational influences on static and moving bodies of that Great Machine "really" worked. As he wrote in his famous *Philosophiae Naturalis Principia Mathematica*:

> ...*I have not been able to discover the cause of these properties of gravity from phenomena, and I frame no hypotheses...it is good enough that gravity does really exist, and act accordingly to the laws which we have explained, and abundantly serves to account for all the motions of the celestial bodies...*[246]

Newton recognized that the very idea of gravitational forces reaching across space seemed to be foolish. He wrote to fellow scholar Richard Bently:

> ...*that one body may act upon another at a distance through a vacuum without the mediation of anything else, by and through which their action and force may be conveyed from one to another, is to me so great an absurdity that, I believe, no man who has in philosophic matters a competent faculty of thinking could ever fall into it.*[247]

Nevertheless, as Einstein pointed out, quantum mechanics doesn't replace Newtonian physics:

> ...*creating a new theory is not like destroying an old barn and erecting a skyscraper in its place. It is rather like climbing a mountain, gaining new and wider views, discovering unexpected connections between our starting point and its rich environment. But the point from which we started out still exists and can be seen,*

although it appears smaller and forms a tiny part of
our broad view gained by the mastery of the obstacles
on our adventurous way up.[248]

Stretching Minds—Thinking Small

Although Newtonian physics works wonderfully well to describe and predict events in our "everyday world," it cannot account for phenomena in the subatomic realm which appear to be governed by very different rules.

How small is subatomic? First, we can't even actually "see" an atom, much less, like Einstein's unopenable watch, view what is inside. All scientists can do is speculate about what is there based upon certain observations regarding how atoms tend to behave...which, in turn depends upon specific means and methods by which they are observed.

Quantum mechanics has changed the way scientists previously visualized the atom as being much like a tiny model of our Solar System with a Sun-like nucleus in the center. The subatomic nucleus was envisioned to contain nearly all of the atom's mass in the form of positively-charged particles (protons)...along with particles about the same size as the protons but without a charge (neutrons). Hydrogen, a lone exception, is the only atom with no neutrons in its nucleus.

Orbiting the nucleus, like planets orbit the Sun, are electrons containing almost no mass (compared with the nucleus), each having one negative charge. The number of electrons and protons is always the same so that the atom, as a whole, has no charge.

The new quantum theory model presents a vision which is quite different both in reference to substance and scale.

As Henry Stapp explained to the Atomic Energy Commission:

...an elementary particle is not a structure built out of independently existing unananalyzable entities, but rather a web of relationships between elements whose meanings arise wholly from their relationships to the whole...It is, in essence, a set of relationships that reach outward to other things. [249]

Size comparisons of subatomic particles with our Solar System are also dramatically different, whereby distances between an atomic nucleus and its electrons are far greater. According to Ernest Rutherford, who created a model of the atom in 1911, the space occupied by an atom compared with its orbiting electrons are "like a few flies in a cathedral."

Even that model is now obsolete. As described by Gary Zukav, the difference between the atomic level and subatomic level is as great as the difference between the atomic level and the entire planet.

Zukav writes:

It would be impossible to see the nucleus of an atom the size of a grape. In fact, it would be impossible to see the nucleus of an atom the size of a room. To see a nucleus the size of an atom, the atom would have to be as high as a fourteen-story building! [250]

For another comparison, Zukav asks us to imagine an atom as the size of a grain of sand in the center of the dome of Saint Peter's basilica in the Vatican, with electrons the size of dust particles revolving around its outer edge. However, unlike dust particles which can be visualized as "things," quantum mechanics views subatomic particles only as "tendencies to exist" or "tendencies to happen" which can only be "seen" in the form of mathematical probabilities.

Subatomic "particles" aren't actually real particles made of "stuff," yet for convenience are statistically measured as quanta in terms of energy units in the same way as particles. These quanta unceasingly change measurable appearances from energy to mass and back, although "within a common identity."

In 1900, Max Planck was the first physicist to calculate the sizes of "energy packets" (quanta) in various waves of light frequency (color) using his mathematical invention famously known as "Planck's constant." All of those packets of color, red for example, have the same size.

It should be noted that those "waves" of light can also be measured as energy "particles" which don't contain any physical "stuff." Depending upon which equipment we select to observe it, some experiments show that light is wave-like, while others show that it is a particle-like phenomenon.

This "wave-particle duality" paradox presents a perplexing dilemma for scientists who like tidy and definitive answers. Thomas Young's 1903 experiments showed that light must be wave-like, while Einstein "proved" that it is particle-like.

Einstein's theory proposed that light is comprised of tiny particles (photons) analogous to a stream of bullets, whereby energy itself, is quantized. He termed this a "photoelectric effect."

As Planck described Einstein's theory:

> ...the photons (the 'drops' of energy) do not grow smaller as the energy of the ray grows less; what happens is that their magnitude remains unchanged and they follow each other at greater intervals.[251]

Einstein was not able to dispute the contradiction between light as a wave versus light as quanta, but simply took the contradiction as something which would probably be understood later. Nevertheless, while he is far more famous for two revolutionary theories of relativity, both were based upon his discoveries regarding the quantum nature of light which earned him a Nobel Prize.

In 1913, Danish physicist Niels Bohr came up with an explanation that also earned him a Nobel Prize. Bohr speculated that electrons revolve around the nucleus of an atom at specific distances and in precise orbits, or "shells." When an atom such as hydrogen is excited with heat or white light, it causes an electron to jump into one of the outer shells. How far it jumps depends upon how much energy it receives. The electron eventually returns back to shell number one and emits energy in the form of light.

It was Einstein's fascination with the mysterious nature of light that led to his discovery that $E=mc^2$ (where energy is proportional to mass multiplied by the extraordinarily huge number of the speed of light squared). While that equation appears to be remarkably short and simple, it has since enabled humanity to harness the power contained in tiny atoms both to power prosperity and to annihilate itself.

The first of Einstein's breakthrough discoveries, his Special Theory of Relativity, affirms that as with quantum mechanics, appearances of events are relative and dependent upon the observers.

This theory fundamentally tells us three things. First, a moving object measures shorter in the direction of motion as its velocity increases until it reaches the speed of light and disappears. Second, the mass of a moving object measures greater as its velocity increases, until it becomes infinite at the speed of light. Third, moving clocks run more slowly as their velocities increase, until they reach the speed of light.

Here, space and time are not two separate things, but together form space-time where energy and mass are actually different forms of the same thing. How these mass versus energy determinations are measured is influenced by how fast the object and observer are moving relative to one another.

To a very high-velocity space traveler, her wristwatch (if it is a good one), appears to keep perfect time...ticking off sixty seconds each minute. Yet as she accelerates faster and faster, and if her watch also simultaneously communicated its recorded time back to Earth, the reception intervals between seconds, minutes, hours, days and years would grow longer. Ultimately, centuries might pass on Earth during but a few years of her high-velocity experience.

Einstein's remarkable theory is based upon the similarly astounding constancy of the 186,000 miles per second speed that light travels irrespective of any and all observers. Whether measured as a wave or a particle, or whether the velocity of a photon is measured while moving away from or towards an observer, that constant never varies.

Imagine, in contrast, that someone walking at a speed of two miles per hour onboard a train traveling 60 miles per hour is clocked through a window by an observer as it passes a boarding station. If that person is walking in the same direction the train is moving, her measured velocity would be 62 miles per hour...58 if she were walking toward the caboose.

Now compare this with clocking the velocity of a photon fired from the front of that train detected at a stationary target many miles ahead. Logic would predict that by adding the velocity of the train to that of the photon, accurate measurements would record a slightly higher net photon speed. That simply doesn't happen...not even for a photon fired by a rocket ship traveling at 100,000 miles per second as clocked at a recording station on another planet.

Thinking Outside the Cave

Plato's allegory *Phaedo* likens our understanding of the objects and phenomena by which we perceive the world to the experience of emerging from a dark cave into sunlight where only vague shadows of what lies beyond that prison are cast dimly upon the wall. Those shadow forms of perception are both non-physical and non-mental, existing nowhere in time, space, mind or matter.

Quantum mechanics and Einstein's Special and General Theories of Relativity beckon us to move our minds beyond caves of previous time-space references.

Briefly summarized, using light velocity as a measurement constant, Einstein's Special Theory of Relativity demonstrates that two events which happen at the same time in one frame of reference may occur at different times when seen from another frame of reference.

Einstein's realization that moving clocks change their rhythm led Einstein to the conclusion that "now," "sooner," "later," and "simultaneous" are relative terms which depend upon the state of motion of the observer. This seems counterintuitive, particularly since the time differences are much too small for those of us who live low-velocity Earthbound existences.

Meanwhile, classical Newtonian laws work just fine until we reach velocities approaching the speed of light. That one-dimensional view of time is entirely separate from our three-dimensional perception of space through which we can locate all objects, ourselves included, in a statically measurable coordinate matrix. [252]

Einstein's space-time continuum is very different, wherein time is fully integrated as a fourth dimension of reality. Although we can't actually "see" that dimension, it serves to define relationships expressible through Pythagorean-like diagrams and mathematical constructions which can be experimentally verified. Those diagrams have not only extended our sense of reality beyond our sensory experiences, but beyond our traditional perceptions of what constitutes common sense as well.

Larry Bell

As Gary Zukav observes:

The General Theory of Relativity shows us that our minds follow different rules than the real world does.

Rational minds operate on impressions they receive from limited perspectives, just as those imprisoned in Plato's cave do, to form structures which determine what they will and will not accept freely. This limited perspective is based upon human sensory information which perceives a three-dimensional coordinate system within tiny time and place references in the Universe.

Einstein discovered that such observational laws are valid only in certain regions of space where we reside. As our experience expands, we encounter more difficulty superimposing that reality upon other expanses where the rules no longer work.

General Relativity extends Einstein's Special Relativity theory, which applied only to coordinate systems moving uniformly relatively to each other, in order to examine phenomenon seen from two different frames of reference where one is moving uniformly and the other is moving non-uniformly. In other words, it describes events which occur in a coordinate system that is moving non-uniformly in terms which are meaningful to an observer in a coordinate system which is moving uniformly.

For example, imagine that the cable supporting an elevator in a very tall building snaps so that the compartment plummets downward. The people inside are unaware that this has happened because they can't look outside. According to Newton's Law of Gravity, the cabin accelerates as it falls...therefore its motion is not uniform.

Something strange happens within the cabin. Under normal conditions, an object dropped by someone, a pen or handkerchief for example, would fall towards the floor. Gravity would "pull" it there, just as it ordinarily holds the passengers to the floor. In this falling elevator case, however, they observe that the dropped objects won't fall, but simply hang in the air. If one were given a push, it would go straight forward until it hit an inside wall of the cabin.

To the observers inside the falling cabin who are experiencing an "inertial coordinate system," there are no forces acting upon any objects around them. Nevertheless, rules of Newton's physics still apply...an object at rest remains at rest, an object in motion remains in motion, and for every reaction, there is an equal and opposite reaction. If one of the passengers pushed a handkerchief, the handkerchief would seem to push back...but with a force too small to be readily detected.

Sadly, the force they will experience when the elevator cabin reaches the bottom of its shaft is quite a different matter altogether. It's probably better that the clueless passengers aren't aware of this abrupt and final end point.

Einstein concluded from such a thought experiment that gravity is equivalent to acceleration...a realization which led to his General Theory of Relativity. This entailed two ways of envisioning mass. One is gravitational mass, or the "weight" of an object that might be measured on a balance scale...the amount of force the Earth appears to tug on the object. The second type of mass is inertial mass...a measure of the resistance of an object to acceleration or deceleration (which is simply negative acceleration). This is why a pen and feather dropped in a vacuum with no air resistance would fall at exactly the same velocity.

Einstein wasn't the first to discover that inertial mass and gravitational mass are equivalent; this was recognized three hundred years earlier, but was disregarded as merely a coincidence. Einstein decided that it was just too much of a coincidence to be ignored.

He reasoned that his Special Theory of Relativity, which

deals with un-accelerated (uniform) motion, was inadequate to describe much of what is going on in most of our Universe. Included are remote regions of space which are far from centers of gravity, as well as within very small subatomic regions of space…the domain of quantum mechanics.

Einstein's visualized the Universe as a relatively flat plane which is curved by large masses such as celestial bodies which cause "bumps." The larger the masses, the larger the flat space-time "distortions." A mass the size of a star causes a relatively big bump, compared with orbiting planets which take the easiest paths around them.

Planets and other objects in our Solar System move as they do not because of gravity exerted upon them as a distance from the Sun, but rather because of the terrain of the neighborhood they are traveling through. English astronomer, physicist and mathematician Sir Arthur Stanley Eddington drew an analogy involving a big sunfish he whimsically, and perhaps appropriately, named "Albert."

As we peer from our boat into the clear water, we observe that all smaller fish appear to be repelled from a point near the sandy lake bottom. They swim either to the left or right of it, but never over it. When we look closer, we notice that Albert has buried himself in the sand and has created a sizeable mound exactly at that spot. As the fish approach, they are simply following the easiest available path around Albert's mound.

Eddington offered this analogy to illustrate that if we could visualize Einstein's space-time continuum model, we would understand that planets do not move around the Sun because of "forces between them," but rather because of the geography (geometry) along their pathways. We can't directly see that geometry because it is four-dimensional, while our sensory experience is limited to only three dimensions.

Imagine life in a flat world of two-dimensional people who have only height and width and no concept of a third dimension.

A straight line between them would appear as a wall which they can walk around but never step over in a mysterious (to them) third dimension. Spheres would not exist in their experiences… only circles. In a flat world, which they can only exist within— not on the surface of—two individuals setting off in opposite directions would never meet again.

Another way to help visualize influences of gravity (acceleration) upon space-time is to imagine a coordinate grid marked upon a stretched membrane of rubber with all lines straight, and all time clocks synchronized.

Wherever there is a large "piece of matter" such as the Sun, it distorts (curves) the space-time continuum membrane so that planets are deflected from straight line paths. Like the fish in Eddington's analogy, they take the easiest path around it.

Einstein's General Theory of Relativity seems both beautifully elegant and enormously challenging to comprehend. On one hand, it informs us that the presence of mass/energy determines the geometry of space, and that simultaneously, the geometry of space determines the motion of mass/energy. Planets (chunks of matter) which had previously been regarded to be held in orbits around the Sun by gravitational attraction (force fields), are more realistically described as taking easiest paths through the curved space-time topography.

Yet just as that gravitational attraction exists only as the equivalent of motion, there is also no real "thing" as "matter," which exists only as a curvature in the space-time continuum. There is really not even such a thing as "energy," which only exists as mass operating in, and simultaneously influences space-time curvature.

And, to top it off, this can only really be described using very complex mathematics, where a fourth dimension—time— exists only in theoretical equations. Nonetheless, so far, it all works.

Minds over Matters

So what if matter is only illusory after all? Does it really matter?

And if time is merely a non-linear contrivance—no previous "past" leading to a present "now" followed by a future and unknowable "when"—will this change normal routines such as having to get bills paid "on time"? Don't try that particularly dangerous experiment at home. Should we perhaps just reconcile ourselves to be satisfied to live in a three-dimensional world, or at least one that gives every outward appearance to our five senses of being one? After all, since that fourth dimension primarily exists in mathematical theorems and multi-world hypotheses, it won't change pragmatic realities and responsibilities which demand our single-world attention.

Sure, but isn't it also interesting to contemplate how some of those subatomic mysteries connect with a really big Universe of metaphysical potentials which simultaneously exist in both the "in here" within each of us and the "out there" which we are all part of? Consider, for example, that distinctions between organic (living) and inorganic (inanimate) stuff are meaningless at the subatomic level. As Gary Zukav points out:

> Some biologists believe that a single plant cell carries within it the capability to reproduce the entire plant. Similarly, the philosophical implication of quantum mechanics is that all of the things in our Universe (including us) that appear to exist independently are actually parts of one all-encompassing organic pattern, and that no parts of that pattern are ever really separate from it or each other." [253]

And how is it possible for those incredibly teensy particles and/or waves to instantaneously "know" what decisions are being made elsewhere and anywhere—then appear to "exist" here and there at the same space-time? Might this imply that being both here and there at the same time indicates that all particles—the ones that make up you and me very much included—are integrally connected within an in here/out there Universe of "everywhere"?

Is there such a "thing" as a conscious Universe which cannot be consciously accessed through our five senses alone? Physicist E.H. Walker has speculated that even photons may be conscious:

> *Consciousness may be associated with all quantum processes...since everything that occurs is ultimately the result of one or more quantum mechanical events, the Universe is 'inhabited' by an almost unlimited number of rather discrete conscious, usually unthinking entities that are responsible for the detailed working of the Universe.*[254]

Quantum theory delves bravely into such ideas, while simultaneously suggesting that all ideas regarding "absolute truths" are illusory. As Gary Zukav explains, "All attempts to describe 'reality' are relegated to the realm of metaphysical speculation." Zukav describes this scientific and mental paradox:

> *The mind is such that it deals only with ideas. It is not possible for the mind to relate to anything other than ideas. Therefore, it is not correct to think that the mind actually can ponder reality. All the mind can ponder is its ideas about reality. (Whether or not that is the way reality actually is, is a metaphysical issue.) Therefore, whether or not something is true is not a matter of how closely it corresponds to the absolute truth, but of how consistent it is with our experience.*[255]

Larry Bell

Henry Pierce Stapp summed up the foundational philosophy, saying:

> [Quantum mechanics] was essentially a rejection of the presumption that nature could be understood in terms of elementary space-time realities. According to the new view, the complete description of nature at the atomic level was given by probability functions that referred, not to understanding microscopic space-time realities, but rather to the macroscopic objects of sense experience. The theoretical structure did not extend down and anchor itself on fundamental space-time realities. Instead, it turned back and anchored itself in the concrete sense realities that form the basis of social life...This pragmatic description is to be contrasted with descriptions that attempt to peer 'behind the scenes' and tell us what is 'really happening.' [256]

As science peers behind those scenes, a growing body of evidence indicates that the distinction between the "in here" and the "out there" is an illusion.

As Gary Zukav observes:

> Now, after three centuries, the Scientists have returned with their discoveries. They are as perplexed as we are (those who have given thought to what is happening). 'We are not sure,' they tell us, 'but we have accumulated evidence which indicates that the key to understanding the Universe is you.'

Zukav concludes: "If the new physics has led us anywhere, it is back to ourselves." [257]

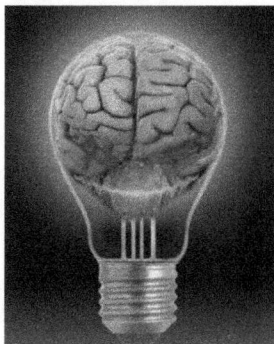

Thinking Hard and Fast

DO UNCERTAINTY PRINCIPLES and other quantum mechanics observations have any relevant correlations with how we actually think and make decisions? Daniel Kahneman, who received a 2002 Nobel Prize in Economics, and his former (now-deceased) colleague Amos Tversky seem to think so.

This is what they wrote in a 1974 Science journal article titled *Judgment under Uncertainty: Heuristics and Biases*:

> *Many decisions are based on beliefs concerning the likelihood of uncertain events such as the outcome of an election, the guilt of a defendant or the future value of the dollar. These beliefs are usually expressed in statements such as 'I think that...', 'chances are...', 'it is unlikely that...', and so forth. Occasionally, beliefs concerning uncertain events are expressed in numerical form as odds or subjective possibilities. What determines such beliefs? How do people assess the probability of an uncertain event or the value of an uncertain quantity?*
>
> *...the subjective assessment of probability resembles the subjective assessment of physical*

quantities such as distance or size. These judgments are all based on data of limited validity, which are processed according to heuristic rules. For example, the apparent distance of an object is determined in part by its clarity. The more sharply the object is seen, the closer it appears to be. This rule has some validity, because in any given scene the more distant objects are seen less sharply than nearer objects. However, the reliance on this rule leads to systematic errors in the estimation of distance. Specifically, distances are overestimated when visibility is poor because the contours of objects are blurred. On the other hand, distances are underestimated when visibility is good because the objects are seen sharply. Thus, the reliance on clarity as an indication of distance leads to common biases. Such biases are also found in the intuitive judgment of probability.[258]

Systems of Thought

Daniel Kahneman's popular New York Times bestseller book *Thinking Fast and Slow* also presents insights into two fundamental "systems" of mental awareness that influence our individual tendencies to view a particular situation one way or another.[259]

Kahneman characterizes patterns of thinking into separate modes: a System 1 that operates automatically (quickly, intuitively and impulsively); and a System 2 which is "heuristic" (slow, contemplative and judgmental). While not expressed in these terms by the author, we might therefore associate System 1 as characterizing a right-brain-dominant mode, and associating System 2 with left-brain tendencies.

As Kahneman further explains, System 1 detects and observes simple relationships such as "they are all alike" and "the son is much taller than the father." While this mode excels at integrating information about one thing, it doesn't deal well with multiple distinct topics at once...or at processing purely statistical information.[260, 261]

Kahneman points out that the main function of System 1 is to maintain and update a model of your personal world which represents what is normal in it:

> The model is constructed by associations that link ideas of circumstances, events, actions and outcomes that co-occur with some regularity, either at the same time or within a relatively short interval. As these links are formed and strengthened, the pattern of associated ideas comes to represent the structure of events in your life, and it determines your interpretation of the present as well as your expectations of the future.[262]

Heuristic thinking, (slow thinking) on the other hand, is more attentive to what is going on around it. And whereas it articulates reasoned choices and judgments and moderates System 1 impulses and behaviors from overt expression, it is often susceptible to endorsing or rationalizing questionable ideas and feelings generated by System 1.

Viewed separately, both systems have basic problems and strengths. Although System 1 is the origin of much of what we do wrong, it is also the origin of what we do right—which is most of what we do.[263]

System 1 encourages us to view the world as more tidy, predictable and coherent than it really is. It supports comforting illusions that past experiences can enable us to predict and control the future. This is often necessary to reduce the anxieties we would experience if we allowed ourselves to fully acknowledge disturbing uncertainties of existence. Without reassurances from System 1, we would tend to avoid worthwhile, yet problematic, enterprises which reward confidence and courage.[264]

System 2 checks System 1 to help keep it from making foolish and dangerous choices. One way it does this is to unconsciously substitute a response to an easier problem. As George Polya wrote in his book *How to Solve It:* "If you can't solve a problem, then there is an easier problem you can solve: find it." [265]

Kahneman summarizes tendencies of both systems we are likely to recognize from time to time in almost everyone... ourselves included.[266]

System 1:

- Operates automatically and quickly, with little or no effort, and with no sense of voluntary control.

- Generates impressions, feelings and inclinations; when endorsed by System 2, these become beliefs, attitudes and intentions.

- Distinguishes the surprising from the normal; it infers and invents causes and intentions.

System 2:

- Frames decision problems narrowly, in isolation from one another; it focuses on existing evidence, and ignores absent evidence.

- Generates a limited set of assessments; it neglects ambiguity and suppresses doubt; it sometimes substitutes an easier question for a difficult one.

- Is often biased to believe and confirm; it links a sense of cognitive ease to illusions of truth and pleasant feelings.

Research by psychologists Keith Stanovich at the University of Toronto and Richard West at James Madison University, Virginia corroborates the concept of "two minds" posited by Daniel Kahneman and Amos Tversky. In Stanovich's book *Rationality and the Reflective Mind* he refers to "algorithmic" thinking (System 2) as slow thinking which demands computation, as compared with "reflective" thinking (System 1) which involves more superficial thinking.[267, 268]

Stanovich and West were particularly interested in determining differences among individuals that influence why some are more susceptible to biases than others. Here, System 1 and System 2 thinkers both express certain vulnerabilities.

Stanovich observes that whereas algorithmic thinkers tend to perform best on intelligence tests (such as IQ exams), this doesn't necessarily indicate that they are more rational or immune to biases. A truly rational person tends to be more "engaged." However, a superficial thinker may also have a tendency to apply biased "lazy mind" thinking to answer questions with their first idea that comes to mind without checking the facts and assumptions.

Kahneman provides a simple "bat-and-ball" puzzle to test people's tendency to answer questions with the first idea that comes to mind without checking it:[269]

- A bat and ball cost $1.10

- The bat costs one dollar more than the ball.

- How much does the ball cost?

The answer number that probably intuitively comes to your mind is 10 cents...wrong! Doing the math: if the ball costs 10 cents, then the total cost would be $1.20 ($0.10 for the ball, and $1.10 for the bat). The correct answer is 5 cents.

Don't feel too badly. Many thousands of university students, including 50 percent of those at Harvard, MIT and Princeton, gave the same intuitive incorrect answer.

Here's another puzzle:[270]

- All roses are flowers. Some flowers fade quickly.

- Therefore, some roses fade quickly.

A large majority of responders bought into this flawed syllogism. It is possible that there are no roses among the flowers that fade quickly.

Daniel Kahneman points out that biases introduced by either fast or slow thinking can't readily be turned off. On many occasions, the lazy System 2 will simply adopt the suggestions of System 1 and move on.[271, 272]

The best we can do is learn to recognize situations in which we make mistakes and try harder to avoid them when the stakes are high. It's easier to recognize other people's mistakes than our own.

Exercising Successful Intuition

Our intuition draws upon memories and biases gained through past experiences which engage and integrate immediate and deliberative thinking processes. Here, Kahneman observes that expertise born out of mental practice plays an important role in honing accurate and balanced intuitive judgments and choices.

Kahneman reminds us that we have intuitive feelings and opinions about almost everything that comes our way. We like or distrust people long before we know much about them; we trust or distrust strangers without knowing why; we feel that an enterprise is bound to succeed without analyzing it.

Whether we state them or not, we often have overly confident answers to questions that we don't completely understand, relying on evidence that we can neither explain nor defend. We also fool ourselves by constructing flimsy accounts of the past failures and successes, believing they are true.[273, 274]

System 1 readily indulges narrative fallacies borne out of attempts to make sense of the world through explanatory stories we find compelling and simple. As Kahneman observes, these perceptions favor pictures of reality which are concrete rather than abstract; assign larger roles to talent, stupidity, and intentions rather than luck; and focus upon a few striking examples that happened, rather than on the countless events that failed to happen.

Whereas some predictive judgments rely largely on precise System 2 calculations and explicit analyses, others involve System 1 in two main varieties. One form of these intuitions draws primarily upon skill and expertise acquired through repeated experience. (Chess masters and physicians are examples.) The other type, which is sometimes subjectively indistinguishable from the first, arises from oversimplifying a complex issue, such as by substituting an easier answer in response to a more difficult question that was asked.[275]

Most valid intuitions develop when experts have learned to recognize familiar elements in new situations, and then to act in a manner that is appropriate. And whereas System 1 excels at observing patterns and relationships upon which intuition relies, it does not (cannot) allow for information it does not have. Information that is not retrieved (even unconsciously) from memory might just as well not exist.[276]

Our memories record vast repertories of knowledge and skills acquired throughout our lifetime of practice which we apply through intuition to guide us through analogous circumstances and challenges. Kahneman emphasizes that the acquisition of skills most particularly requires a regular environment, an adequate opportunity to practice, and rapid and unequivocal feedback about the correctness of thoughts and actions.[277]

Henry Simon, who studied chess masters, observed that following thousands of hours of practice they came to see pieces on the board differently from the rest of us. He wrote:

> The situation has provided a clue; this clue has given the expert access to information stored in his memory, and the information provides the answer. Intuition is nothing more than recognition.[278]

Accordingly, Daniel Kahneman reminds us that whereas "expert" intuition strikes us as magical, it is not. Indeed, he writes:

> ...each of us performs feats of intuitive expertise many times each day. Most of us are pitch-perfect in detecting anger in the first word of a telephone call, recognize as we enter a room that we were the subject of the conversation, and quickly react to subtle signs that the driver of the car in the next lane is dangerous.[279]

Thanks to our fast-thinking System 1 functions, many of these intuitive judgments are instantaneous. This is when our associative memory takes control to distinguish surprising from normal events in a fraction of a second, recognizes the causal nature of the abnormal surprise, and automatically searches for the best response.

Associative memory involves a vast network of ideas which might be thought of as "nodes," which link together according to categories we unconsciously ascribe to them. However, instead of imagining as psychologists once did that our minds go through conscious ideas one at a time, the current view of associative memory perceives a great deal happening all at once.

While each new idea simultaneously activates many others, only a few of them register on our consciousness. As Kahneman notes, most of the work of associative thinking is silent, hidden from our conscious selves.[280]

How does the information that supports intuition get "stored" in memory? According to Daniel Kahneman, certain types of intuitions are acquired very quickly.

For example, we have inherited a survival facility from our ancestors, along with bad personal experiences and shared lessons, to know when to be afraid. We are born prepared to avoid hazards and to fear spiders. We are also likely to tense up when we approach a spot in which an unpleasant event has occurred, even when there is no reason to expect it will happen again.[281, 282]

Fear can be learned quite easily through information and warnings from others. An example is a fireman who has acquired a "sixth sense" of danger through discussions of experiences of others which prompted him to think about types of fires he was not involved in, and to mentally rehearse what the cues might be, and how best to react.

People tend to access the relative importance of issues by the ease with which they are retrieved from memory. Frequently mentioned topics populate the mind even as others slip away from awareness…a fact that is certainly not lost on the consciousness of advertisers and politicians.[283]

Exercising our deliberatively analytical System 2 functions can truly involve thinking harder than we might imagine. Such mental effort invariably causes our pupils to dilate…sometimes as much as 50 percent more than when we are resting.

Psychologist Eckhard Hess has described pupils as windows into the soul. Writing a Scientific American article, he told of market bazaar shoppers wearing dark glasses to hide dilated pupils which would alert merchants they negotiated prices with of high interest in their products.

Energy Food for Thought

Mental stress burns up lots of energy fuel. Just like electric circuits in your home can become overloaded and trip fuses which shut off power, overtaxed mental facilities can also shut down. Fortunately, our brains do this selectively, ensuring that the analytical system controlling our most important activities gets all the reserves it needs.

System 1 takes over in emergencies, assigning total priority to self-protective actions such as responding to immediate driving hazards. "Spare capacity" is then allocated on a second-by-second basis to other tasks requiring priority attention.[284]

Changing brain activity patterns demonstrate that mental energy demands decrease as skills at related tasks increase. A "law of least effort" applies to cognitive thinking in solving difficult problems, just as it does to physical task exertion by seasoned athletes.

Switching working memory repeatedly from one task to another under time pressure is particularly effortful. People who test well on abilities to do this are likely to perform well in such activities as air traffic control and military pilots.[285, 286]

Concentrated mental effort directed to even a single task tends to limit our brain's available energy budget to directly associated activities. If we go beyond that budget we fail, which is why it is difficult or impossible to conduct several activities at once.

We cannot compute the product of 17x24 while making a left turn in dense traffic...don't try. Still, we can probably carry on a conversation with a passenger while driving on an empty highway, or perhaps read a story to a child while thinking about something else.[287]

An example of this difficulty is illustrated by a short *Invisible Gorilla* research film produced by Christopher Chabris and Daniel Simons which simply features two teams passing basketballs—one team wearing white shirts, the other wearing black. Viewers are instructed to count the number of passes made by the white team, ignoring those in black.

Halfway through the video, a woman wearing a gorilla suit appears, crosses the court, thumps her chest and moves on. The gorilla is in full view for nine seconds.

Of the many thousands of people have seen the video, about half have never noticed anything unusual. Being told to ignore one of the teams apparently caused mental blindness. In fact, even after being told, many who failed to see the gorilla were certain that it wasn't there. They couldn't imagine having missed it.

Very strong mental effort is required to simultaneously retain several ideas that require separate or combined actions. System 2 alone has the capacity to follow external instructions, to compare objects on several attributes and to make deliberate choices between options.

Accordingly, Nobel laureate economist Daniel Kahneman notes that people tend to eventually gravitate to least demanding and "economical" courses of action where effort is a cost, acquisition of related skill is driven by the balance of cost benefits and laziness is built deep into our human nature. [288, 289, 290]

Research by social psychologist Roy Baumeister and his colleagues at Florida State University proves that the term "mental energy" is more than just a metaphor. Writing in the *Proceedings of the National Academy of Sciences,* Baumeister noted that the human nervous system actually consumes more glucose than most other parts of the body, and that effortful mental activity requiring self-control appears to be especially expensive in the currency of glucose.

Referring to this glucose drop as "ego depletion," Baumeister equates it as being similar to the experience of a runner who draws down glucose stored in her muscles during a sprint. He and his team tested this correlation by giving a volunteer group lemonade sweetened with sugar following a challenging cognitive task and prior to preceding with a second task. A second control group was given lemonade sweetened with Splenda.

Neither group was told which sweetener they had ingested. As predicted, the control group experienced ego depletion during the second task, whereas restoring the level of available sugar in the brains of the first group prevented deterioration of their performance.[291]

The Baumeister study demonstrated that any significant effort of will or self-control required do something is tiring. As a result, ego depletion during the course of such exertions typically makes one less motivated or able to immediately take on another demanding task, or even to continue an existing one.

For illustration, Baumeister's team documented decisions by eight Israeli judges who spent full and tiring days reviewing applications for parole.

The cases were presented in random order, and the heavy caseload only allowed the judges spent an average of 6 minutes deciding each one. Of these, only 35 percent of the total requests were approved.

The study authors recorded exact times of each decision, along with the times of the judges' morning, lunch, and afternoon meal breaks. They then plotted the proportion of requests against the time since their last food break.

The results indicated high incidences of good news for parole applicants whose cases were reviewed soon after meal periods...a 65 percent approval rate. There was not welcome news for most of the applicants who were reviewed during the two hours or so until the judges' next meals when the approval rates dropped steadily to about zero. Fatigue and hunger were both assumed to have influenced the results.

Effortless Progress

Thinking smart doesn't necessarily have to be hard work. In fact, doesn't it seem that many of your best ideas come to mind when you are most relaxed and in a reflective mood?

Economist Daniel Kahneman points out that our more relaxed ideas and decisions may often be better than when we consciously work our thinking minds too hard. He observes that people who are cognitively very busy are more likely to make superficial judgments in social situations through weakened self-control. A sleepless night or a few drinks, for example, can have the same disrupting effect by overloading short-term memory.[292, 293]

So if the highly generalized System 1 mental shotgun approach makes it easier to generate quick answers to difficult questions without imposing much hard work on our lazy System 2, maybe that isn't always so bad. And considering our frequent overconfidence in believing things we really know very little about, the fact that we are still around to learn from these occasions suggests that none of those errors were fatal...at least not yet.[294]

In any case, if System 1 oversimplification of issues sometimes gets us into trouble, tendencies leaning too far in the other direction can as well. Kahneman writes:

> *Experts try to be clever, think outside the box, and consider complex combinations of features in making predictions. Complexity may work in the odd case, but far more often than not it reduces validity. Simple studies have shown that human decision makers are inferior to a prediction formula even when they are given the score suggested by the formula! They feel they can overrule the formula because they have additional information about the case, but they are*

wrong more often than not.[295]

Our most productive and innovative thinking often seems effortless. We happily engage in this for many hours at a time, doing what we truly care about and enjoy without consciously "thinking" or using "willpower" at all.

Creative performance researcher Mihaly Czikszentmihalyi refers to this as being in a "flow." He describes people in this mental mode as experiencing "...a state of effortless concentration so deep that they lose their sense of time, of themselves, of their problems." Descriptions of the joy expressed by people in this state are so compelling, that Czikszentmihalyi calls it an "optimal experience." [296, 297]

So maybe try to relax. Take at least an occasional break to vacation in that state of bliss where time zones, self-consciousness and problems cease to exist.

Learning from Machines

WHEREAS THE COMPUTATIONAL power of the human brain is largely prewired by evolution, artificial intelligence (AI) capacities arising from revolutionary computer technology power and applications are growing exponentially.

As Christof Koch, chief scientist and president of the Allen Institute of Brain Science in Seattle predicts, sweeping societal and economic influences of AI signal a fourth industrial revolution. He observes:

> The first, powered by the steam engine, moved us from agriculture to urban societies. The second, powered by electricity, ushered in mass production and created consumer culture. The third, centered on computers and the internet, shifted the economy from manufacturing into services.

Koch points out that before modern farm equipment and tractors came along, it took 30 times more people to farm one hundred acres that it does today. This has resulted in producing more food for growing populations at affordable prices.

And while the Model T turned out the lights on many

professions including blacksmiths and carriage makers, its introduction of affordable automobiles through mass production created huge new demands for labor created by the steel industry, glass industry, rubber industry, textile trade and oil and gas.

Koch also recognizes that many people understandably...

> *Worry that (AI) will do great harm to society—putting people out of work, adding to inequality and removing warfare from human control, and even posing an existential risk to the long-term future of Homo sapiens.*

At the same time, he reminds us that all of the previous technical revolutions profoundly increased human productivity, welfare and lifespans.[298]

Dystopian visions of massive AI-driven job losses are premature. Throughout history, employment adapted as machines gradually replaced more and more aspects of labor over time. While once again, this fourth revolution will eliminate some jobs, it will also create opportunities for new ones that will require and enable more people to think smarter.

In any case, there is no way to turn back the clock of progress where even Einstein's space-time continuum takes on a new dimension of meaning. Unlike speed of light, there are no known theoretical limits to computational intelligence.

Artificial Intelligence as Competitor and Companion

The concept of "thinking machines," which was first hypothesized during a 1956 meeting of scientists, mathematicians and engineers at Dartmouth College, is no longer theoretical. Moreover, those machines are already beginning to outthink some top human experts in certain very complicated mental challenges.

- By 1997, a "Deep Blue" IBM computer defeated the reigning world chess champion, Gary Kasparov.

- In 2011, "Watson," another IBM computer, beat all humans in the quiz show *Jeopardy*.

- In 2016, an "AlphaGo" algorithm developed by "DeepMind," a London AI company, dispatched Lee Sedol, a top player in ancient and complex board game "Go." The algorithm was originally trained on 160,000 games from a database of previously-played games.

The program was later upgraded to "AlphaGo Zero," which taught itself by playing four million games against itself entirely by trial and error. AlphaGo Zero subsequently annihilated its parent, AlphaGo, 100 games to zero. It accomplished learning capacity in less than one month what would have required a decade or two of training it takes a human to become a highly skilled Go master.

- In 2017, "Libratus" software developed at Carnegie Mellon University beat four top players over a 20-day tournament of No-Limit Texas Hold'em poker. The code doesn't need to bluff...it just outthinks humans.[299]

In addition to embarrassingly besting us in fun and games, AI is also competing with more practical roles we have naturally assumed needed us. Few occupations, including a major percent of highly-trained legal and medical diagnostic services, are immune from competitive AI and concomitant robotic automation workplace challenges.

A 2016 McKinsey Global Institute study estimated that between 10 and 50 percent of all U.S. job tasks could be automated using existing robotic technology. In about 60 percent of 800 occupations surveyed, at least 30 percent of those primary activities can be replaced by software. Some jobs, such as drivers, retail workers and fast-food employees, may become entirely obsolete.

Automated vehicles can be expected to replace many of the estimated one of every twelve American males—more than 10 million—who are currently employed as drivers. By 2005, AI had already learned to drive an autonomous vehicle over a 132-mile off-road course in the Navada-California desert in under seven hours. In 2017, Uber used an automated 18-wheeler to deliver 50,000 cans of Budweiser from Fort Collins to Colorado Springs, Colorado. The driver spent most of his time sitting in the sleeper cabin monitoring the system's performance.

Significant AI impacts upon air transport can also be anticipated. Expanding use of drone technologies is likely to result in a lessened need for pilots for military and private aviation.

Robotic systems currently developed to support human work activities will ultimately replace many of them altogether. Greg Creed, CEO of Yum Brands, which owns Taco Bell, KFC and Pizza Hut, says that he expects that "by the mid-2020s" automation will take the place of most food service workers.

"Semi-automated masons" (SAMs) produced by the Construction Robotics company can now lay bricks at least three times faster than humans. They work in tandem with bricklayers who finish the corners and scrape off excess mortar.

Automated servants have come into our homes to perform such domestic tasks as cleaning swimming pools, mowing lawns, and cleaning floors. Others provide us with patient and informed responses to questions regarding the best traffic route to take to virtually anywhere and a limitless variety of other topics.

Don't be surprised to see interactive human-mimicking

next-generation versions of Amazon's "Alexa," Microsoft's "Cortana" and Google's "Google Assistant" increasingly serving as virtual substitutes for actual two- and four-legged companions. Many can already anticipate what you may wish to discuss based upon your past information requests. Within a decade, their conversations and voices will become indistinguishable from fellow humans who can be counted upon to tell you what you really want to hear.[300]

Do be advised, however, that we may be wise not to trust them to hold those friendly conversations confidential. In addition to being developed to retrieve information, arrange appointments, provide directions, play favorite music and remind us of scheduled appointments, they can also be used to whisper our personal secrets to others behind our backs.

Just as our online activities, including emails, searches and website visits are continuously monitored and stored, voice assistants can do the same. Whether spoken or typed, those messages leave behind a steady trail of recorded snippets which are accessible to uninvited eavesdroppers. That data record revealing our special interests, habits and preferences can then be used to target us for advertising or other purposes.

As *Comparitech* security review website founder Richard Patterson warns:

> *While users can take a few precautions to lessen the impact on privacy, there's no way to use a voice assistant and maintain complete privacy.*[301]

Patterson points out that host companies can even listen in to everything that is going on in our surroundings when we imagine them to be sleeping.

Whenever a user initiates a voice assistant request with a "wake-up" word or phrase, such as "Alexa" or "Okay, Google," the device instantly begins recording audio clips which are processed for responses by the operating company's server. This sound activation feature means that virtual assistants are constantly capable of listening and recording…even when the device is not engaged in an active conversation with its user.

Marc Laliberte, an information security threat analyst at network security company WatchGuard Technologies warns that:

> These devices should not be operational in locations where potentially sensitive information is verbally passed.

Laliberte also advises that limited access can help people from tampering with the system.

> Privacy concerns arise when someone other than the voice assistant's owner uses the device, as most devices can't distinguish between different people's voices.[302]

Quantum Computing Leaps Forward

Information security threats have rocketed up to national levels as the result of staggeringly large processing capacities afforded by rapidly accelerating quantum computer (QC) advancements. As University of Maryland researcher Christopher Moore testified at an October 2017 House Science Committee hearing on "American Leadership in Quantum Technology," merely 300 atoms under full quantum computer control might potentially store more pieces of information than the number of atoms that exist in the entire Universe.[303]

Such implausible features are made possible by equally incomprehensible subatomic-scale phenomena. Unlike current computers which process tiny "bits" of data in a linear sequence as either a one or a zero, at the seemingly weird subatomic scale, a quantum bit (or "qubit") can be both a zero and a one at the same time. As a result, rather than growing linearly, adding more qubits expands computing power exponentially.

Just as AI promises to transform an endless variety of peaceful information and problem-solving tasks, its vast capacity to out-think conventional computers presents enormously troubling cybersecurity challenges. In addition to overwhelming cryptographic codes used to protect top secret data, it can also be weaponized for conduct of armed conflicts at much larger scales and higher speeds than humans can comprehend or react to.

International foes and friends are racing to achieve QC supremacy which can defeat all current-generation defenses against military, information security, banking and utility infrastructure system cyberattacks. The first hostile nation to win this race will be able to open the encrypted secrets of every country, company and person on the planet; dominate global information-technology and the global financial systems; compromise the safety of medical, food and water services; put transportation and energy infrastructures at risk; and threaten domestic and military security systems.

Researchers Daniel Bernstein at the Technische Universiteit Eindhoven and Tanja Lange at the University of Illinois, Chicago stressed this urgency in a September 2017 report in the scientific journal Nature, noting: "We are in a race against time to deploy post-quantum cryptography before quantum computers arrive." They predict that "Many commonly used cryptosystems will be completely broken once large quantum computers exist." [304]

Writing in the *Wall Street Journal*, Committee for Justice President Curt Levy and Ryan Hagemann at the Niskanen Center posit a challenge in ensuring ways to ensure that future AI algorithms with minds of their own remain accountable to transparent oversight.

The authors' greatest concern isn't that advanced

computers we create will go rogue and turn against us like HAL 9000 in *2001: A Space Odyssey*. They foresee a greater threat that AI complexity enables developers to secretly "rig" a system to the advantage of special interests, such as to manipulate a corporate operating program to reveal trade secrets to outside competitors.[305]

QC progress now continues to rapidly accelerate following a three-decade scientific siesta since the concept was first proposed by Russian mathematician Yuri Manin in 1980:

- D-Wave Systems, a company based in Burnaby, British Columbia demonstrated a special- function 16-qubit QC in 2007 at the Mountain View, California Computer History Museum.

- In 2011, D-Wave Systems sold its first 128-qubit commercial system ("D-Wave One") to the Lockheed Martin Quantum Computing Center located at the University of Southern California. The companies have since entered into multi- year agreements which have led to the development of more powerful D-Wave Two and D-Wave 2X systems.

- In 2013, Google established a Quantum Artificial Intelligence Laboratory (QAIL) at NASA's Ames Research Center at Moffett Field, California in collaboration with the Universities Space Research Association (USRA).

- In 2015, QAIL publicly displayed a 10-foot-tall D-Wave 2X unit chilled at 180 times colder than deep space which is expected to operate 100 million times faster than any conventional computer.

- IBM has recently announced an initiative to build a

commercially-available "IBM Q" along with an Application Program Interface (API) to enable customers and programmers to begin building interfaces between the company's existing five-qubit cloud-based computer and conventional computers.

A New Era of Neurotechnology

Is artificial intelligence different from "the real thing" that goes on in our brains? Apart from our claims to unique spiritual, sensate and social qualities, can our human species keep up with—or perhaps even survive—exponentially growing artificial thinking machines and automated surrogates which are already outsmarting and outworking us in many areas of human endeavor?

Or on the other hand, might we not only learn from those products of our own innovation, but even interface AI systems with human minds to expand cognition and consciousness? Christof Koch believes that we can.

He urges:

> There is one way to deal with this growing threat to our way of life. Instead of limiting further research into AI, we should turn it into an exciting new direction. To keep up with the machines we're creating, we must move quickly to upgrade our own organic computing machines: We must create technologies to enhance the processing and learning capabilities of the human brain.[306]

Koch offers some early, yet promising neurotechnology examples that apply to present-day computational systems:

- Transcranial direct current stimulation: This

noninvasive brain technology induces a weak electric field in the cortex underlying the skull. Research in animals and humans suggests that this may enhance neuro-plasticity, the process in which the brain improves its performance when an action is repeated over and over. Users wear headphones that gently stimulate the motor cortex while performing simple activities such as lifting weights, swinging a golf club or playing a piano.

- Electroencephalogram (EEG): Electrodes built into a headset detect brain waves during deep sleep. The device then plays low sounds that enhance the depth and strength of those waves, leading to more restful sleep.

This noninvasive technology is presently limited because those billions of tiny nerve cells that generate brain waves are quite remote from the scalp, allowing only faint echoes of neuronal chatter to be picked up. Christof Koch concludes: "We aren't anywhere close to selectively silencing or amplifying the activity of small cliques of neurons."

- Neurosurgical Implants: Ultimately, to boost brain power we need to directly listen to and control individual neurons and atoms of perception, action, memory and consciousness. This currently requires some neurosurgery to penetrate the scull and access brain tissue. The good news is that brain-machine implant interfaces are happening faster than expected.

Nancy Smith was injured in a car accident which left her as a tetraplegic who can only move her shoulder and head. Neurosurgeons and neuroscientists implanted a tiny "bed of nails" in the region of her cortex to encode her intention to grasp a cup or press piano keys. Algorithms decode her neural signals and pass instruction to a musical synthesizer so that she can play music in her mind.

Bill Kochevar was paralyzed below the shoulders following a bicycle accident. A Cleveland-based team of doctors and neuroscientists placed electrodes into his left motor cortex that read out electrical tremors of about 100 neurons. From these they decoded and transmitted his intentions to reach out and grasp objects by electronically stimulating muscles in his arm. While crude, it enables Kochevar to eat and drink by himself.

There are more than 50 patients with such neuronal listening devices installed in their brains. Current and future applications include direct brain stimulation for obsessive-compulsive disorder, treatment-resistant depression, essential tremor, Parkinson's disease, epilepsy, stroke recovery and even blindness.

Christof Koch visualized that new neurotechnology developments may help patients recover lost functionality, including driving a car with their minds, plus a great deal more. He contemplates:

> My hope is that someday, a person could visualize a concept—say, the US Constitution. An implant in his visual cortex would read this image, wirelessly access the relevant online Wikipedia page and then write its content back into the visual cortex, so that he can read the webpage with his mind's eye. All of this would happen at the speed of thought.[307]

Koch continues:

> Another implant could translate a vague thought into a precise and error-free piece of digital code, turning

anyone into a programmer. People could set their brains to keep focus on a task for hours on end, or control the length or depth of their sleep at will.

Koch's vision brings a literal new meaning to the notions of "getting our heads together on an idea" and "sharing thoughts." As he imagines this, he suggests:

> *Another exciting prospect is melding two or more brains into a single conscious mind by direct neuron-to-neuron links—similar to the corpus callosum, the bundle of two hundred million fibers that link the two cortical hemispheres of a person's brain. This entity could call upon the memories and skills of its member brains but would act as one 'group' consciousness, with a single, integrated purpose to coordinate highly complex activities across many bodies.*

Christof Koch believes that humankind is at the threshold of a transformational new era that merges unlimited capacities of thinking machines and biological minds to revolutionize the entire meaning of "intelligence:"

> *While the 20th century was the century of physics—think of the atomic bomb, the laser, the transistor—the 21st will be the century of the brain—the most complex piece of highly excitable matter in the known Universe.*

Ultimately, our intelligent machines may even influence us to reinvent ourselves to equip us with "bigger brains" that will be needed to keep pace with our inventions.

Confronting Uncertainties and Fears

ONE OF MY former graduate students in the space architecture program I founded at the University of Houston rehabilitated and reinvented himself through sheer willpower following a devastating vehicular injury. His extraordinary courage and achievement serve as a personal inspiration in my life which I will share with you.

Eric was one of a great many delightfully bright, enthusiastic and idealistic young people who I have had the enormous pleasure to work with throughout my nearly five decades of teaching. Although he enjoyed his time here, he looked forward to returning to Belgium to be reunited with his friends and family following graduation.

Then, after fulfilling his military obligation, he would embark upon the professional aerospace design career that he dreamed of.

Things didn't work out at all as he had planned.

The week after completing his studies, Eric was severely injured in a car accident while vacationing with his brother and a pal. He was in a deep coma when I visited him in a Houston hospital.

His father had flown in to be with him, and his doctor gave

us terrible news. Eric had sustained extensive brain damage, along with severe traumas to other internal organs and limbs. It appeared extremely doubtful that he would regain consciousness, and even if he did, would likely never be able to talk, dress and feed himself, or lead a normal life in any respect.

Eric's father accepted that dismal diagnosis graciously and bravely, but said he would not abandon hope for a much fuller recovery. I tried to act optimistic too, yet lacked full conviction.

Eric's mental will to overcome that setback has proven that prognosis to be very wrong on all accounts. Since that tragic time, he has visited me in Houston on at least three occasions. Although he walks and talks with some labor, has lost the use of one arm, has impaired vision, tires readily and has also had to adjust and adapt to other daunting challenges, his mind is not only functioning—it is truly marvelous.

Eric has matured into an individual of truly admirable awareness and insights who speaks again and again about good ways that the accident has changed his life. He reflects about how, through that experience, he discovered the great importance of love he has received from his family and friends. He reminds us never to take the incredible gift of life for granted.

Eric expressed gratitude that a need to compensate for an inability to manually draw design concepts and construction details motivated him to become highly proficient with computerized graphic systems.

These new skills enabled him to create successful business offices in Belgium and New York which offer those services internationally. He recently visited Houston again to meet with a local client.

Hearing Eric tell it, that accident was a lucky event. And he's demonstrated that there's every good reason to believe him.

Whole-Brain Planning for Extreme Conditions

The Sasakawa International Center for Space Architecture (SICSA) program that Eric attended emphasizes holistic problem-solving research, planning and design for habitats in space, and also for extreme environments on Earth. Included are human facility and infrastructure requirements in remote polar stations, offshore underwater and surface locations and transportable shelters to accommodate victims of natural and man-made disasters.

Independently supported by outside gift and research funds since its inception in 1987, SICSA offers two companion degree-granting options through the University of Houston's Cullen College of Engineering: a Master of Science in Space Architecture; and a joint Master of Science Space Architecture-Aerospace Engineering degree.

SICSA's central priority is to educate interdisciplinary groups of advanced students, including those who are previously from non-aerospace backgrounds, to develop comprehensive knowledge, skills and connect-the-dot analytical thinking needed to solve complex problems demanding well-coordinated "big picture" approaches. Participants come from a variety of undergraduate and graduate-level backgrounds, including: aerospace, mechanical, and civil engineering; architecture and industrial design; and human factors and biomedical fields.

Realistic planning for extreme conditions in space and on Earth requires those involved to imagine themselves in unique and often life-and death-defining circumstances they have never personally experienced. In doing so, they must learn to apply holistic extreme thinking which combines lessons gained from those who have actually experienced such conditions with an imaginative ability to project oneself into real-life responses to everything which can possibly (and probably) go wrong.

In keeping with this objective, I have introduced a short "extreme experience diary" assignment into a special workshop I teach. Its purpose is to encourage students to revisit challenging experiences they have survived in order to more fully understand and appreciate how they managed to cope with their personal uncertainties and fears.

The brief exercise asks each student to write a diary entry recreating an extreme experience in their life as if they were writing it today. In doing so, they are asked to recognize that the meaning of the term "extreme" is relative to each individual's outlooks and experiences. It is not intended as a competition to win a "worst case scenario" prize. Instead, it urges them to reexamine aspects of their personal coping skills that can be expanded and reapplied to new challenges.

I will share just a few of their responses:

Dongwook K: South Korean Sentry on DMZ Patrol Duty

It was AM 1:35 in the evening when Corporal Kim and Private Lee alerted me to replace them for sentry duty. I rapidly wake up and put on my combat uniform and jacket. Also, Private Seo starts to get ready to go on sentry with me.

Before we leave the door, he and I have to take rifles and fully-loaded magazines. We walk to outside…it is too cold! My glasses are covered with frost and I start coughing due to breathing cold air.

The area where I am stationed is one of the toughest of the 15 GP [Guard Post] infantries, GP001. The region here is surrounded by mountains and has high altitudes.

I wipe the glasses and now I see the ground covered by snow. I have been here one year, but every time I go out for sentry I get nervous. A few weeks ago, a North Korean guard shop toward a South Korea sentry.

Private Seo and I start to move from GP001 to 01 sentry. It takes an hour to get there. Since the path is covered by snow, I have to sweep the pathway. I start sweating. Carrying a gun and wearing a bullet-proof vest makes me slow and tired.

We finally get to the next sentry. I point my gun toward the North Korea territory and start to look at the DMZ with its telescope. I do not see any movement. It is quiet and dark. The only visible things are orange lights along a ten feet high fence.

A few minutes later, Private Seo hears a sound behind trees. We aim our guns to those trees and wait. After a few seconds, a family of hogs come through the trees. Since it is not allowed to hunt or kill animals in the DMZ, wild animals freely go around the area. Every time I see them, they seem threatening due to body size...as big as a small car. Surprisingly, they are surviving in the DMZ without stepping on undiscovered mines. I believe they have very sensitive noses to detect mines, but I often see exploded bodies of hogs.

Private Seo and I have returned to GP001 before dawn after work hours. I wait for breakfast and start eating. Since the weather is cold, the hot soup gets cold quickly.

After I eat breakfast, I finally go to sleep. The sleep hours were just four. Sergeant Kim forces us to do our daily work. I have to dig the ground. It is so hard to dig it because the land is frozen. I'm not able to dig it, but I keep digging until I can reach two feet deep.

I have only six months left until I finish my duties. I feel a day as long as one year.

The cold environment and isolation from the outside makes everyone to have hope, but some to keep saying "it is life of prison."

To compare with North Korea side, we are living in luxurious space and environment. One time I saw them through a very precise telescope. I could see what they were doing and where they were hidden and did aim at us. And they have no trees on their mountains. They use all the trees to make fire.

I just thank to God that I am on the South side of Korea.

Lee M: The Fear of Wonder

Before boarding the plane, I immediately asked myself if this was what I wanted to do. Although the seat had been booked and the hotel reserved, a slight hesitation clouded my mind.

I boarded the plane and took off for Europe. Being a United States native and never actually having set foot on other soil around the world, this was the greatest yet daring moment for me. There I was, all by myself, with a curious mind that put me in a lot of danger. It was my first time traveling by myself out of the country.

There was a short period before boarding the plane that I did not want to go. I did not know what was out there. The rest of the world was always viewed through pictures and videos. I only believed it existed because of what I saw on the screen. It was all make-believe; I would be traveling to a blank place in space. I always thought that traveling to a place like New York and California was foreign enough for me. Now I was going to a place that even the language is unfamiliar to me. I was finally on my own.

The trip for me was a requirement, not only for my degree, but also for my life. I believed it would broaden my perspective. It was sort of a life retreat that I needed to reflect on my goals.

The beginning preparation was stressful and rushed. I made a last minute decision to go on this study abroad trip a week before the application was due. It was a last push that I decided to accept this challenge. I told myself that this would be a careless decision. Whatever happens, happens.

That was why I was so hesitant to board the plane. I thought that I had made a decision that I hadn't considered all the way through. I felt like I did not have a lot of preparation time. If anything were to happen in the far off land, I would be in deep water. In the end, I went.

My fear became true at the beginning of the trip. I had a short layover in Turkey that I barely missed. The signs were confusing while the chaos of people in the same situation didn't help. When I finally set forth in Rome, the stress was at its peak. I did not have any sort of communication, nor did I speak Italian. I had to find help from a transit worker who barely spoke English and managed to buy a ticket that took me to AirBnb. On the train ride I looked out the window. I began searching for any make-believe in the landscape and buildings. Ironically, I wanted the foreign place to be fake so that I would wake up from a dream.

It was overwhelming and unbelievable that I was in another place across the world. Everything I saw on television and pictures before were right in front of my eyes. It was all real. The hilly landscape, tall stony pines, mopeds.

I told myself that this was real. I was finally in another country all by myself. Whereas I had previously regarded it to be a survival situation, I now agreed with myself that it was more of an adventure.

When I finally reached Airbdb and set foot out of the train I realized that this was to be more than just a school trip. It would be a memorable trip. Although many of my fears along the way came true, the destination of experience was to be well worth it.

It was interesting to finally get past the first phase of hesitation and fear and finally accept that I was somewhere across the world. I made a daring decision to travel on my own in a foreign place. With no idea what I was going to expect, it was forever an extreme, yet memorable place in my life. It could be a stepping stone toward even more daring things.

In the end, it was an unfamiliar wonder.

Maria H: Diary of a Refugee

After three hours of being half-asleep, always in fear for my siblings Ali and Yara, I woke up in that meadow this morning, completely soaked and full of mud—again the tent didn't resist the heavy rain last night. No wonder as it is the third day in a row we couldn't find a proper place to sleep. I always tried to get shelter for Ali and Yara in the villages we passed by, but there are thousands of us. People are scared and won't let us in.

But today, everything will get better—it's gonna be the day me and my family will finally reach freedom! Freedom of regimes, freedom of war, freedom of being—that was my first thought this morning, as every morning since we escaped from war a month ago. It is this thought that keeps me going—even in desperate months without water, food or a place to sleep.

Today we are lucky. A group of Serbian civilians provided some voluntary food donations. Thank God we were in front of the queue and finished our meal before anyone of the back rows got angry and made us share.

Ali suffers from a cold, He is also feverish and in very bad condition. But probably it's me who suffers even more. I feel like a cruel punisher who makes him walk all day long although it won't help him cure.

Meanwhile, my feet are one open sore—some blisters got infected and I don't have something for disinfection...I thought as we'd reach the Hungarian border by the night, as a European Union member, they might have some basic medical care provided for us...

But I should have known better. As we finally reached the border by 10:00 PM, they did not at all welcome us with open arms. Instead, they've built a 5 meter high barbwire fence controlled by the military to protect themselves from us. It was a tragedy of course, most of our men went crazy, attacked and shouted at the officers, tried to cut holes in the fence, flailed around and were finally pushed back by force. A lot of them were injured by airsoft guns.

Ali and Yara were crying. They couldn't understand how we've finally reached our destination but weren't welcomed at all. I was close to tears as well. Why would a country like Hungary, which is blessed with freedom and wealth not help us in our misery? Why would they not even treat us like human beings and care for us at least until a solution has been found?

By a speaker we were told that there is no opportunity to pass the border. Not today, not tomorrow, and not in the near future. When somebody asked what we were supposed to do now, some of the officers just told us, "Go home, idiot!"

Of course, this statement caused another attack wave by our people. Meanwhile, I decided to better search for a place to sleep in the nearby forest and to make a plan for our escape tomorrow. An increasing number of gunshots kept me awake in fear.

Maybe tomorrow will be better.

Larry Bell

Brenda C: Shaken Childhood Memories of an Earthquake

I am an international student from El Salvador, a third world country with a tropical climate, beaches and volcanoes. El Salvador is the smallest and also the most densely populated country in Central America. As of 2015, the country had a population of approximately 6.38 million, consisting largely of Mestizos of European and indigenous American descent.

I lived in my country for 20 years and grew up with such circumstances as hurricanes and earthquakes. The 2001 earthquake that my family experienced when I was seven years old left an impression that has haunted me ever since.

I remember that my family was sitting in the living room watching the Disney Channel, and the house started to shake hard. My brother and I started to scream and cry.

My mom and dad were trying to open the door to go to the street, but the door was moving so hard that we had to be inside until the earthquake finished. After that we went to the street with all our neighbors. I remember being confused, because it was my first real experience with such a disaster.

The night of the earthquake we slept in the garage (we took our beds out of our rooms). An earthquake is not a one-time event. After the main one there are duplicates in minor scale, but as a 7-year old, all of them felt exactly the same way.

Nothing was normal that year. My school classes did not start until February (our school year is from January to October). My church was destroyed by the earthquake so they started doing the services in a tent each Sunday. A part of the school suffered serious damage as well and therefore they had to rearrange the classrooms for all students.

In my town, there was a major landslide that put underground an entire section of a neighborhood with the families inside. I remember that a lot of people died there. Some of my friends are still alive because they were somewhere else that day, but their moms, dads, sisters and brothers died inside their houses.

Mental health became a big concern. I remember listening to stories about how the world was ending that year and how under the houses was water that with another earthquake of that magnitude everyone that was still alive was going to die.

Those are things that as a seven year old girl I observed from that period. The following years I remember being paranoid and mentally preparing each 13th of each month an earthquake was going to happen.

Every time an earthquake happened, I started to run, scream and cry. It took me a while to get over those panic attacks as I grew up. I think I was 19 years old when I got used to earthquakes.

I live in El Salvador knowing as "El pais de las hamacas"—or in English "The country of the hammocks", because of the frequent earthquakes or "temblores". You have an idea how extreme conditions are going to be, but it is totally different when you are experiencing them in real life.

Austin K: Surviving a Bumpy Road

Since the 4th grade, my brothers, father and I have taken week-long camping trips out to various parts of Texas such as Palo Doro and the Guadalupe Mountains. This past year we were in the Chihuahuan Desert.

Everything began relatively uneventful other than my younger brother bumping his head on a cactus. Then on day three that all changed.

We drove out to a secluded trailhead to go for a hike about 40 miles away from our campsite to a natural spring. On the way, I sat on the bed of our truck. The road was a little bumpy out there, but the warmth of the Sun and the cool breeze negated any discomfort from the road.

We arrived at the trailhead, hiked out six miles through desert brush, then on to an empty creek bed that gradually became more and more green as we walked the last two miles to the spring. The view when we arrived in the small humid canyon was almost surreal as to how much the world around us changed as we got closer to water.

After a short break for lunch, we headed back to the truck. It was now late afternoon and we all wanted to get back to camp before dark to start dinner. Heading back, I sat in the truck back again and relaxed as we drove along. About 20 minutes later there was as huge jolt. I felt myself flying...and then everything went black.

I still don't know how much time had passed before I awoke in a panic, in the dark, very cold, and in dirt about ten feet from the side of the road. Suddenly pain hit me, an awful headache that made every other sensation unbearable.

After rising slowly and carefully to my feet, I stumbled into a thorny plant that cut my arm and staggered back toward the road. I had no idea where I was. All I knew was that I needed to go to a hospital, and that there wasn't really a way I knew of to get there.

I sat down on the road shivering in tears and scared. I tried to gather myself, walked over to the brush, and began to gather twigs to make a signal fire. The more I moved, the dizzier I became.

Just before I pulled the flint from my pocket to start a fire I became to feel very sick. It was all I could to eventually compose myself enough to start the fire. Then, with the sense of a small victory, I sat next to that fire to attempt to contemplate exactly where I was.

I looked up into the sky at the stars and felt small and helpless. As the fire started to die, I tried to get up to gather more twigs, but as I got up a blackness began to take over my mind. I fell towards a large rock. My only thought was my life might then be ended.

I dreamed that there were was a hurricane and lightning in the desert. Instead, that wind, sound and light turned out to be a search and rescue helicopter. The next morning, I awoke in an El Paso hospital bed, confused but very thankful that I was still alive.

Kevin G: Day in the Life of a Homeless Youth

I felt filthy and tired. It had been a week since I had been in school. I was forced to make a decision whether I would show up to school dirty, or find a place to stay where I could take a bath.

It had been a week of couch surfing from house to house and I was running out of friends who would take me in as my welcome was well worn out, I feared that my grades were falling apart too, and that my attendance was riding the edge of having to repeat the school year all over again.

It didn't seem fair that my mom had chosen to take care of her mother instead of us, and in doing so, had left. Or that I had to take care of my brother because he lost his job. Working at Burger King had left me exhausted, and I was afraid that I would not make it much longer. My time was running out.

The people at school began to wonder where I was. When I did show up, the clothes I wore repeatedly gave it away. Sometimes instead of going to class, I hid in the locker room to get some rest in safety and peace.

My AP teacher began to notice. She reached out to me and began to tell me about a future where I didn't have to live like this. She said that the first step would be to join a shelter. It was hard to admit that I was officially homeless, but that was truly the first step.

Today, I'm waiting to start a four-year university on a scholarship. I still don't tell people that I'm homeless. It's not because of pride as before. It's not that I don't think that they'll understand either. It's only that I think they won't know how to handle it.

Skip Brown: An Extremely Isolated Example

If this truly was a "worst case" mental challenge coping competition, circumstances experienced by another individual who never received a college degree would be a strong candidate. His diary, of sorts, was compiled from excerpts taken from his correspondence with me from a very extreme environment of a man-made kind.

John "Skip" Brown at that time was a forty-year-old black-American death row inmate at Holmesburg Prison in Philadelphia who had originally contacted me asking if I might be able arrange with NASA to have him put on a one-way experimental mission to Mars. He wrote that rather than simply being warehoused as so many other inmates were waiting for execution, he wished to give up his life for some meaningful purpose.

Skip had been an avid space enthusiast since he had built his first model of the X-15 rocket plane. That interest led him to follow international space developments.

We corresponded over many years about special psychological challenges of long term missions...dealing with isolation from familiar comforts and social relationships in particular. The following excerpts taken from several of his letters were presented by one of my graduate students at a large SICSA-sponsored international conference on design for extreme environments conference I hosted in 1991:

As an inmate at Holmesburg Prison for more than one year and still counting, I am living under isolated conditions which are equivalent in many respects to a mission to Mars and beyond. I would like to offer some of my experiences and thoughts to surviving long periods of isolation for consideration at the International Design for Extreme Environments Assembly (IDEEA One). Unfortunately, I will not be able to attend.

Isolation conditions here at Holmesburg are no joke. The prison was locked-down for two months on a full time basis beginning last year in December after a fifth inmate was stabbed to death. This means that we were locked in our cells 24 hours per day except for times we were let out for showers, medical attention, visitors, and to see a social worker. This past February the rules were changed to lock-down the prison on a "part-time" 24 hour per day status to test how the inmates behaved.

I have carefully observed inmates after they went through 32 hours on lock-down and would not trust them on a trip to mars with me. One big problem at Holmesburg is to find the right cell partner. Since many inmates are emotional, due to mental and other personal problems you have to be very careful who you pick. Or else!

I have had six cell mates before I went in the "hole" (which I discuss later), and four of them had serious problems. For manned space missions to Mars, crew selection is very important.

The key to surviving in prison or on a trip to Mars is to keep yourself busy. I do this by studying space science and by maintaining correspondence with space organizations I belong to. I keep very busy reading and fantasizing about Mars and the Universe beyond.

When we are locked-in I hold classes in my cell, teaching basic science, psychology and cosmology. I am self-taught in these areas at first became interested in astronomy at age eleven. When I was on the outside I drove a tractor-trailer to earn money for my astronomy and planetary book collection. Other inmates pay me for teaching them so that I can earn money for research materials. My cell is my science laboratory.

My hours are very long each day in my cell. I spend much of my time trying to get the feeling of what it would be like to go to Mars. I "log in" at least to 24 hour days and often test my endurance to see if I can stay awake for 24 hours. When I "max out" I can sleep for nine or ten straight hours and wake up, take a cold shower, drink coffee, and sit on my bunk and plan my day.

In my studies I have found that most humans have the ability to adapt to prison life. In spite of the fact that the prison is overcrowded and tension is in the air, only a few inmates have "snapped out". The two inmates who hung themselves last year were both white. This prison is about 95 percent Afro-Americans like myself. We have only a few Asian and Spanish inmates.

Inmates are under tremendous stress to survive and this is a very dangerous place. You have to watch your back at all times. Other inmates respect the fact that I am into space science and this keeps some of the tension down. They call me "Professor".

I even have a project on prolonged isolation and stress research that involves the social work program here. The Captain called me into his office to meet with me personally and talk about my inmate isolation project which he thinks is unique. Earning respect in some ways makes it easier to deal with isolation.

Thinking Whole

I raised my ability to cope with isolation when I was put into the hole for fourteen days. This occurred because of a dangerous cell mate during lock-up. It may serve as an example of what can happen when one member of a space crew becomes mentally and physically dangerous or otherwise unable to cope with challenges of a mission. This particular inmate who attacked me had been transferred here from a prison called Camp Hill because of a major riot that burned the entire complex to the ground. It was the worst in Pennsylvania history.

After five years in prison for pulling a stick-up he was under great stress and had a very nasty attitude when the guards put him in my cell. The argument started over a small matter of a damned light bulb. In short, I was studying when he wanted to sleep. Following the argument we were both taken to the hospital. Luckily for me, I just came out with a busted lip, swollen leg, and a few bumps and bruises. Small things can lead to big problems when people are under stress.

I told the guards that I wanted to stay in the hole because of my isolation project. I had my own cell down there, so that I didn't have to worry about other problem inmates. I had books to read, a radio, telephone and shower time, plenty of food, and clean clothes. It wasn't too bad, not like the old days. I found that frustration only really gets to me when I can't meet certain personal conditions. I have learned to live with it.

There are a lot of people in jail not doing anything with their lives. For example, there are about 650,000 black Afro-American males locked up in the prison system nationwide out of a total of about one million. News reports often refer to this as 'warehousing' inmates. It is a terrible waste of human lives and resources.

I have interviewed at least 400 prison inmates, and many have told me that they wouldn't mind being used in space experiments. Instead of using rats and jellyfish onboard the shuttle med-lab, for example, inmates would like to know if they could be used in these experiments. If you think this is a good idea, please write me and give me your opinion. I will volunteer.

Since this writing, Skip was transferred to that Camp Hill Prison in Camp Hill, Pennsylvania. He reported that because of the previous riots he was on 24 hour lock-down, and that conditions were far worse than at Holmesburg.

Despite these hardships, Skip reported that he continued to gather data for his isolation study and to follow space activities.

A representative from Holmesburg Prison attended AICSA's IDEEA One conference where Skip's "paper" was presented, noting that he had become quite a celebrity for attaining this professional recognition. I have not received any communications from Skip for several years and can only imagine that he might have made that final celestial trip far beyond Earth after all.

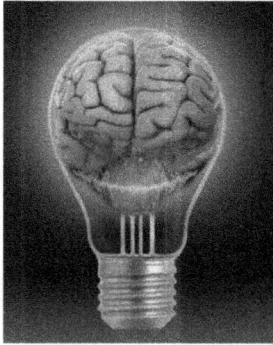

Part Four: The Evolution and Elevation of Creativity

ADAPTIVE POWERS OF imagination that enabled John "Skip" Brown to survive many years of emotional isolation and hardship on death row have enabled our Homo sapiens ancestors to prevail over extreme conditions that overwhelmed their Homo erectus predecessors. Even more, these uniquely human faculties have enriched our lives, for without imagination, the very essence of social culture is unimaginable.

Imaginative "creativity" defies boundaries of any singular scientific phenomena or, authoritative perspective. As described in the blog *Psychology Wiki,* it has been "attributed variously to divine intervention, cognitive processes, the social environment, personality traits, and chance ('accident or serendipity'), genius, mental illness and humor." [308]

True creativity cannot occur without whole brain mindfulness. Anything less would invariably produce only half-baked ideas. It would also be a terrible waste. As Thomas Edison, an indisputably creative fellow reportedly remarked, "The chief function of the body is to carry the brain around."

Creativity is imagination put to purposeful ends of the creator. Although exactly how that happens is as a highly individual and subjectively evaluated matter, it is clearly a topic of interests that sells many books and other print publications. I can therefore only wish that this one will be included...although hopefully not according to a genre category described by Stephen Asma, author of *The Evolution of Imagination*.

As Chicago Columbia College professor Asma observes:

> *Books about creativity have tended to fall into one of three genres. On the one hand, there have been breathless and over-reaching feel-good paeans to famous entrepreneurs and successful CEO creatives. This kind of book is crammed with amusing but shallow factoids and over-interpreted fMRI studies, all wrapped up in a vaguely inspirational glaze.*

"Next," he continues,

> *We have the how-to books that give artists a series of exercises to unblock their creative flow. These books are either therapeutic or instructive, or both, and seek to nurture the joy of our inner prodigy.*

Asma concludes:

> *The third genre is the impenetrable academic buffer, chock-full of erudite and cryptic references to Foucault and the hegemonic phallocentric horizon of being, but otherwise devoid of illumination.*[309]

Imaginary Wonders

AS PHILOSOPHY PROFESSOR Stephen Asma (who is also an accomplished jazz musician), both asks and answers:

> *Why do we have imagination? One major answer is functional and utilitarian...evolutionary adaptation, for example. The other is because it provides some of the highest human pleasure and joy. The fantasy view of imagination tilts in this direction (though fantasy can also be recruited for adaptive survival ends).*[310]

Immanuel Kant and Aristotle viewed the primary role of imagination as an unconscious faculty that gathers and synthesizes sensory perceptions into coherent and universally applicable representations. Kant tended to regard imagination primarily as a synthesizer of sensibility and understanding...as a form of judgment rather than one of fantasy or creativity. In his treatise *Poetics*, Aristotle praised artistic forms of imagination for shaping a version of real events such that a higher truth emerged.[311]

British naturalist Charles Darwin saw imagination as a faculty that created brilliant and novel results by uniting former images and ideas. Applying this to his personal life, he reflected:

> *I attain the highest level of adaptive imagination when I have voluntary control over the uniting impressions and scenarios—when I can conduct internal simulations of possible outcomes (using impressions, folk physics, and variable conditions).*[312]

Darwin wrote in his famous work, *Descent of Man*:

> *The value of the products of our imagination depends of course on the number, accuracy and clearness of our impressions, on our judgment and taste in selecting or rejecting the involuntary combinations, and to a certain extent on our power of voluntarily combining them.*[313]

Viennese psychiatrist Sigmund Freud envisioned imagination hard at work in the dark poetics of dreams as a necessary release system for antisocial desires. And while it may be tantalizingly seductive to occasionally attempt to correlate and interpret particularly provocative dreams with triggering causes and profound "meanings," such mental theater is often likely to reflect more nonsense than neuroses.

As Stephen Asma points out, our dreams are frequently more emotional than intellectual. Unlike more logical, sequential and linear contemplation in our waking life, they represent highly intuitive and image-based forms of thinking and feeling. Since dreams do not signal to the subject whether the experience is real or a figment—the senses can frequently be tricked.[314]

Asma characterizes dreams as:

> *Improvisations in the sense that they are autonomous,*

> *uncontrolled narratives with loose cause-and-effect*
> *sequencing. In fact, some dreams may only be 'brain*
> *noise'—the hum and flicker of a big wet machine in*
> *rest phase.*

During deep rapid eye movement (REM) periods of sleep, storms of neuronal firing sweep through the brain, while the neural systems most active during awakened times cease firing completely.

The mentally restorative quality of sleep we experience may be influenced by our individual levels of calming and relaxing serotonin. Many mathematicians and scientists report getting their "aha moments" after they have relaxed their conscious pursuit of a solution. When the problem sinks down into the unconscious, it continues to have a life, as it were—a private life that consciousness is not privy to.[315]

Whole Brain Imaginings

Aristotle described imagination as:

> *A faculty in humans (and most other animals) that*
> *produces, stores, and recalls the images used in a*
> *variety of cognitive and volitional activities.*

This faculty serves as a driving force for smarter, non-cliché thinking in a great variety of human endeavors. Included are the visual, literary and performing arts; science and engineering; marketing and economics; and ethics and government. While often annotated with lightbulb metaphors, lightning flashes, sparks and other combustion symbols, many of those insights quietly emerge without drama or fanfare.

Stephen Asma describes imagination from a whole-brain sensory perspective as:

Larry Bell

An embodied voluntary simulation system that draws upon perceptual, affective, and memory elements, for the purpose of creating works that adaptively investigate external and internal resources.

In addition to being an extrinsically useful "adaptive investigation system," imagination also possesses a capacity to experience significant intrinsic value in joy of play and states of wonder. This second system accomplishes its synthetic work through mechanisms which are distributed across various regions that access and control cognition and modes of communication.

Imaginative play enables us to take ideas "off-line" and rehearse them before taking action. Einstein reputedly said that "play is the highest form of research," claiming that his mind engaged in a kind of "combinatory play" or "associative play" just before his major breakthroughs. His local analysis would follow after this synthesizing creative phase. [316]

Einstein also said: "I am not enough of an artist to draw freely upon my imagination. Imagination is more important than knowledge. Knowledge is limited. Imagination encircles the world." Or as Harvard psychiatrist Arnold H. Modell puts it, our minds have the ability to create a "second universe"—an internal environment of possibilities that exists concurrently with the stubborn physical world. [317]

Our imaginative powers increase as we repeatedly exert voluntary control over many downstream modes of cognition and culture (e.g., through technology, innovation, storytelling, music, etc.). These events involve the manipulation of information-rich perception, memories, image schemas and bodily gestures born out of emotional needs and social experiences.

Here, our evolved present day human intellect can be viewed as both a product and servant of our social life. Our improvising imagination—our early intellect—gave us the behavioral and mental scaffolding to organize and manage our experiences. In fact, this began to occur long before human imagination invented language and word concepts.

How Imaginative Humans Got Big Heads

Anthropologist Robin Dunbar has gone so far as to attribute a rapid expansion in the size of the human neocortex (broadly characterized as the "rational brain") with increased cognitive demands of cultural learning. He reasons that as groups became larger and more closely organized during the Middle Pleistocene period between 800,000 and 200,000 years ago, it became more cognitively demanding to keep track of many complex social relationships. This imposed requirements for increased mental processing power to build better memories, representational abilities and even language.[318, 319]

In the 1960s, neurologist Paul MacLean proposed that our modern brain contains three distinct evolutionary stratum layers collectively referred to as the "triune brain" which he correlated as being analogous to an archaeological site. He surmised that each of these brains operates like "three interconnected biological computers, [each] with its own special intelligence, its own subjectivity, its own sense of time and space and its own memory."

Although various aspects of MacLean's brain model are debated by neuroscientists today as being overly simplistic, it may be useful to provide a general reference to help visualize why and how our mental faculties have been shaped by external challenges and influences.[320]

According to MacLean, the oldest layer of the triune brain, the "reptilian complex," comprised of the thalamus, cerebellum and basal ganglia, maintains functions like circulation and respiration, motor control and motivational or appetitive drive (in the higher regions of the basal ganglia). All vertebrates have similar systems.

A middle layer, the "limbic system," enables the emotional and memory aspects of the mammal mind. This region includes the amygdala, hippocampus, midbrain and especially the periaqueductal gray (PAG) area.

The third and most recent final brain layer, the neocortex, is a six-layered sheet-like structure in the roof of the forebrain that is found only in mammals. This region, which is immense in humans compared with other primates, is deeply grooved to maximize surface area. It contains various functional lobes: the frontal lobe (planning, calculating); the parietal lobe (touch, etc.); the occipital lobe (vision, etc.); and the temporal lobe (auditory, etc.).

Our enormous human cortex (and particularly the outsized prefrontal cortex), enables us to hold and manipulate sophisticated concepts. Although we can't match a jaguar in a foot race, we can easily outrun all other animals in agile mental simulations.

A key role of the prefrontal cortex to act as a filter system for self-control of emotions and ethical decision making is well documented. MRI brain scans on subjects now in their forties have revealed that strongly disciplined people had more active prefrontal cortex areas, and the majority of the weaker-willed subjects had more active limbic regions (e.g., the ventral striatum).[321, 322]

Our modern neocortex mushroomed to its current size less than one million years ago. This is a remarkably short time considering our future-looking, tool-wielding symbol-juggling human family broke off from the great apes in Africa at least six million years earlier.

Nevertheless, Stephen Asma argues that more of the heavy lifting in human creativity is borne by the emotional brain (limbic system), rather than by the rational brain (neocortex). He attributes this emotional construct as the primary imaginative prerequisite that caused Homo sapiens to emerge from fellow primate origins.

Throughout most of hominid history, our ancestral brain sizes, proportional to overall bodies, were approximately the same as other apes. Skull sizes of contemporary chimpanzees and Australopithecus, an extinct hominin that lived between 3.0 and 2.9 million years ago, averaged around 450 milliliters.

Paleolithic records reveal that as Homo erectus emerged, the neocortex began expanding significantly, and by 1.8 million years ago, brains were averaging around 600 milliliters. This evolution is presumed to reflect an increased tissue volume, in turn attended by neural system wiring changes that augmented processing power for functional tasks. There was a particularly prominent increase in the Broca's area, the part of the frontal lobe that is correlated with language.

A big mental capacity jump during the Middle Pleistocene period between 800,000 and 200,000 years ago doubled average hominid brain sizes. Anthropologist Rick Potts, who directs the Human Origins Program at the Smithsonian Natural History Museum, has attributed this exploded size and complexity to survival requirements imposed by intense climate changes.[323]

Radical temperature fluctuations and geological transformations between 800,000 and 200,000 years ago caused intense adaptation pressures involving thinking patterns, behaviors and even social strategies. Habituations that had previously worked well for those living in jungle environs became ineffective in the woodland fringe environments, on the grassland savannah or on the coasts.

Unfamiliar environmental and unstable situations during that period may have forced Homo erectus to slow down in order to analyze and strategically plan new solutions where purely habit-based strategies no longer worked. Basic survival required a more powerful information processor with better memory, reasoning abilities and social skills needed for rapid adaption to unfamiliar environmental and resource conditions.

Our successful Homo sapiens ancestors became adept at dealing with these challenges, while the Neanderthal, our close genetic Eurasian cousins (sharing about 90 percent of the same genes) were not. Although they too used tools, buried their dead, built fires, and were bigger and stronger than our ancestors, failures to adapt to climate change ended their existence.

As their world became colder between 50,000 and 40,000 years ago, the sapiens expanded their food hunting and gathering territories into growing tundra environments, while Neanderthals retreated into shrinking forests.

Physiological variances in body types help to explain these different strategies. Larger, stronger and physically more robust physiques of Neanderthals fit well in the context of forest ambush-style hunting which took down large animals with heavy short-range weapons. This contrasted with the leaner, faster, and more aerobic physiologies of Homo sapiens who emerged out of Africa. The bodies of our African ancestors better fit the needs of plains hunting, which required lighter weapons and long-range pursuit running.[324]

Homo sapiens responded not only by innovating lighter projectiles such as spears, but also by creating better clothing shelter "technologies" for the colder regions. Neanderthals failed in applying comparable cultural flexibility to move beyond experience-based strategies and tried-and-true customs.[325]

Our fortunate ancestral cognitive and social inheritance has led to increasingly faster-paced innovations.

Imagine that while 11 millennia passed between the Agricultural Revolution and the Industrial Revolution, it only took only 120 to get from the Industrial Revolution to the light bulb. Humans landed on the Moon 90 years later. Twenty-two years after that came the World Wide Web. A mere nine years later, the human genome was fully sequenced.[326]

Inventing Ourselves and Our World

There is real truth in the notion that creative people constantly reinvent themselves. As fresh experiences etch new neural pathways, plasticity enables our human brain to constantly reconfigure its own circuitry as an unceasing work in progress. This mental agility enables expansive dimensions of innovative thinking which other animals lack.

My neuroscientist friend, David Eagleman, describes how this came about in his coauthored book with composer Anthony Brandt titled *The Runaway Species: How Human Creativity Remakes the World*. He explains that the mass expansion of the human cortex "unhooked huge swaths of neurons from early chemical signals—hence these areas could form more flexible connections."

These many "uncommitted" neurons make us capable of mediated behaviors involving thought and foresight, such as understanding a poem, navigating a difficult conversation with a friend or generating a new solution to a problem.[327]

As David Eagleman puts it, "mediated behavior is how we generate novelty. It's the neurological basis for creativity." This type of flexible-wiring behavior contrasts with the sort of automated "push-button" thinking that becomes more hard-wired through experience.

For example, the expertise is acquired when the sculptor chisels, when the architect builds a model or when the scientist conducts an experiment. This practiced dexterity is also important to make new mediated outcomes possible.[328]

Automatized behaviors tend to operate in an autopilot mode without having to consciously think about them at all.

Honeybees, for example, depend entirely upon prewired networks, whereby a stimulus triggers the same reaction every time. Without having to contemplate the best among all various options, they are programmed to "land on blue flower, land on

251

yellow flower, attack, fly away." This automated mode applies even when they are exploring new territories.

Bees behave this way because neurons in their brains are fixed into place, passing signals from input to output like firefighters passing water pails in a bucket brigade. Those brigades begin to form before birth according to chemical signals which determine routings of neural connections between the different brain regions associated with movement, hearing, vision, smell and so on.[329]

Eagleman observes that we have quite a lot of bee in us:

> ...even as we learn new skills, we tend to streamline them into habits rapidly. We burn the task into fast pathways in the neural circuitry.

He adds:

> The most rapid conduit becomes favored over other solutions, minimizing the brain's chance of making an error. Neurons that are not required for that task are no longer triggered.

Of course, we also have a lot more brain cells working for us than bees do.

Whereas bee brains have about one million neurons, the human brain has about one hundred billion. In addition to quantity, we also have a big advantage in quality...with large numbers of our cells dedicated to sensory functions ("what's out there?") and actions ("this is what I'm going to do").

This enables us to take in a situation, chew on it, think through alternatives and, if necessary, take action.

The Evolutionary Art of Language and Innovation

Stephen Asma adds still another vital ingredient of sapiens' rapid evolutionary success. He writes:

> *Most evolutionary psychologists claim that the cause of [the Homo sapiens'] cognitive fluidity was the development of language (in the late Pleistocene), because language provides an obvious syntactical/ grammatical system for manipulating representations.*

Asma contemplates:

> *I try, for example, to imagine what it was like to be a conscious being before language (either a Homo erectus man or a contemporary Homo sapiens baby), I run straight into the fact that my mind is already deeply structured by language. It is difficult to peek around the veil of language to see the pre-linguistic operating system at work.* [330]

Eric Kandel literally visualizes an answer to Asma's dilemma. In his book *The Age of Insight*, he writes:

> *Perhaps in human evolution the ability to express ourselves in art—in pictorial language—preceded the ability to express ourselves in spoken language.* [331]

Lacking true language, and prior to pictorial images, our pre-sapiens ancestors in Africa and Eurasia around 500,000 years ago probably communicated with one another by gesture and mimicry. This view is consistent with anthropologist records revealing that bands of hunter-gatherers communicated by means of gestures, facial expressions and mime.[332]

In contrast with tool-making, innovation in the human visual art tradition exploded in a very short and recent period. The earliest forms of pre-figurative decorative design reach back to about 140,000 years ago.[333]

Oldwan stone implements, including simple choppers and pounders, continued with little innovation for about a million years between 2.6 and 1.8 million years ago. Subsequent tool-making industries, such as the Acheulean (1.7-0.2 MYA) and Mousterian (30,000-40,000 MYA), were more innovative and diverse. Nevertheless, they advanced very gradually and conservatively compared with the appearance and spread of visual technologies.

Production of simple hand axes that were flaked repeatedly to a create a biface symmetrical point remained basically the same for over a million years before evolving to create other adaptive tools like spear points, arrowheads, and stone knives. In contrast, cave paintings, such as the Chauvet Cave in the Georges de l'Ardèche, France dating back 30,000 years ago, demonstrate that human minds could convert three-dimensional animals (e.g., a bison or bear) into two-dimensional line representations.[334]

Stone-sculpted Venus figurines which appeared across Europe, from Portugal to Russia, between 28,000 and 21,000 years ago all had a remarkably similar style with exaggerated breasts. They are likely to reflect culturally-connected fertility symbols or mother goddess references.

Samuel Taylor Coleridge, English author of the famous poem *Kubla Khan,* posited that the ideal form of imagination occurs when art invites the viewer or listener to experience fresh insight and edification. He argued that the goal is not to convey literal understanding of nature...although understanding may be a welcome by-product. Understanding—even science—

is pedestrian when compared with the ideal expressive world of imagination.[335]

Plato, on the other hand, as reflected in his *Republic, Book VIII*, was highly suspicious of any imagery that didn't qualify as testable fact. This prejudice against images—born out of Plato's Pythagorean, revealed clear distrust of imagination gained and expressed through the senses. For Plato, whose paradigm of knowledge is math, artists were merely playing around with surfaces of things, not the things themselves, and certainly not the essences (forms) of things.[336]

Stephen Asma observes that, as with Plato and Aristotle, many philosophers throughout history intentionally or inadvertently demote "imagination" to become a sort of "weak knowledge," making it derivative or secondary to "real knowledge." In doing so, they have tended to think of real knowledge as "a process of seeing through the particular cases to the universal rules or laws that govern them."

Modern culture owes its very existence to imaginative innovation, a uniquely human cognitive process that synthesizes and acts upon observations, musings and theories to produce new or modified insights and products. As da Vinci, Einstein, Edison and countless other scientific and technical theorists, inventors and practitioners have demonstrated, innovation born of imagination is no longer viewed as the exclusive domain of the fine arts.

Asma points out that this imaginative process involves the whole brain. He writes:

> *There is no imagination organ buried in the neuroanatomical structures of the brain. Several candidates for location have come and gone, most popular of which is the idea that the right hemisphere houses imagination. But data suggest no clear localization of creativity, and the most that can be*

said with confidence is that communication between brain regions is very high in imaginative people.

There may be a solid scientific basis to defend "scatter-brained ideas" after all. Those mental communications interconnect information processing centers which are distributed throughout many locations. That creative network includes centers within the emotional brain (limbic system), memory system and motor system that interact with the rational brain (neocortical deliberation system).[337]

Underlying this cognitive realm, humans have a much older "simulation system" built up from sensory-motor mimicry and associated learning which operates outside of our creative consciousness. Our brain plasticity wires and strengthens preferential neural pathways through repeated network thought associations according to the adage that "neurons that fire together, wire together." This open-ended system supports what we recognize as emotional intelligence from which higher order evolution of social and adaptive problem-solving emerged.[338]

Stephen Asma disavows common tendencies for some evolutionary psychologists to reduce the creative mind to a set of domain-specific problem-solving computing circuits which are then projected into this Pleistocene era. He cites modular notions, for example, that there are specialized hard-wired mind circuits for avoiding poisonous plants, for detecting people who cheat or for finding a fertile mate.

Instead, Asma argues that the human improvising mind is the very opposite of a collection of hardwired modules or circuits which are dedicated to highly specialized functions. Instead, it functions more like a multimedia processor that blends pictures and propositions, memories and real-time experiences and sounds, stories and feelings. In doing so, imagination is not just a passive spectator of images and memories...it also constructs new knowledge and new behavioral norms.

In contrast to acting as a passive computational processor of existing images and memories, imagination proactively constructs unrealized possibilities. Asma characterizes this process as a kind of internal talking, where a particular thought is bound by language structures and functions which bring together representations (like memories and concepts) into novel combinations which are governed by linguistic grammar. This often occurs in the form of rapid blather.

Why Computers Can't Outthink Us

Imaginative human thinking processes differ in fundamental ways from operations of algorithm-based computer programs. These computer programs channel data through logical syntax systems to arrive at outputs. Although artificial intelligence can indisputably outperform great human chess players, such advantages lie in an ability to link together mind-numbing numbers of ideas and images rather than by deriving or inferring original ideas from non-programmed data sources.

Computers are terrifically good at remembering and keeping track of things—they have much better memories than we do. On the other hand, they aren't good at coming up with new ways to organize, modify and apply those things for alternate purposes...to innovate.

Unlike computers, the human brain doesn't just passively take in experience data, but instead constantly works to convert the sensory information it receives in order to imagine how everything connects together. The fruit of that mental labor can produce new realities.

Some of those new realities are born of a human "sixth sense," more commonly referred to as "intuition." While the best description of intuition is arguable, philosophers and theologians have tended to traditionally characterize it as an idea that doesn't enter our awareness through the five senses.

The five senses are gateways of empirical knowledge. However, such events that produce wonderful but rare "ah ha!" revelations often occur when we least expect them...times when we are engaged in unfocused, associational states of mind which constitute raw elements of later, more organized, imaginative compositions.

As David Eagleman writes:

> The basic software of the brain—which drinks in the milieu and procreates new versions—gives rise to everything that surrounds us; streetlights, nations, symphonies, laws, sonnets, prosthetic arms, smartphones, ceiling fans, skyscrapers, boats, kites, laptops, ketchup bottles, auto-driving cars.

Computer software doesn't attempt to make sense out of the information data we put into it. It really has no reason to care one way or another whether a particular image is a chipmunk or a cathedral, whether it is oriented upside down or sideways, or whether it was taken in Spain or in your backyard.

As smart as digital assistants like Siri appear to be at instantly pulling up facts regarding just about anything, knowing how to direct us along highways and side roads to obscure, remote locations and patiently rerouting us when we don't follow her instructions, she literally has nothing better to do with her time...no life of her own at all. Don't expect her to go home and use the recipe she found for you to whip up a batch of cookies for her digital family.

Siri and other computer software programs operate on "closed-world assumptions" we feed into them, where a statement presented to be true always is, and where a statement that is not known to be true is always presumed to be false. They only know what we tell them in order to perform a task that we dictate. It never occurs to them to argue or improvise. They give us back exactly what we put in, garbage or whatever.

Some people seem to live in closed worlds too. In doing so, they miss out in opening their lives to wonderful potentials and joys of imagination. Or as David Eagleman put it, "to constantly peer over the fence of today into the vistas of tomorrow." [339]

Eagleman observed that when operating within a closed-world constraint:

> We tend to assume that, whatever we know, that's essentially where things end; mentally we're tethered to our contemporary world. The future is imagined to be much like the present, even though the limitations of this approach become clear with a glance at the past.

The human capacity to think forward beyond the past enables us to contemplate dangerous consequences as well as positive rewards of future decisions. As the philosopher Karl Popper said, this capacity to simulate possible futures "allows our hypotheses to die in our stead." For example, we run a simulation of the future ("what would happen if I stepped off this cliff?"), and then adjust our future behavior accordingly (take a step backward). [340]

Growing with the Flow

Philosopher Stephen Asma, also an improvisational jazz musician who has played with such notables as Miles Davis, Bo Diddley, Buddy Guy and Otis Rush, points out a need for creative artists to be able to clear their minds in order to get "in the zone." This involves finding ways to enter "Zen moments" of being fully present in an egoless state. He notes that:

> Buddhist artists have been doing this for thousands of
> years, producing amazing poetry, ink drawings,
> calligraphy, bonsai, ikebana, sculpture, and so on.[341]

Asma acknowledges that this egoless state also presents a
paradox. He observes that in order to be fully in the "here and
now:"

> I must actually shut off all imaginative creation of
> the future (what could be), and the re-creation of the
> past (what was), as well as the imaginative
> possibilities of the alternative present.

He continues:

> The present moment is a singularly unimaginative
> place. In Chan (Zen) Buddhism, the artist celebrates
> this empty (no self) moment, even as she drags ink
> across rice paper. In contrast, Tibetan Buddhism
> celebrates a creative visualization tradition that is
> deeply imaginative and filled with rich narratives and
> images about past, present, and future beings of
> various power and influence.

Other psychologists of creativity, like Mihaly Csikzentmihalyi,
have also glorified this condition of creativity as "flow."
According to Csikzentmihalyi, these experiences occur when
there is a balance between challenges and skills, and when action
and awareness merge, self-consciousness disappears, time
becomes distorted and the activity becomes an end in itself with
inherent rewards.[342]

In this true meditative state, the past is already gone, and
thinking about the future becomes a subjective exercise in
imagining nonexistent events. Nevertheless, we also live in co-

present simultaneous possible worlds made up of "almosts" and "what ifs" and "maybes" which are in various processes of happening. Imagination expressed through intuition is required to help us prepare for them too.

As David Eagleman points out, "We are masters at generating alternative realities, taking what is and transforming it into a panoply of what-ifs." He attributes much of this capability to what he terms a "creative economy" of thinking which catalogs and stores important past lessons so that we don't need to devote needless energy relearning them.[343]

Eagleman observes that navigating the human world is a difficult and energy-expensive endeavor that requires moving around and using a lot of brainpower. It conserves a lot of that energy when we can make correct short-cut predictions:

> When you know that edible bugs can be found beneath certain types of rocks, it saves turning over all rocks. The better we predict, the less energy it costs us. Repetition makes us more confident in our forecasts and more efficient in our actions.[344]

Repetition also presents downside problems when we allow creative thinking to ebb. David Eagleman and his co-author Anthony Brandt remind us that too much familiarity through repetition often breeds indifference.

Waning attention causes us to put less effort into understanding something better, exploring new ideas and weighing alternative solutions. They note: "This is why marriage needs to be constantly rekindled. This is why you'll only laugh so many times at the same joke."

Our innovative spirit introduces surprises that keep us awake to new experiences and possibilities. Surprise engages us. Surprise allows us to escape autopilot. Surprise gratifies us.

All of this requires our minds to conduct perpetual

balancing acts. As Eagleman and Brandt describe the situation:

> On one hand, brains try to save energy by predicting
> away the world; on the other hand, they seek the
> intoxication of surprise. We don't want to live in an
> infinite loop, but we also don't want to be surprised
> all the time.[345]

Exiting Comfort Zones

ENGLISH ACTOR DAN Stevens regards the personal "comfort zone" as the great enemy of creativity, He advises: "Moving beyond it necessitates intuition, which in turn configures new perspectives and conquers fears."

British celebrity chef, Heston Blumenthal, observes:

> *As we get older, we tend to become more risk averse because we find reasons why things won't work. When you are a kid you think everything is possible, and I think with creativity it is important to keep that naivety.*

While much creative thinking occurs subconsciously, we can often give ourselves a boost in situations that require ingenuity and flexible thinking. Sometimes this requires getting outside of our comfort zones of tried-and-true experiences, ready-made methods and popularly-assumed perspectives.

Originality requires breaking some molds, including those we have allowed to crystallize around our own mindsets. Conversely, and also true, Hungarian-British author and journalist Arthur Koestler defined creativity as *"breaking of habits through originality."* Inventor Charles Kettering characterized innovation as to "Get off Route 35."

David Eagleman and Anthony Brandt remind us that the very origins of originality typically consciously or subconsciously draw upon raw materials provided by past experiences. Just like the massive programs running silently in computers, our inventiveness typically runs in the background, outside of our direct awareness. We consciously or unconsciously transform catalogued materials into new or modified forms by bending, breaking and blending them.[346]

Bending refers to remodeling a preexisting idea or object archetypes into a different version. For example, by changing its shape or size to fit another purpose. They note that this bending takes endless forms, including chorographers who bend human forms of dancers to fit themes and movements of performances, and recording artists who create their own renditions of popular music.

Eagleman and Brandt describe breaking as taking an existing concept or thing apart and reassembling the fragments in new ways. An example is when biochemist Frederick Singer figured out how to chop complex insulin molecules into shorter, more manageable, pieces for sequencing the composite amino acids in order to figure out the overall insulin molecule architecture. His "jigsaw" method, which earned Singer a 1958 Nobel Prize, is still used to map the structure of proteins.

Blending entails combining two or more concept sources in novel ways. This often involves weaving together different threads of knowledge from the natural world to produce designs and structures that follow the same patterns and principles. As with bending and breaking, this blending can be observed in virtually all aspects of human creation and activity: in art, literature and music; in metaphors used in everyday communication; and in sciences such as chemistry and metallurgy.

Authors Eagleman and Brandt hark back to chronicle a great leap forward in human civilization which occurred around 3,300 BC when Mesopotamians first blended copper and tin to begin a revolutionary Bronze Age of weaponry, sculpture, pottery and coinage. Whereas each of the components which had been separately used thousands of years earlier are relatively soft, when mixed together, they are harder than wrought iron.[347]

Eagleman and Brandt conclude that we bend, break and blend everything we observe, and that those tools allow us to extrapolate far beyond the reality around us. Much of this bending, breaking and blending ideas occurs at times when we don't realize it is going on. Yet whenever conscious or not, these cognitive processes apply to all areas and practitioners of creativity that break standard molds of thought to reveal previously unseen patterns, relationships and possibilities.

American entrepreneur, business magnate, inventor and college drop-out Steve Jobs described creativity as "just connecting things." He explained:

> *When you ask creative people how they did something, they feel a little guilty because they didn't really do it. They just saw something. It seemed obvious to them after a while; that's because they were able to connect experiences they've had and synthesize new things.*

You may have observed that not all of those creative new things we think up receive the sort of deserved enthusiastic responses we have hoped for. Thinking "out of the box" often smacks of unwelcome nonconformity to prevailing and popularly accepted conventions and standards. These "new" ideas are often openly resisted by closed mind-sets.

Social scientists Diego Gambetta and Steffen Hertog

characterize a potentially dangerous form of mind-set that seems to be opposite of the improviser...one that is thin-skinned and easily bruised when preconceived expectations are not met. Ironically, they found this closed-mind condition to be particularly common among engineering students who we might naturally imagine to be among the most inventive populations. The researchers even controversially suggested that engineering programs might foster such mind-sets through intensive emphasis on decontextualized knowledge.[348]

Philosophy professor Stephen Asma emphasizes that an improvising mind-set readily accepts risks of failure. The true improviser gets knocked down ten times, and gets up eleven.

American engineer, inventor, Delco founder and General Motors research director Charles Kettering advised that true inventors don't take either formal education or fear of failing very seriously. He wrote:

> You see, from the time a person is six years old until he graduates from college he has to take three or four examinations a year. If he flunks once, he is out. But an inventor is almost always failing. He tries and fails maybe a thousand times. If he succeeds once, then he's in. These things are diametrically opposite. We often say that the biggest job we have, is to teach a newly hired employee how to fail intelligently. We have to train him to experiment over and over and to keep on trying and failing until he learns what will work.

Hungarian-British author and journalist Arthur Koestle believed that a truly creative education comes from within. He wrote:

> Creative activity could be described as a type of learning process where teacher and pupil are located

in the same individual.

Novelist W. Somerset Maugham wrote that "Tradition is a guide and not a jailer." The past may be revered, but it is not untouchable. Still, all too often, education at all levels focuses excessively backwards on received knowledge and established results to the neglect of forward views toward a better world that students can design, build, and inhabit.

Psychologist Stephen Nachmanovitch writes:

> *Education must tap into the close relationship between play and exploration; there must be permission to explore and express. There must be validation of the exploratory spirit, which by definition takes us out of the tried, the tested, and the homogeneous.*[349]

As for winning public validation, Eagleman and Brandt point out that the act of creation is only half of the story: the other half is the community into which the creation lands. The novelty of any innovation alone is insufficient. Influence and impact also requires resonance with one's society.[350]

History demonstrates that willingness and motivation to innovate can be encouraged by robust cultures that afford significant shock absorption from failures. Philosopher, sociologist and psychologist George Herbert Mead cited the American experience as evidence.

Mead wrote that unlike early Europeans and Asians, Americans "Did not think of themselves as arising out of a society." On the contrary, Mead explained: "the pioneer was creating communities and ceaselessly legislating changes within them. The communities came from him, not he from the community."

He concluded that such a spirit of independence may be "a

crucial prerequisite for having a whole culture that happily sanctions dreaming." [351]

Breaking Molds—Remolding Possibilities

Our wonderful minds enable us to experience aspects of our present world through our senses, to reach beyond boundaries and limitations others take for granted, to envision alternate futures and to remodel realities to match imagined possibilities. In short, they empower us to convert fictions to facts, and what-ifs to what-is's.

Psychologist/writer Edward de Bono credited with originating the term "lateral thinking" believes:

> *Creativity involves breaking out of established patterns in order to look at things in a different way."* *He counsels that "One very important aspect of motivation is the willingness to stop and look at things no one else bothered to look at. This simple process of focusing on things that are taken for granted is a powerful source of creativity.*

De Bono advises that:

> *We need creativity in order to break free of temporary structures that have been set up by a particular sequence of experience.*

Here:

> *Creativity is a great motivator because it makes people interested in what they are doing. Creativity gives the possibility of some sort of achievement to everyone. Creativity makes life more fun and interesting.*

As previously discussed, these remarkable abilities involve our whole brain. Granted, endless models map our brains into separate territories where *"this"* region does *"this,"* whereas *"that"* region does *"that."*

Some "experts" primarily associate creativity (or innovation) with right brain activity. Others attribute predominate responsibility for creative capacity to "divergent thinking" processes mediated by the frontal cortex lobe where idea generation occurs. While true in part, such models give far too little credit to a most important aspect of our highly integrated neural architecture that enables adaptive and innovative thought.

As David Eagleman describes this, creative whole brain thinking arises from sweeping collaboration and distant neural networks "such that no brain region works alone; instead, like a society, regions work in constant hubbub of crosstalk and negotiation and cooperation." [352]

Creativity to overcome fear and mental inertia involves acting upon our curiosity and confidence to open our minds to new modal possibilities.

As English screenwriter and producer John Cleese, who co-founded the popular *Monty Python* comedy troupe, explains:

> We all operate in two contrasting modes, which might be called open and closed. The open mode is more relaxed, more receptive, more exploratory, more democratic, more playful and more humorous. The closed mode is the tighter, more rigid, more hierarchical, more tunnel-visioned.

Cleese observes:

> Most people, unfortunately spend most of their time in the closed mode. Not that the closed mode cannot be

helpful. If you are leaping a ravine, the moment of takeoff is a bad time for considering alternative strategies. When you charge the enemy machine-gun post, don't waste energy trying to see the funny side of it. Do it in the 'closed' mode. But the moment the action is over, try to return to the 'open' mode—to open your mind again to all the feedback from our action that enables us to tell whether the action has been successful, or whether further action is needed to improve on what we have done. In other words, we must return to the open mode, because in that mode we are the most aware, most receptive, most creative, and therefore at our most intelligent.

Albert Einstein stressed that "The true sign of intelligence is not knowledge, but imagination." He also posited that:

To raise new questions, new possibilities, to regard old problems from a new angle, requires creative imagination and marks real advances in science.

Hungarian biochemist Albert von Szent-Gyorgyi, who discovered Vitamin C and who won the Nobel Prize in 1937, characterized this creative imagining as recognizing possibilities that others have simply overlooked: "Discovery consists of seeing what everybody has seen and thinking what nobody has thought."

Educational author George Kneller notes that such discoveries or reflective insights often appear to us at moments when we take time to reexamine our thinking to consider what circumstances or assumptions might be misconstrued. Kneller observes:

Creativity, as has been said, consists largely of

rearranging what we know in order to find out what we do not know. Hence, to think creatively, we must be able to look afresh at what we normally take for granted.

Creating New Connections

International business advisor and author Margaret Hefferman attributes great creative importance to pattern recognition...most particularly in her corporate field, as an ability to discern patterns in tons of data. She observes:

> *Your mind collects that data by taking note of random details and anomalies easily seen every day: quirks and changes that, eventually, add up to insights.*

Venezuelan-American filmmaker and public speaker Jason Silva agrees, observing:

> *Creativity and insight almost always involve an experience of pattern recognition; the Eureka moment in which we perceive the interconnection between disparate concepts or ideas to reveal something new.*

In her book *Breakthrough Creativity: Achieving Top Performance Using the Eight Creative Talents*, Lynne C. Levesque emphasizes that creative people are unafraid to challenge the status quo:

> *To be creative you have to contribute something different from what you've done before. Your results need not be original to the world; few results truly meet that criterion. In fact, most results are built on the work of others.*

Creativity springs much less a desire to be different than from a willingness to be different in pursuit of something fresh or better. The well-known writer, reporter and political commentator Walter Lippman famously quipped: "When all think alike, then no one is thinking."

As the late American jazz composer and bandleader Charles Mingus pointed out:

> *Anybody can plan weird; that's easy. What's harder is to be simple as Bach. Making the simple awesomely simple, that's creativity.*

German-American architect Helmut Jahn also expressed this quest for essential simplicity, stating: "Creativity has more to do with the elimination of the inessential than with inventing something new."

Making Ideas Happen

FORMER HARVARD BUSINESS School professor and Harvard Business Review editor Theodore Levitt offers an important distinction between creativity and innovation, whereby: "Creativity is thinking up new things. Innovation is doing new things."

With regard to the former, American vocalist Judy Collins shares that:

> *I think people who are creative are the luckiest people on Earth. I know that there are no shortcuts, but you must keep your faith in something Greater than You, and keep doing what you love, and you will find the way to get it out of the world.*

W. Arthur ("Skip") Porter, a Texas business executive who served as Oklahoma Secretary of Science and Technology, characterized "The innovation point [as] the pivotal point when talented and motivated people seek the opportunity to act on their ideas and dreams."

Where do these individual ideas come from, and why do some materialize into innovations, while others who are probably even better never gain traction? Some prominent creative-innovative achievers reflect upon important success determinates.

Boundless Curiosity

Leo Burnett, founder of the Leo Burnett Worldwide Inc. advertising company, has observed, as I also have, that: "Curiosity about life in all of its aspects, I think, is still the secret of great creative people."

As highlighted in the introduction, whole-brain thinking is expressed in everyday life through curiosity that compels our interest in how and why natural and man-made things work the way they do...interconnected relationships between ourselves and others...patterns and rhythms observed in nature...spiritual lessons and explorations that motivate higher purposes and values...inspirations experienced through image forms, literature and stories of the past, music...everything combined that our whole minds can contemplate.

Albert Einstein, whose revolutionary theory of general relativity exemplified holistic thinking, purportedly said: "I have no special talent. I am only passionately curious." Nor was science his only passionate interest. He is also broadly quoted as saying:

> If I were not a physicist, I would probably be a musician. I often think in music. I live my daydreams in music. I see my life in terms of music...I get most joy in life out of music.

Einstein is only one among legions of creative iconic figures with multiple passions. Former British Prime Minister Winston Churchill, who won Nobel Prize for Literature in 1953, reflected: "If it weren't for painting, I wouldn't live. I wouldn't bear the extra strain of things."

On the business side, the late hard-hitting advertising executive Carl Ally, who helped promote the growth of some corporate firms such as Federal Express and MCI into industry giants, concluded that "The creative person wants to be a know-it-all." This is someone who "wants to know about all kinds of things: ancient history, nineteenth-century mathematics, current manufacturing techniques, flower arranging, and hog futures."

Ally added:

> Because he never knows when these ideas might come together to form a new idea. It may happen six minutes later or six months, or six years down the road. But he has faith that it will happen.

Bold Confidence

The late American scientist and inventor Edwin H. Land, who co-founded the Polaroid Corporation, once said: "The essential part of creativity is not being afraid to fail."

We can observe that people around us who are most fear-tolerant appear to run the gambit from those with a naïve tendency to ignore the likelihood and consequences of failures—to self-reliant risk-willing innovators who recognize and act upon opportunities that most other people let pass by.

These two opposite-appearing personality types aren't necessarily mutually exclusive. Many highly successful proactive innovators exhibit both of these characteristics. Referring to the former tendency, maintaining a child-like mind, Pablo Picasso said: "Every child is an artist, the problem is staying an artist when you grow up."

Overcoming that problem can be a big challenge. As Bucky Fuller observed, "Everyone is born a genius but the process of living de-geniuses them."

English writer and poet Samuel Johnson said, "Self-confidence is the first requisite to great undertakings." This fundamentally involves believing in possibilities...overcoming doubts of failure...remaining open to new experiences...being too busy working and learning to limit boundaries of investigation and thought. It is an attitude that says: "I can do this thing...I can make this work out...this will be a worthwhile contribution and exciting learning experience."

We can readily detect confident people. They tend to be relaxed, focused and positive. Their self-assurance stems from emotional feelings about how they see and value themselves, rather than upon all-consuming concerns about how others see them. Self-confident people know themselves, recognize their own strengths, and acknowledge their weaknesses as opportunities for improvement.

French philosopher, playwright, novelist, literary critic and political activist Jean-Paul Sartre warned, "If you are lonely when you're alone, you are in bad company."

How we psychologically view and value ourselves greatly influences our performance in areas of life...very much including the business world. Those who only feel good about themselves through recognition and approval by others are consigned never to be free.

Poor self-esteem virtually guarantees defeat and failure. Without it, we're unlikely to take the risk of giving everything necessary we've got to the challenge at hand. Or as nine-time Olympic gold medal winning track and field athlete Carl Lewis expressed it, "If you don't have confidence, you'll always find a way not to win."

As Albert Bandura, a psychologist at Stanford University, writes:

Perceived self-efficacy is defined as people's beliefs about their capabilities to produce designated levels of performance. Self-beliefs determine how people feel, think, motivate themselves and behave.

Bandura reports that people with lots of confidence in their abilities approach difficult tasks as challenges to be mastered, rather than as threats to be avoided. They set challenging goals for themselves, and maintain strong commitments to achieving them. They persevere and quickly recover after setbacks. They attribute failures to insufficient efforts, knowledge and skills that they believe are attainable.

Sometimes we judge ourselves too harshly. We get caught up in vicious cycles of declining confidence and performance. We get discouraged and engage in negative self-talk.

John Assaraf, *New York Times* bestselling author of *Having it All,* writes that while we may not always be aware of it, we constantly create and repeat self-affirmations. He explains:

> *The problem is, we typically don't pay attention to exactly what those affirmations are saying. Often we go through the day giving ourselves all sorts of contradictory, or even negative messages. We may project confidence to the world around us, while our inner dialogue says...I hope this works. I am so nervous about this. I hope I don't blow it. Affirmations are self-fulfilling prophecies. If we say, 'This is never going to work...then chances are excellent it never will.*

Entrepreneurs recognize and accept that risks of painful setbacks and failures are very real. They realize through experience that failing can often be another step in a new and better direction. They keep moving forward, and learning in the process. They look for and see a big, bright, colorful picture that others see only as a problem or obstacle.

Two business people face the same tough conditions but respond to them entirely differently. One views the situation as a threat that causes stress and anxiety. The other sees the same conditions as a challenge that motivates and excites them.

Steve Jobs cautions:

> *Your time is limited, so don't waste it living someone else's life. Don't be trapped by dogma—which is living with the results of other peoples' thinking. Don't let the noise of others' opinions drown out your inner voice. And most important, have the courage to follow your heart and intuition. They somehow already know what you truly want to become. Everything else is secondary.*

The great American orator and influential politician, William Jennings Bryan, advised that "The way to develop self-confidence is to do the thing you fear and get a record of successful experiences behind you." In doing so, success validates confidence, demonstrating that one's belief in their own judgment and ability is well-founded. Success breeds success.

Marianne Williamson, a four-time New York Times bestselling author and founder of project Angle Food, a meals-on-wheels program serving homebound Los Angeles AIDS patients, inspires us to overcome self- doubts that handicap full lives. She writes:

> *Our deepest fear is not that we are inadequate. Our deepest fear is that we are powerful beyond measure. It is our light, not our darkness that most frightens us. We ask ourselves, 'Who am I to be brilliant, gorgeous, talented, fabulous?' Actually, who are you not to be? You are a child of God. Your playing small*

does not serve the world. There is nothing enlightened about shrinking so that other people won't feel insecure around you. We are all meant to shine, as children do. We were born to make manifest the glory of God that is within us. It's not just in some of us; it's in everyone. And as we let our own light shine, we unconsciously give other people permission to do the same. As we are liberated from our own fear, our presence automatically liberates others.

Determined Commitment

Calvin Coolidge, the 30th President of the United States, a man noted for decisive actions, attributed central importance to dogged determination. He said:

> *Nothing in this world can take the place of persistence. Talent will not: nothing is more common than the unsuccessful men with talent. Genius will not: unrewarded genius is almost a proverb. Education will not: the world is full of educated derelicts. Persistence and determination alone are omnipotent.*

Albert Einstein reportedly said: "It's not that I'm so smart, it's just that I stay with problems longer."

Michelangelo is also credited with modestly describing his genius as more a matter of eternal perseverance and patience, stating: "If people knew how hard I worked to get my mastery, it wouldn't seem so wonderful."

The Merriam-Webster dictionary defines persistence as "the quality that allows someone to continue doing something or trying to do something even though it is difficult or opposed by other people." In other words, it typically requires powerfully determined commitment, often under outright discouraging circumstances.

As characterized by America's 32nd President Franklin Delano Roosevelt: "When you reach the end of your rope, tie a knot in it and hang on."

Examples of successful perseverance are endless. J.K. Rowling lived and raised her young daughter under government assistance in the United Kingdom while writing her first *Harry Potter* book, which was rejected by 12 major publishing houses over a seven-year period.

Henry Ford, who went bankrupt three times before he produced his first successful automobile, said: "Failure is merely an opportunity to more intelligently begin again."

Winston Churchill observed that: "Success consists of going from failure to failure without loss of enthusiasm." He emphasized: "Continuous effort—not strength or intelligence—is the key to unlocking our potential."

Famed American architect, systems theorist and inventor Buckminster ("Bucky") Fuller, said:

> *I'm not a genius. I'm just a tremendous bundle of experience…Most of my advances are by mistake. You uncover what is when you get rid of what isn't.*

He also reflected: "How often I found where I should be going only by setting out for somewhere else."

Thomas Edison, as quoted in a 1921 interview by B.C. Forbes for *American Magazine*, said:

> *I never allow myself to become discouraged under any circumstances. I recall that after we had conducted thousands of experiments on a certain project without solving the problem, one of my associates after we had conducted the crowning experiment and it had proved*

a failure, expressed discouragement and disgust over our having failed to find out anything. I cheerily assured him that we had learned something. For we had learned for a certainty that the thing couldn't be done that way. And we would have to try some other way. We sometimes learn a lot from our failures if we have put into the effort the best thought and work we are capable of.

Professional basketball star, performer, businessman and chairman of the Charlotte Hornets Michael Jordan cautions that sometimes we're inclined to expect winning results too soon. He has said: "I've failed over and over again in my life...that is why I succeed."

The idea, of course, is to learn from mistakes...what went wrong...what parts succeeded...rather than perpetuate them.

South-African-American business magnate, inventor and SpaceX founder-CEO Elon Musk stresses the importance of constant performance reassessments and adjustments in personal and corporate life:

I think it's very important to have a feedback loop, where you're constantly thinking about what you've done and how you could be doing it better. I think that's the single best piece of advice: constantly think about how you could be doing things better and questioning yourself.

Douglas Hofstadter, Pulitzer Prize-winning author for cognitive sciences ("Hofstadter's Law") plus composer, artist, calligrapher, physicist and programmer, summarizes the general process:

You make decisions, take actions, affect the world,

*receive feedback from the world, incorporate it into
yourself, then the updated 'you' makes more
decisions, and so forth, round and round.*

Obstinate Persistence

We can readily observe that highly recognized innovative
achievements often occur following repeated unsuccessful
attempts by people with tendencies to obstinately persevere in a
course of action in spite of difficulty or opposition.

Consider, for example, that day in 1879, when Thomas
Edison applied electricity to a fine thread of carbon thread that
he twisted into a horseshoe shape. Although the filament glowed
steady and bright, he recognized that it was inadequate to
market as a commercially viable bulb.

"Ransacking nature's warehouse," Edison set out to
experiment with alternative filament materials including various
plants, pulp, cellulose, flour paste, tissue paper and synthetic
cellulose.[353]

Edison later said:

> *I speak without exaggeration when I say that I have
> constructed 3,000 different theories in connection
> with the electric light, each one of them reasonable
> and apparently likely to be true. Yet only in two cases
> did my experiments prove the truth of my theory.*

Not all of Edison's ideas panned out that great…he wanted to
offer the middle-class public a much more affordable piano than
a Steinway. The one he designed in the 1930s out of concrete
for the Lauter Piano Company failed miserably. Weighing
literally a ton, its sound quality was also far inferior.[354]

As American astronomer, cosmologist, astrophysicist and
astrobiologist Carl Sagan advised:

> *Skeptical scrutiny is the means, in both science and religion, by which deep thought can be winnowed from deep nonsense.* [355]

Nevertheless, some idea seedlings just require a lot of patient nurturing before they bear fruit. James Dyson's invention of the first successful bag-less vacuum cleaner required 5,127 prototypes and fifteen years before going to market. He reported:

> *There are countless times an inventor can give up on an idea. By the time I made my fifteenth prototype, my third child was born. By 2,627, my wife and I were really counting our pennies. By 3,727, my wife was giving art lessons for some extra cash. These were tough times, but each failure brought me closer to solving the problem.* [356]

David Eagleman and Anthony Brandt remind us that failed ideas aren't really wasted. Many of them serve as fodder for other concepts and creations:

> *Innovation takes wing when the brain generates not just one new scheme, but many, and sketches those ideas to different distances from what is already known and accepted. Risk-taking and fearlessness in the face of error propel those imaginative thoughts.* [357]

American author Roger von Oech, whose focus has been on the study of creativity, observes:

> *It's easy to come up with new ideas; the hard part is letting go of what worked for you two years ago, but will soon be out of date.* [358]

Larry Bell

Linus Pauling, one of the founders of the fields of quantum chemistry and molecular biology, reportedly advised: "The best way to have a good idea is to have a lot of ideas." [359]

Leonardo da Vinci persistently distrusted his first solution to any problem as being the result of an overlearned routine. David Eagleman explained that this is because as a forest of interconnectivity, the brain is built for efficiency which "tends to land on the most well-trodden answer first."

And as British molecular biologist, biophysicist and neuroscientist Francis Hampton Compton Crick reportedly once said:

> *The dangerous man is the one with only one theory, because he'll fight to the death for it...the stronger approach is to have lots of ideas and let most of them die.* [360]

Part Five: Inspiration from My Friends

ONE OF THE great blessings in my life has been to count many remarkably creative and innovative super achievers among my personal friends and working affiliations.

Some of these individuals have gained prominent global and national distinctions, some have advanced truly important but less publicly recognized professional contributions and many, many more have quietly inspired my life and those of countless others as brilliant examples.

Source: Joanne Herring

Joanne King Herring (L), the true-life heroine portrayed by Julia Roberts (R) in the movie Charlie Wilson's War, who arranged for vital arms support for Afghanistan freedom fighters to defeat Soviet forces during the '80s.

Source: Joanne Herring

Open source stock photo

Open source stock photo

Jane Goodall has dedicated her entire life to environmental stewardship in devoted efforts to protect chimpanzees and other wild animal populations and through the establishment of her Roots and Shoots educational programs.

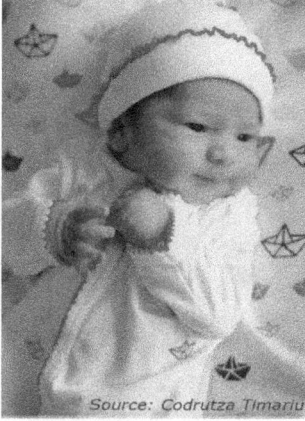

Source: Codrutza Timariu

Dr. Eddie Yosowitz is among countless dedicated health care professionals who share our happiest and most difficult times. He helped to make the joyous arrival of Thomas (L) possible.

Source: Dr. Eddie Yosowitz

Sculptor Dennis Kowal urges us to appreciate the importance of fully living and loving whatever we do.

Source: Dennis Kowal

Source: Dennis Kowal

Architect Victor Lundy's works evoke timeless inevitability of belonging in each setting.

The Westport Unitarian Church communicates a sense of perfect eternal natural harmony.

The US Tax Court in Washington, DC combines a bold exterior and elegant interior.

Ballerina Nao Kusuzaki teaches that artists can break rules only after first learning them.

Larry Bell

US Weather Satellite Service founder Fred Singer is a hero to many who honor his unwavering commitment and significant contributions to advance science.

Apollo 7 Astronaut Walter Cunningham emphasizes the importance of comprehensive problem-solving teamwork that produces verifiable results.

290

Three aerospace greats: Burt Rutan (L), Max Faget (M) and Buzz Aldrin (R).

Burt Rutan's historic aircraft designs include Voyager, the first aircraft to fly non-stop around the globe without refueling, and SpaceShip One (L), the first privately-funded craft to enter the edge of space twice within two weeks.

Max Faget's many innovative NASA concepts include key features of the Mercury, Gemini and Apollo capsules.

Buzz Aldrin, Neil Armstrong commemoration and the author at Purdue University.

Gemini/Apollo Astronaut Buzz Aldrin is a former Korean War fighter pilot, an MIT Ph.D, and active space mission designer.

Neil Armstrong was a board member of a private space company I co-founded with Max Faget and two other partners.

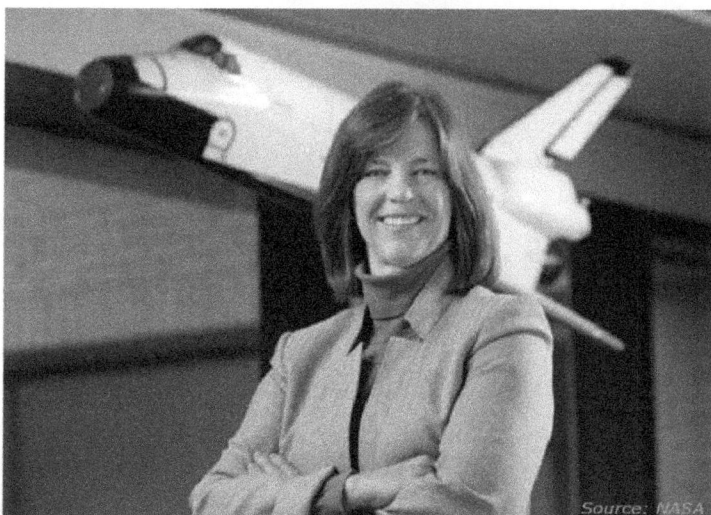

Astronaut Dr. Bonnie Dunbar who flew five Space Shuttle missions fortunately disregarded earlier comments from anyone who said space is not for women.

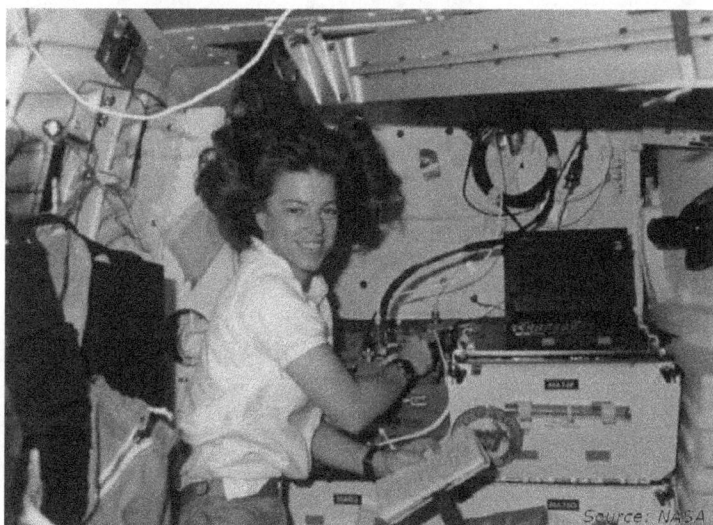

Bonnie says: "you never think of making history while you're there. If you're doing that, you're not putting all your brain cells where they need to be."

Larry Bell

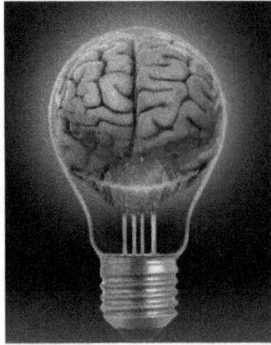

The Humanitarians

Joanne King Herring: Beautiful Diplomacy

JOANNE KING HERRING thinks whole and lives whole. Throughout trying times and triumphs she ceaselessly champions charitable causes with the same generous concern, thoughtful intellect, candid honesty, and beautiful ageless grace that she brings to her many personal friendships.

Joanne's humanitarian passion is exemplified in the blockbuster movie *Charlie Wilson's War* which chronicles her crucial assistance to Afghanistan freedom fighters in defeating Soviet forces during the 1980s. Actress Julia Roberts portrayed part of Joanne's true-life role in this semi-secret war opposite Tom Hanks whose real character was Texas Congressman Charlie Wilson.

After Pakistan's President Zia Ul-Haq told Joanne that poorly-armed Afghan soldiers were fighting against Soviet forces with the goal of using Afghanistan to dominate the entire Middle East, she became determined to take a first-hand look at the situation. She managed to sneak into Afghanistan with a small crew, including professional combat photographer, Robin King, to film devastating Soviet helicopter attacks and interviews with besieged tribal leaders. That film was shown to every influential politician who would look and listen. One who did, was Charlie Wilson, a Democrat Congressman from Lufkin, Texas who served on the House Appropriations Committee.

Joanne personally persuaded the Saudi Arabians to fully match the billions of U.S. dollars Congressman Wilson channeled into support for Afghanistan fighters who successfully crushed Soviet military aspirations. As she observes:

> *We were breaking every rule, but we had to do it because we had to stop the Soviets in Afghanistan. Because their ultimate objective was the Strait of Hormuz, through which 80 percent of the world's oil passed daily. The US was not energy independent. Our economy would be seriously threatened. I was sure this was true. When I told US policy makers, the bored look in their eyes changed to understanding and belief. That's when America turned!*

Representative Wilson, who came to love Joanne with hopes of marrying her said, "Joanne is a very difficult woman to say no to." Those who know her will find that observation to be endearingly true.

Joanne attributes her strong sense of purpose and determination to deep religious moorings:

> *I am now sure that every experience, to follow, both good and bad, was God preparing me to work with the Afghans against the Soviet Union. I must now continue to work to help them survive because the Soviet Union has returned. They are selling drugs in return for arms which will be used against those fighting for freedom worldwide.*

Reminding us how valiantly the Afghans fought and died to

defeat one of the greatest war machines in history, the Soviet Union, she implores, "Now, we must help them win the peace."

Joanne believes that "solving poverty world-wide is the answer to global peace." Moreover, she has proven through a program she initiated in village of 20,000 people in a war-torn region of Afghanistan that it could survive alone if provided five elements simultaneously: food, water, healthcare, education and jobs. For eight years, it has not only flourished is the capital of its province, but has established its own citizen army. The Taliban does not come within 50 miles of them.

Joanne wants to replicate this approach throughout other troubled and struggling regions of Afghanistan and the world:

> This village success was achieved for just $450,000…half the cost of keeping one American soldier in the field one year. That accomplishment has excited other countries. George Clooney has expressed the desire to initiate this program in Africa. India and Pakistan are also interested.

She adds,

> The United States has been at war 16 years in Afghanistan. Instead of wasting billions of dollars, if the U.S. had funded all 119 villages in Afghanistan, the country would be free of the terrorists today, and our own children would not be there.

Joanne Herring has won hard-fought personal and charitable achievements throughout her entire life. She was born as Joanne Johnson on July 3, 1929…the only child of a Houston family that set very high standards for success, intelligence, good works, and good manners.

The Johnson home was in a prestigious and clubby River

Oaks neighborhood. Her father was the first player All American player chosen from the Southwest Conference. He also beat the famed Olympic gold medalist Jim Thorpe as first pro football pick. Nevertheless, he was discouraged from a professional athletic career by Joanne's grandfather who believed polo was more dignified.

Although the Johnsons spoiled Joanne, their lofty expectations in virtually everything also made Joanne's early years discouraging. She viewed herself as unattractive, lonely with no friends, and "dumb," achieving only average grades. Dyslexic symptoms when she read caused letters and numbers to "jump around on the pages."

An inspirational teacher who saw Joanne's academic capabilities much differently encouraged Joanne to compete for acceptance to the National Honor Society. At age 15, she succeeded.

That wasn't the only dramatic development to elevate her low self-esteem. In a family that valued physical attractiveness, Joanne shed her self-perceived ugly duckling image to grow into a beautiful swan. Classmates noticed this as well, and those friendless lonely days were over for good. During an era when high school dances were held in school gymnasiums with girls on one side—many boys on the other side lined up for chances to dance with her. She became popularly nicknamed "one-step Johnson."

Joanne had a good singing voice. At age 17 she starred as princess in the *Student Prince* musical with the Houston Summertime Light Opera.

At age 20, Joanne was selected in a MGM audition to play a lead role with Clark Gable in *Across the Wide Missouri*. Her parents were against her participation in the movie business. They asked her: "Why involve yourself in that disgusting business when all the perks are available in marriage. Marry a rich boy." And she soon did.

That same year, Joanne experienced a spinal tumor. Upon being warned that an operation could be fatal or lead to permanent paralysis, she chose to accept those enormous risks. Crediting her strong faith in God, and against big statistical odds, she fully recovered.

Girls in those days were encouraged to study home economics or prepare for teaching careers. While attending the University of Texas in Austin, Joanne discovered broader personal capabilities. She recalls:

> *The tragedy of dyslexia taught me to develop an almost photographic memory and an analytical mind which was essential for me in the future in working with heads of state, especially men. It was a man's world.*

Joanne dropped out of college to marry Robert King, a very successful Houston real estate developer who met her parents' demanding standards of social and financial acceptability. Later, during a major market collapse he went broke and sold everything, including five large residential subdivisions.

In the meantime, Joanne had launched a successful career as hostess of a popular Houston television program. Her introduction to media audiences began at age 33 in a fund-raising promotion for a woman's home charity which she co-founded with her grandmother. That interview led to a 15-year-long *Joanne King Show* series featuring informative topic discussions with prominent public figures. Her program ranked sixth highest in the nation in viewer numbers, an experience that taught her be comfortable in addressing large audiences and highly successful people.

Joanne had hoped unsuccessfully that her television income would reduce financial strains which added to other more personal problems in her marriage to Robert King. After their divorce, she became a single working mother with two children. She recalls: "This taught me humility, and to care about people in need. I understood their problems."

Joanne's captivating persona, genuine southern charm and fashion model good looks spread to gain international recognition. In her mid-30s, while economically struggling to cover basic family expenses, Joanne was broadly welcomed into the arms and palaces of European high society. Her Grande Dame celebrity status earned her invitations to the most ritzy royalty galas, where top designers lavished her wardrobe with free costumes befitting those high profile occasions. Government-sponsored tourism industry promotions featured documentaries *Joanne Herring in Spain, Italy, France and Africa*.

Joanne's gracious beauty, intelligence and captivating social skills drew the admiration and romantic interest of Texas billionaire Robert Herring, founder of Houston Natural Gas which later became ENRON. The two deeply respected each other, married, and became an influential duo until his loss to lung cancer in 1981 before ENRON's demise. Together, they made dozens of trips to the Middle East for oil and gas deals, including 17 trips to Saudi Arabia where she met the royal family who were hugely instrumental in the war against the Soviet Union. Joanne reflects: "God provided once again."

Her travels with Bob Herring launched Joanne on a new Jet Set trajectory to international celebrity status which served to advance her increasingly proactive anti-communist passion. As Joanne reflects:

> *The aristocratic contacts I made at parties provided exactly the right person at exactly the right time and place to provide exactly the right tools to help in the war to end communism.*

The kings, queens and heads of state that she met during the making of these documentaries liked her, and felt she understood both their problems and the world's. This catapulted her from being a media star to becoming useful to those in power. They consulted her. The President of Pakistan and the King of Morocco realized the communist domino theory was endangering their countries. Her intellectual friendship with them and other powerful figures in France and the Middle East led to the decision that the Soviets must be stopped in Afghanistan.

America was engaged in the danger of communist incursions in our own hemisphere, and did not feel we could take on Afghanistan.

Recognizing her business and political acumen, highly-placed government officials, including King Hassan II of Morocco, President Zia Ul-Haq of Pakistan, and other powerful leaders in France and the Middle East sought her advice. The highest position she could accept without losing her U.S. citizenship was honorary counsel to Pakistan and Morocco, simultaneously.

At the risk of being invaded, the President Zia Ul-Haq allowed the arms arranged for by Joanne and Charlie Wilson to pass through Pakistan to the Mujahedeen in landlocked Afghanistan. Pakistan President Perez Musharraf who followed Zia Ul-Haq said:

> I know Joanne Herring to be a most dynamic and inspiring personality. Her deep commitment to alleviate and assuage the sufferings of people of our region has touched me.

While working with Pakistan, Joanne energized and transformed the cottage industry by enlisting influential friends in the fashion industry to help poor Pakistani villagers redesign their handmade crafts, including rugs, fabrics, and copper and silver goods, for

Western consumer markets. Her entire purpose was to have the money benefit the villagers. She sadly quit when upon realizing that greedy local bureaucrats and middlemen were skimming profits, but this experience was to provide the insight and experience making it possible for her village in Afghanistan to become successful and self-supporting.

U.S. Secretary of State James Baker whose immense help fueled her success in Afghanistan and in the fall of Soviet Union said: "I have known Joanne all my life. She walks where others fear to tread and never quits. She is a flash of light in a dark world."

And as President George W. Bush similarly recognized: "Joanne Herring is an extraordinary woman who was and still is a real catalyst in our world."

Joanne's public contributions have earned her numerous national and international honors. Among these, she was nominated along with Wilson and CIA officer Gustav ("Gust") Avrakotos, both now deceased, for the Congressional Gold Medal...the highest civilian honor bestowed by Congress. She was also granted the title of *Knight* by Order of the Crown in Belgium; *Dame* by Order of St. Francis in Italy; and appointment as *Ambassador-at-Large,* along with the *Quaid-e-Azam Award,* the highest honor bestowed by the nation of Pakistan.

Joanne is a highly-recognized tour de force on national and state levels as well. She co-chaired the Special Olympics in New York City with Henry Kissinger and was elected to the Texas Hall of Fame.

Joanne's example teaches us that successes we value most often come with achievements earned through persistent hard work:

> *I have found life to be one difficult situation after another. Nothing I have ever done has been without heartache and sacrifice. I am no different from*

anybody else. Success is never easy. If you want to win, you must always roll up your sleeves and work while others play. My mantra is work longer and harder than anyone else, and with God's help you'll win.

Sharing a related experience that applies to everyone, she recalls:

I was at a Home Depot, parked near a Rolls Royce. He said, 'Like my car?' And I said 'Oh Yes!' And he said. 'I always wanted one. That's why I became a plumber.' The point is, a plumber is a hugely successful job if you make it one.

That's a standard that Joanne has continued to follow throughout her entire charitable life…to do whatever it takes to make it count as the best damn one possible.

Jane Goodall: Life Lessons from Primates

Primatologist Jane Goodall is a marvelous spokesperson, teacher and role model demonstrating a compassionate and selfless devotion to environmental stewardship. Moreover, her very authentically thoughtful, engagingly personal and enthusiastically captivating demeanor reveals no self-awareness of much-deserved global celebrity whatsoever.

My wife Nancy and I first became acquainted with Jane at an Explorer's Club event in West Texas, where her discussion of experiences with a community of chimpanzees in African bush country was the keynote attraction. Jane also spoke about goals and activities of the non-profit Roots and Shoots program she founded in 1991. The organization addresses wide-ranging environmental, conservation and humanitarian issues.

Thinking Whole

We subsequently hosted a follow-up meeting and presentation event in Jane's honor at our Houston home. The life experiences and lessons she has shared with all of us are inspiring.

Jane was born in London in 1932. Lacking finances for college tuition, she attended secretarial school, worked briefly for a London documentary film company, and later, waited tables to save money for a dreamed ocean passage to Kenya.

Upon reaching Nairobi, Jane secured a provident secretarial position with the famous paleoanthropologist Louis Leaky, whose pioneering research into human origins led him to take a strong interest in studies of great apes. Recognizing her passion for animals and the makings of a good scientist, he arranged for her to conduct field observations of primates in Tanzania. Her influential mentor underwrote the trip by selling rights to print first pictures to a British weekly publication.

Jane arrived in Gombe, Tanzania at age 28, possessing no college degree and no research experience. Having previously only known fictional representations of Africa presented by Tarzan movies and Dr. Dolittle books, she was to encounter, and immediately fall in love with, a challenging new land of Malaria, parasites, snakes, storms...and yes, chimpanzees.

Those close engagements with wild chimpanzees which have continued throughout her life have been consequential in raising public appreciation of their many human-like qualities, along with their vulnerability to destructive human encroachments on their habitats.

Jane taught us, for example, that some chimpanzees are toolmakers, fashioning fishing probes with a particular brush-tipped design used to extract termites from their mounds. Mothers teach these skills to their offspring.

Upon first hearing about this discovery, Louis Leaky sent a return telegram to Jane, writing: "now we must redefine tool, redefine man, or accept chimpanzees as human." Leaky also sent

303

a letter to the National Geographic Society, saying:

> *I feel it is important to draw attention to the fact that the work which Jane Goodall has done, with research grants, from the Society, has been so important as to necessitate a complete review of scientific thought about how to define man himself.*

Other observations of chimpanzee behaviors were devastatingly upsetting to her. Coupled with a 1975 cannibalistic infanticide, a violent four-year-long conflict between two communities in northern and southern regions of the Gombe Stream Park revealed that a very "dark side" also existed in their nature. She wrote in her memoir:

> *For several years I struggled to come to terms with this new knowledge. Often when I woke in the night, horrific pictures sprang unbidden to my mind—Satan [one of the apes], cupping his hand below Sniff's chin to drink the blood that welled from a great wound on his face; old Rodolf, usually so benign, standing upright to hurl a four-pound rock at Godi's prostrate body; Jomeo tearing a strip of skin from Dé's thigh; Figan, charging and hitting, again and again, the stricken, quivering body of Goliath, one of his childhood heroes.*[361]

While emotionally dispiriting, the savage war between two formerly united chimpanzee communities did not alter her devotion to serving as their tireless advocate. To this end, Jane has established several primate sanctuaries, including an outdoor facility at Stanford University, has mentored generations of primate and other environmental scientists, and has founded effective charitable fundraising and teaching organizations to promote conservation consciousness.

Jane's Roots & Shoots initiatives bring together youth from preschool to university age to identify and work on problems in their own communities affecting people, animals or the environment. Founded in 1991, the organization currently has chapters in more than 140 countries, with over 8,000 local groups and nearly 150,000 annual worldwide participants.

Jane Goodall's life is a testament to what passion can accomplish. She demonstrated that a woman with no previous college education or research experience can impact science, advance public consciousness about important issues, create and lead substantial educational and conservation initiatives and can even become the first person without an undergraduate degree to earn a PhD at Cambridge University.

Jane attributes her courage and motivation to act upon her passions to motherly confidence: "My mother used to tell me, 'Jane, if you really want something, you work hard enough, you take advantage of opportunities, you never give up, you will find a way.'" [362]

She has a life-long passion to make the natural world more humane for all creatures. Well into her 80s, Jane's continues a 300-day annual travel schedule to lobby governments, visit schools and give speeches.

Dr. Eddie Yosowitz: Introducing New Lives

Obstetrician-gynecologist, Dr. Eddie Yosowitz, is an inspirational example among countless unheralded health care professionals who provide aid and comfort during trying periods in our lives and those of loved ones. He also embodies inventive thinking and humanitarian values which find self-enrichment through non-medical contributions to others.

Eddie was born in 1942 in Vincennes, Indiana. His father, Joseph Yosowitz, owned a dress shop on the banks of the

Wabash River. His mother, Sally, worked at his side. She was a lovely woman, and a bright light in Eddie's life.

As a youth, Eddie helped in his father's store where his colorblindness represented a significant merchandizing and sales disadvantage. This was not the sort of business he envisioned as a career opportunity. A strained relationship with his father further capped any interest in future family business prospects.

Eddie had a much closer relationship with his grandfather, Benjamin Yosowitz, who owned a dry goods store and worked as a tailor on the opposite side of the Wabash. "Benny", as he was known by everyone, originally emigrated from Poland in the 1920s. Together with Jenny, a mail order bride from Chicago, the couple repaired clothes for workers in near-by southern Illinois oil fields.

Benny has represented an important role model throughout Eddie's life. Despite prevalent anti-Semitic attitudes at the time, it seemed that nearly everyone in the community loved and respected him.

Eddie delights in telling a particular story about his grandfather's ability to survive difficult situations:

> Back in the 1940s, a Ku Klux Klan rally involving many of the oil field workers smashed windows on Benny's store. When I asked him whether he was frightened by that experience, he replied 'no, they all knew me and put food in my mouth. They were only showing off their club. Besides, it only cost me 50 cents to replace each of those broken windows and I charged each of them $2 dollars for their sheets.'

Like his grandfather, Eddie has a strong independent nature. At age 17, he left a note for his father and boarded a Greyhound bus for South Haven in southern Michigan. As he recalls, "I was scared, but other than the $20 dollars my mother had given me,

I was determined to be successful on my own."

Eddie got a job waiting tables and singing in a Jewish resort night club, just as his mother once had. Living very frugally, he managed to save most of his tip money for college, and was accepted at Indiana University.

Lacking sufficient savings to wait longer, Eddie applied for medical school at Indiana University after completing only three undergraduate college years. Upon receiving a written response stating that he would be listed as an alternate for admission, he immediately decided to plead his case for full acceptance in person.

The very day he received the letter, Eddie drove his jalopy car to see the Dean of Admissions Mahoney who had written it. Arriving announced, his audacity paid off. Impressed with Eddie's determination, Dean Mahoney not only agreed to have him enrolled, but also championed his subsequent professional progress.

Eddie attributes his interest in medicine to the influence of a Dr. Sam Chattin, a Vincennes family practice physician. Dr. Chattin was also the father of a beautiful teen age daughter whom Eddie was dating at the time.

Dr. Chattin introduced Eddie to his home library containing a large collection of books covering a wide variety of medical and biological subjects. Eddie's obvious fascination to learn more about these topics influenced Dr. Chattin to invite Eddie to join him on his medical rounds and house calls.

Those mentoring experiences fundamentally changed Eddie's life. Through Dr. Chattin, he discovered great honor and value in serving as a trusted family counselor and respected community contributor. Through Dr. Chattin, Eddie saw a person who was actually capable of saving people's lives.

Fuller realization that saving lives requires hard work and dedication was influenced by another important mentor. Catholic Sister Susanne, a young no-nonsense instructor at a high school-level Ford Foundation-sponsored science seminar, told him: "Eddie Yosowitz, you won't make it as a doctor. You're smart enough, but you're just not disciplined enough."

Asking for an opportunity to prove otherwise, Sister Susanne agreed to give him some very difficult, time-demanding science assignments. Eddie seriously and successfully applied himself to the challenge, and Sister Susanne never forgot. Several years later, she wrote to congratulate him upon reading about a "Yosowitz cuff" invention that Eddie had created during the 1970s to prevent fatal premature births. The device holds the baby inside an "incompetent cervix" until it reaches a viable development stage to survive outside the womb.

Eddie reflects:

> As I think about it, here I am, a Jewish guy who owes much to the important influences of two Catholic mentors...Dean Mahoney and Sister Susanne. Now I want my life to be a conduit of decency from them and my grandparents and other family.

Following graduation from Indiana University medical school, Eddie was accepted for several different residency programs. He chose to move to Houston for three reasons.

First, he identified with a "surgeon's personality type", a desire to deal with immediate medical issues...to get it done decisively with quick results. Houston was "surgeon country", the home of famed heart surgeons Denton Cooley and Michael DeBakey.

Second, Houston had a large Jewish population. He saw it as a welcoming community to raise a family.

Third, Eddie loved baseball. The Houston Astros had just moved into a magnificent dome structure referred to as "the eighth wonder of the world."

The new Dr. Yosowitz entered a three-year residency at

Baylor University's obstetrics-gynecology program which included two Houston hospitals that prioritized services for low-income residents. He remains proud of the fact that hard work earned him the status of being chosen as "chief resident" among the ten participants in his program.

Following his Baylor residency, Eddie served for two years as a U.S. Air Force major during the Viet Nam War. He was stationed at Sheppard Air Force Base in Wichita Falls, Texas, where he took care of pilot and prisoners of war families.

In 1994, observing that the less personalized nature of large hospital employment structures was changing, Dr. Yosowitz founded a more cost-effective treatment center, the Women's Specialists of Houston (WSOH). He named the term "specialists" in remembrance of something his mother had once told him: "She said when she gave me that $20 that I was special, and she never lied!"

The new venture was financed, in part, using money provided by a five-year option Eddie granted to Houston's St Luke's Hospital in exchange for a discount on the sale price if and when they purchased the organization. Although St Luke's ultimately passed on the option, WSOH grew and prospered. Houston's Texas Childrens' Hospital purchased the practice in 2007.

Dr. Eddie Yosowitz is grateful and proud to note that despite some very challenging incidents in delivering more than 10,000 babies over 33 years of practice, he has never lost a mother. He cites one very difficult case as an example:

> A medically-distressed woman arrived at the operating room in an advanced labor stage on a 4th of July. Due to the holiday, the hospital was functioning with only a small skeletal staff. Making matters even worse, the available interns in attendance were new in the practice, with limited experience.

A life and death crisis soon ensued for both mother and baby:

> The woman cried out in intense pain as we moved her onto the operating table. Her complexion turned pallid, and she registered almost no pulse. It was clear that needed a C section to rescue the infant, but I didn't know the cause of the problem. I then discovered that for some unknown reason her uterus had spontaneously ruptured. The baby was actually floating in amniotic fluid and blood outside the uterus!

Eddie recalls:

> I said to myself, this woman may bleed to death if I don't immediately prevent this from happening. I'm the only the only one here that can save her...something I have prepared for all my life. Now, dammit! Do what you are trained to do!

He did that, and the mother and baby survived.

He later learned, the new mother hadn't thought to report a minor car accident a few days before. It became apparent that pressure from her car safety belt had caused her uterus to weaken, and in labor, it ruptured.

Eddie expresses as his greatest satisfactions:

> To deliver healthy babies to people who really want them and will take loving care of them...to share precious moments in individual and family lives...and to realize that those new children have full lives ahead.

There is a generational satisfaction to his service as well: "I have

delivered children of parents I helped bring into the world."
He adds:

> *I also share terribly difficult and sad times with individuals and their loved ones. The hardest of all is to have to inform patients of distressing laboratory test results, such as evidence of cancer, or indications that the baby they have excitedly waited for has a poor prognosis for survival. It's particularly troubling when I see people who might have curtailed a cancer if only they had been examined earlier by an informed physician.*

Yet Eddie Yosowitz is far more than a competent physician. He also directs his whole-brain thinking and innovative talents to a variety of creative and public-minded non-medical pursuits. He credits two of these, book writing and music composing, to his now-deceased mother.

Eddie reflects upon wonderful made-up stories she told him and his sisters and brother as children:

> *There was one where Kingfish of the Sea would outsmart Sharkey the bank robber. We couldn't wait to learn how the next episode would turn out as mother said...'and then tomorrow...'*

Eddie has donated all proceeds from three children's books he has written to charity. He also freely contributes time to read and discuss life lessons they address at predominately low-income family public schools throughout southeast Texas. The sessions typically engage about 600 students ranging from second through fifth grade levels.

All of the books address important moral themes, for example,

> *You don't have to be what everyone else wants you to be...choose your own life; value and pursue your dreams; and don't let doubts or physical attributes hold you back from successes.*

Eddie applies this same philosophy to his own personal experience:

> *I realize that if I'm not always the smartest person in a crowd, I will make the commitment and will expend the energy to accomplish goals I set in life. We all have the potentials to do this.*

Some of the topics raised by those students reveal very troubling family and personal circumstances. Eddie cites an example of a young girl wanting to know how to deal with an irresponsible parent: "My dad and I used to do drugs together." He notes that such issues represent tragic commentaries on our times.

Eddie Yosowitz also generously devotes time to community appointed him to an unpaid position with the Department of Aged and Disabled Services (DADS). He currently serves on Texas Governor Greg Abbot's Infectious Disease Task Force which is aimed at eradicating illnesses caused by the Zika and West Nile viruses.

I will conclude this tribute to Dr. Eddie Yosowitz and fellow health care professionals by sharing a personal experience.

The wife of a young couple that Nancy and I first came to know when walking their dog of a similarly rare breed to ours through our neighborhood had virtually given up hope of conceiving a much desired child. Discouraged by prognoses from previous medical examinations, Nancy referred her to our long-time friend, Dr. Yosowitz, who identified and mitigated the infertility problem.

With great credit to Eddie, and perhaps at least nodding appreciation to our dogs that originally brought us all together, a beautiful new boy has entered the world who otherwise wouldn't be here.

Can you possibly imagine a more marvelous gift?

Larry Bell

The Visualists

Dennis Kowal: Sculpting New Realities

I FIRST MET Dennis Kowal a half-century ago when I enrolled in his sculpture class at the University of Illinois in Urbana-Champaign. He was a young professor and a deservedly respected practicing artist within an outstandingly distinguished faculty. I was a graduate student in industrial design at the time...a program I was subsequently appointed to head over nearly a decade.

Dennis and I are about the same age...at the time of our introduction I had just previously served four years of duty as a U.S. Air Force air traffic controller and had earned a five-year undergraduate degree in architecture. I came to his class with a great desire to expand my design interest and background through ambitious works. Recognizing this, he soon generously suggested that rather than attend his classes, I instead share his personal studio with him.

The two of us became professional colleagues and friends, each separately exhibiting our works in gallery shows. I was mostly doing some rather large carved wood pieces which were being shown and represented by the Distelheim Gallery in Chicago...one was purchased by the Illinois State Museum in

Springfield. Dennis was working primarily in stone and bronze with a national clientele.

Some of Dennis's previous works in solid Corten steel echo patterns of natural form and structure evolved from earlier stone and wood carvings. As much as eleven inches thick, they combine solidity and weight with soft, delicate lichen-like surface textures and earth colors which evoke powerful effects on our senses.

Other materials evoke very different sensations. His carved acrylic pieces, for example, express a light spatial quality conveyed through reflections, refractions and various qualities of light and intensity. He describes these works as "dimensions for exploration" which, like experiencing water, often match his fluid mind frame to pursue a personal aesthetic purpose. Currently, his studio in Sarasota, Florida provides a safe sanctuary for exploration and creation of new acrylics, as well as larger public works in aerospace aluminum with silver surfaces that mimic the ever-changing environment.

The simple, elegant intelligence and integrity expressed in Dennis Kowal's sculpture reflects the same qualities I greatly admire in his personal character. The following dialogue reveals why.

Dennis begins: "Sculpture is what I do—it is my art, my existential joy." He reflects:

> To work from a creative peak is pure joy and energy, as is recognition of beauty by any other means...In the course of things, there are moments magic and mysterious, so sublime as to overwhelm one's total being. That is the furthest, most beautiful, extreme. To aspire to anything else would be to deny one's potential for joy, for transcending the immediacies of day-to-day life.

To this, he adds:

> There is also another level of awareness, coming out
> of periods of quiet, out of depression and futility, as
> out of the eye of a storm, which preludes a burst of
> intuitive energy and visions of a new work, self-
> understanding by what allusions a life is measured.

Dennis reflects back to the time of his 70th birthday when he became obsessed with a simple question:

> What possesses me to construct dialogues about issues
> of my time, i.e., the atomic bomb, the environment,
> war; and in anticipation and related, create sculpture
> for over 60 years; what I call fine art.

Exploring answers to that question, Dennis recalls:

> Works that symbolically reflect concepts that creep
> from my inner, intuitive self. Having had Bulbar
> Polio and celebrating my tenth birthday in the Illinois
> Contagious Disease Hospital, being one of the few
> who survived with comparatively minimal damage,
> cross-eyed for over a year, and my right side weakened
> made manifest the functioning of the right side, left-
> side brain.

That polio experience had a profound influence upon his early life. He became isolated from social contacts as quarantine signs were nailed on trees and doors of his home and as existential fear gripped his small Chicago neighborhood. This frightening circumstance was also difficult for his family. He ponders:

> I often wonder how traumatic those events were for my

parents, and the lingering angst my younger brothers must still harbor regarding what can be describes as collateral damage.

Delirious at home with that disease, Dennis began to romanticize preconceived notions about what constitutes the artistic life. Having learned much by living one, that romance has matured from youthful infatuation to a defining reality. Or as he recently describes this:

> *What is now very clear as my 80th birthday looms is a sense of gratitude, a blessing bestowed upon me for having survived it all, allowing intuitive impulses free reign, recognize mentors…to endlessly study and accumulate the knowledge, develop skills, tools and materials to make a physical reality unrealizable by wishful thinking.*

Those physical realities are products of whole-brain thinking which is both freely meditative and rigorously deliberate. As Dennis describes these process stages:

> *You think—meditate—become possessed by a vague notion—flirt with failure by working on the edge— pushing towards the barest manifestations of a different truth—often turning to drawing to catch fleeting images in sketches that are refined into drawings of implied form—shapes to be made— concept and form become one as a symbol—the implied forms are shapes finely drawn. In time, the work at hand develops its own non-verbal working psyche, which is non-linear; asymmetrical symmetry that is expansive, organic and exclusive.*

Larry Bell

Some of those larger constructions must be conceived within the context of their surrounding settings. As Dennis points out:

> The size of a major public work is by no means arbitrary. How people relate to a given work guides the final dimensions. What results I call 'Human Scale'—the term carries far more meaning than the idea of size alone. For sculpture, unlike any other art form, having the attributes of monumentality and scale is critical to the final aesthetics—no matter the size.

Large pieces, metal works in particular, demand special technical knowledge and experience. Dennis explains:

> Having worked in factories from top to bottom has given me the skills and insights to move forward smoothly, neither ignorant of science and technology nor intimidated by them—an artist must know their craft be it a screwdriver or computer—tools that for me assume the position of a second nature to the more profound issues of my work.

The final visual results of these processes speak in a very special non-verbal dialect. Or as Dennis puts it:

> Using words to communicate with others about visual things is terribly difficult; worse to explain sculpture. We do not use sculpture to explain words. Yet that is the problem. Especially today, when the vicarious experience substitutes for actual participation, words are increasingly a substitute for 'things'.

Those creations often evoke perceptions of familiar, yet nonrepresentational forms born of life patterns. Dennis observes that while many people are most comfortable with art that looks "real," any personal sense of reality is subjective:

> While fishing on Cape Cod with my daughter at sunset, she said to me; 'Dad! You see pictures like this that don't look real—and they are! This doesn't look real, and it is!'

Dennis explains that people are typically most comfortable with artistic works that look like images they recognize because we are all, from birth, learning much about our bodies, others' bodies and everything else in our environment on a very unconscious subliminal level. Consequently, when art has the "look" of reality, we are bringing the whole of our life's experiences to that look and we are comfortable with that experience.

Artists sometimes push observers, and even traditional cultures, out of their comfort zones. Dennis illustrates this by noting the 19th-century sculptor Rodin who did violence to then-accepted sensibilities, as did Erik Satie with his music:

> Rodin saw a different way of depicting the figure, a difference in the scale and the psychology from what he modeled in clay when he moved on to the finish bronzes and even more difficult marbles.

Dennis observes that this situation is similar to much of the artistic work being done today, only on an even more demanding level:

> One can no longer simply rely on ordinary past experiences for understanding. Not only is each artist expressing her or his idiosyncrasies but all of human

art history, everything and anything to their abilities
as an artist; sometimes to the point of being a
professional avante-garde and/or obscurity.

What then, is good-bad? What is creative? What magical?
Whatever? Dennis answers that although rules, as such, are
virtually non-existent for art:

> *We know excellence when we experience it; the*
> *infinite levels of problem-solving, performances, and*
> *the natural manifestations of phenomena; all*
> *included according to one's willingness and capacity*
> *to be receptive, aware and involved; and to notice the*
> *intrinsic value of a thing, situation, or event,*
> *exclusive of whether or not something has been*
> *monetized.*

Expanding personal and external boundaries of expression
entails professional risks. Dennis forewarns:

> *Too often we become trapped by narrow thoughts and*
> *our lives subject to socially-contrived merchandizing*
> *disguised as culture—a marketplace of homogenized*
> *experience serves as a mass community of*
> *consumers...One must pick and choose and have faith*
> *in one's creative autonomy to move out into the larger*
> *world without being intimidated.*

Dennis Kowal describes evolutionary developments in his life
experiences and works as integrally connected and mutually
affirmative:

> *Regardless of material, my sculpture manifests a*
> *refinement of and faith in certain concepts—the most*

absolutely basic being life itself. My works are aware
of entropy and human scale—they are classical and
sensual—symbolic and intuitive—archetypal—
images imbued with historic connotations—they are a
ritual celebration—totems, icons, monoliths,
monuments—affirmations of life.

Dennis urges us to contemplate and appreciate the importance of fully living and loving whatever you do:

Thinking of your life as a whole, an estimated period
of existence during which you will do your 'thing',
noticing the rhythms of days and nights, years, even
centuries, you will evaluate far differently than if you
only see the here and now, the level of one's obsession
(passion) will determine the scope of one's life style—
social involvements, family, possessions,
responsibilities one can truly assume.

Victor Lundy: Creating Eternal Spaces

Victor Lundy readily comes to mind as an architect who exemplifies whole brain thinking. New York Times architecture critic Ada Louise Huxtable has referred to his buildings as putting "heart, hand, and mind working together."

Victor and I both joined the University of Houston's College of Architecture faculty during the late 1970s. I had admired the consistent creative intelligence expressed through his work long before meeting him. These personal and professional attributes have been manifestly evident throughout a lifetime of dedication and achievement.

Born in 1923, Victor and his immigrant family originally lived in New York City where he and his sister attended the public school system. In 1933, his father Alfred, moved the family back to Russia. His mother, Rachael, returned to New York with the children just before their passports expired.

Young Victor expressed an early aptitude for drawing, painting and sculpture. These visual thinking and conceptualization skills have been of fundamental importance to his creative successes. As he has reflected, his entire life devoted to architecture has emphasized making marks—drawing thoughts—painting thoughts.

Victor's beloved art teacher who recognized these talents discouraged him from pursuing an architectural career because she thought he lacked necessary political skills necessary to make it in that profession. Nevertheless, in 1939 he enrolled in the New York University, where his facile illustration abilities were well suited to the school's Ecole des Beaux Arts philosophy of design which placed primary emphasis upon formal aesthetic qualities of a building. There, he excelled at developing effective concept visualizations within characteristically short allocated time periods.

Victor left the comfort and safety of university life in 1942 to enlist in World War Two. Serving in General George Patton's Third Army Infantry, he constantly sketched and annotated war experiences and thoughts in numerous small notebooks he carried in his field pack.

In 1944, Victor nearly lost his arm to a projectile fired from a German Tiger Tank in France. Very fortunately, a highly skilled orthopedic surgeon in an American hospital in England saved his arm, and quite possibly, his life as well. Upon seeing Victor's sketches, the doctor arranged for him to do drawings of operating room procedures, an assignment that kept him out of combat during the remainder of the bloody Battle of the Bulge.

Victor was awarded a Purple Heart for his wound, and later spent a year of recovery in the Washington, DC Walter Reed hospital.

War experiences changed Victor in another way. A

German officer prisoner informed him that the famous architect Walter Gropius was teaching at Harvard. This motivated Victor to meet Gropius, a person remarkably like the officer in aristocratic bearing. He then enrolled at Harvard where he earned undergraduate and graduate degrees.

Whereas Victor's New York University Beaux Art curriculum emphasized poetic European impressionism, the Harvard Gropius philosophy was directed to European modernism which reduced building essence to utmost simplicity of structure. Both qualities are manifestly evident in a rich variety of his projects.

Victor Lundy's architecture combines artistry of light and space with true mastery of construction technologies and reverent use of materials.

A serene example is expressed by his design for the Unitarian Church in Westport, Connecticut. Two soaring arched laminated beam roof elements separated by a long skylight allow light to illuminate the sanctuary. The overall roof form references the spirit of two hands in prayer. Clear glass side walls below visually connect the interior space to a natural outdoor setting.

The Westport Unitarian Church, one of several places of worship he designed between 1956 and 1964, communicates a sense of perfectly belonging in that environment. It evokes a timeless feeling of inevitability that it was always meant to be there, and always should be. It is the product of whole thinking that can imagine and transform a vision of what can be into an appealing reality.

Victor's U.S. Tax Court Building in Washington, DC carries his creative vision of place, purpose, form and structure to an entirely different character and scale. Its timeless balance of bold exterior and elegant beauty of interior spaces earned it distinguished listing recognition on the National Register of Historic Buildings representing our government's finest buildings.

Designed as a "podium for justice," a monumental 4,000-ton cantilevered granite block floats over a glass entrance. Inside, naturally-illuminated, human-scaled courtroom environments afford serene dignity and repose. Carefully crafted traditional materials, including granite, hammered stone and elegant woods, reflect sensitive attention to detail.

Victor Lundy has described his architecture as the "making of form," which entails "solving where to allow light into spaces, and where to keep it out." That making of forms involves close collaborations with engineers to produce delightfully innovative uses and exuberant expressions of materials.

Victor's originality is apparent in the design of cloud-like shade canopies of hanging wood strips he created for the Smithsonian Museum at the National Mall.

Another design produced ten large inflated bulbous-shaped hotdog stand-bathroom structures for the 1964 New York World Fair that were dramatically illuminated at night like hot air balloons.

Some of his projects have required a long time in the making. A prestigious Colombo, Sri Lanka U.S. Embassy commission awarded to his New York office in 1960 required 23 years to complete. The design features granite combined with other traditional materials such as teak wood and ceramic roof tiles.

Throughout his career, Victor Lundy's architecture exemplifies a symbiotic whole-brain reverence for form and structure, the importance of imagination and execution, and the all-crucial inspirational and motivational power of passion to learn and succeed.

As for legacy, he offers some salient advice: "We can do our very best, and then just let it happen."

More comprehensive background and insights regarding the life and works of victor Lundy are provided in a recent book authored by my academic colleague Donna Kacmar; *Victor Lundy: Artist Architect.*[363]

Nao Kusuzaki: Communicating Through Dance

I first met Houston Ballet soloist ballerina Nao Kusuzaki at a private home recital by pianist Kana Mimaki. Throughout her marvelous performance of pieces composed by Franz Liszt, Frédéric Chopin and Claude Debussy, I couldn't help but focus attention upon Nao's perfectly poised, remarkably graceful posture, and intensely attentive presence.

It came as little surprise to learn during a conversation following the performance that Nao Kusuzaki was a professional dancer. Even more, she produces multi-cultural productions that apply rich universal language and structures of dance to provide conceptual platforms for events where artists of different fields can gather and collaborate...places that inspire imagination.

In Nao's words, "The discipline and creativity of dance balances the left and right side of the brain."

Nao Kusuzaki first became exposed to enriching benefits of whole-brain thinking and living through valued examples of both parents. Her father, Kosaku, learned the discipline of responsibility caring for his father who was blind. That grandfather had narrowly missed becoming a casualty of Hiroshima atomic bomb devastation, having fortunately returned to the family home outside the city just before it was destroyed.

Kosaku applied his highly structured and analytical mind to become a neurobiologist researcher of memory. Nao describes him as being demanding of thoughtful standards, but also exercising expectations for Nao and her younger brother, Kisou, in a quiet way. She gratefully recalls: "My father allowed me to try anything, and encouraged me to follow my own interests and dreams."

Nao's mother, Yoko, grew up as the third of four daughters in the picturesque mountainous Shikoku Island in the Ehime Prefecture south of Hiroshima. Both of her parents were teachers.

Nao describes her mother as a free thinker with abundant imagination, but also as someone who instilled a priority to seek and achieve lofty goals. As she puts it:

> *My mother was more of a disciplinarian who brought structure of expectations...always motivating me to reach much higher, and to be critical of myself.*

Recognizing that she was constantly dancing around to music and moving to sound, Yoko took her three-year-old daughter to a ballet school in the Ehime Prefecture. Nao also began piano lessons at age five.

Nao loved dancing in beautiful tutus, but above all, learned the importance of discipline. As she describes the experience, "Ninety percent of my early dance training was about how to behave...the importance of manners and treating other people with respect."

In 1990, Nao's dance career path led to the United States. At age 10, her father's selection for a neurobiology research position at the National Institute of Health moved the family to Washington, DC. There, she became enrolled at a public elementary school, and also at The Washington School of Ballet for children of all ages.

The move appeared to Nao at the time as a mixed blessing and challenging adjustment. While it provided an opportunity to train seriously in ballet, it also left her missing a familiar home and traditions.

Although her father was fluent in English, her unfamiliarity with this new language presented a big problem for Nao at the public school. The ballet school experience, however, proved fortunately very different. She discovered that the language of dance and music is the same everywhere: "I was able to express myself with full freedom."

Exciting professional dancing opportunities were revealed through The Washington School of Ballet's affiliation with The Washington Ballet Company, which performed at large public venues including The Kennedy Center Terrace Theater. That exposure first introduced Nao to the dream of dance as a career. Such an opportunity is rarely possible in Japan...a circumstance she is now determined to change.

Nao's four years of formative experiences with The Washington School of Ballet introduced her to the enormous management complexities and teamwork necessary to stage a professional theatrical event. She observes:

> We can't put on a show by ourselves. We need a director to oversee everything. We need the talent of dancers. We need the backstage crew, including electricians, stage managers, scenic and lighting designers that create the atmosphere. And most of all, we need an audience. We feel the atmosphere created by the audience as well.

Nao adds: "All have to come together from different interest areas."

Other major personal and professional adjustments in Nao's life occurred with subsequent family moves. The first was to Boston at age 14. The second was experienced when she remained with a host family in Boston at age 17 as her parents returned to Japan, where her father took a research position at Hokkaido University. She recalls: "I had one more year left of high school when they left, and I wanted to continue ballet training."

Nao's ambitious and brave goal was to become accepted into a major professional ballet company straight after high school graduation. In 2001, the Boston Ballet company awarded her that opportunity. That experience also raised her performance expectation bar. She reflects:

> *Working for the first time, I was transported to a new world, one that made everything look very easy and effortless...where performers were living that magical illusion on stage.*

Nao first performed in *Serenade*, a one-act piece set to *Serenade for Strings* composed by Tchaikovsky. In *Serenade*, a minimalist design opened audiences to a sense of imagination. This contrasted with another performance in *Giselle* by French composer Adolphe Adam, an emotional drama about betrayal filled with heartbreak.

Later, Nao's dancer dream came true with her guest performance for the role of Odette/Odile, a leading female dancer in *Swan Lake*. Another dream was realized when she held the lead role of Nikiya in a dramatic love story of an Indian temple dancer and her lover, Solar, in *La Bayadere* by French chorographer Marius Petipa set to music of Ludwig Minkus.

While at the Boston Ballet, Nao first met Stanton Welch who was then staging *Madame Butterfly* there. Welch observed Nao's "exquisite lyrical line," and her "wonderful ethereal sense of floating and lightness." In 2004, he invited her to join the Houston Ballet upon becoming its artistic director. She became promoted to soloist in 2008, and realized a long-held dream of dancing in the role of Cio-Cio San in *Madame Butterfly* in 2012.

Nao believes that the Houston Ballet allows more personal interpretation than many other major companies. The company values bringing together a variety of talents, rather than attempting to achieve "the right standard look." Here, there is also a general thematic style difference between classical and contemporary programs.

Classical training emphasizes a very structured approach, where a dancer is primarily an instrument for expressing the choreographer's vision. Contemporary dance more openly enables the dancers to express their ideas and interpretations. Nevertheless, although classical dance may be more constraining, this training constitutes the core vocabulary and discipline for more interpretive contemporary performances. Nao notes:

> *Artists can break the rules after they have learned them well in order to bring new dimensions and opportunities.*

Nao is working to create and meld expressive opportunities afforded by both styles to engage traditional and more experimental audiences. An opportunity to do this was afforded by an invitation by the Asia Society Texas Center in partnership with the Houston Ballet to create and direct a new dance project, which was performed in 2015.

Choreographed by Kenta Kojiri, the piece titled *Tsuru* also featured Nao in the lead dance role of a bird transformed into a woman's form. Drawing upon a Japanese folk tale, *Tsuru* expresses values of Japanese culture while also merging classical and contemporary themes through the common and universal language of dance.

Encouraged by audience's response to the *Tsuru* performance, Nao took the program, along with the dancers and musicians, to Japan. Kana Mimaki, whom I first met along with Nao, was the pianist. Together, they performed excerpts from *Tsuru*, works by Stanton Welch, AM and other classical and contemporary pieces for the public. The event also offered a three-day workshop for middle and high school level students in

Chiba, Houston's "sister city" near Tokyo.

Nao is committed to bringing important lessons and insights gained over 20 years of dance experience to teach and inspire future generations. Most particularly, she says: "I want to create projects that allow for a deepening understanding of Japanese culture."

Nao founded a nonprofit company, the "Creative Minds Collaborative," which espouses the ongoing purpose of introducing and updating present-day Japanese students, performers and audiences with exposure to Western dance culture, and creating a dialogue among artists and their community around the world. Her organization raises funds for events that stage performances and educational workshops that draw and engage artists from various cultures and creative fields.

Nao is a compassionately enterprising leader. She organized a "Dance for Hope," a benefit event at Houston's Hobby Center which provided aid for victims of the tsunami and earthquake that hit Japan in 2011. Houston Ballet colleagues and artistic director Stanton Welch, AM generously donated their time and talents.

Nao Kusuzaki's dance career has taught her much about putting leadership into enterprising practice. As she describes this: "Dance is much more than movements. It connects people. It introduces the discipline of structure." She adds:

> In many ways, a ballet career prepares us to have skills useful in entrepreneurship: clear long-term goal setting and laser focus, the resiliency to keep going when the outlook is not what we expect, and self-reliance.

Nao continues:

> Dance also teaches you cooperation and trust on very

close levels. We know when a colleague is having a troubling day for a variety of possible reasons. When that happens, we anticipate and compensate for their performance. We learn to trust our dance partners with our physical health. As I get tossed around, my partner senses any momentary anxiety and instantaneously adjusts to avoid a bad injury. We work together for emotional support. We help everyone perform at their highest level.

Nao has balanced her dancing career with formal entrepreneurial education studies, recently graduating from the University of Houston's undergraduate management and leadership program. Those studies included French language courses, a key poetic language of ballet. Recalling her early experiences in relocating from native Japan to a foreign U.S. culture, she said: "Learning languages is one of the most fun activities."

Perfecting the universal language of dance clearly tops that list.

The Scientists

Fred Singer: Changing Climate Science

DR. FRED SINGER is an exemplary hero to those of us who honor his unwavering commitment and enormous contributions to advance honest and informed science. In doing so, he has often fearlessly and effectively challenged ideological orthodoxy, just as open inquiry and adherence to sound scientific methods demand. In doing so, he has paid the price for such audacity, responding to disparaging attacks with quiet dignity and well-reasoned factual rebuttals.

Fred is an internationally recognized climate physicist and Distinguished Research Professor at George Mason University. He served as the first director of the U.S. National Weather Satellite Service, and also as vice chairman of the U.S. National Advisory Committee on Oceans and Atmospheres. In addition, he has authored numerous books about climate, energy and environmental issues, including a recent New York Times bestseller, *Unstoppable Global Warming*.

I first became acquainted with Fred through common space exploration interests. During a visit to my office he happened to mention that satellite temperature recordings of the Earth's lower atmosphere were cooling more rapidly, relative to the surface, than greenhouse theory predicts. It would be expected that carbon dioxide would warm the lower atmosphere first, which would then radiate heat back to the surface, the reverse of what was being observed.

Given that our primary conversation was focused upon Mars, not Earth, I didn't give the matter much thought until a year or more later when I was contemplating possible lessons that might be applied from the way natural climate operates on *Spaceship Earth* to the design of artificial life support and energy systems operating beyond our planet. In other words, I began to investigate climate phenomena from holistic references regarding basic principles that govern how natural and technical systems work, how they connect together and how they can be managed to support the most complex systems of all—us humans.

Although I came to appreciate that climate is staggeringly more complex issue than the comparatively simple technical workings of spacecraft systems, it was the very nature of these influences and conditions that led me to question the simplistic and alarmist climate influences attributed to man-made CO_2 emissions by prominent members of the "scientific establishment." This quest for understanding motivated and informed my authorship of two books on the subject: *Climate of Corruption: Politics and Power Behind the Global Warming Hoax* (2012) and *Scared Witless: Prophets and Profits of Climate Doom* (2015).

The second of these books is dedicated to Fred, who along with tens of thousands of other very courageous scientists and writers, who suffered personal attacks and professional penalties for challenging biased research and politically-driven policy agendas. Included are character assassinations that accuse those who speak out as "climate change deniers" who don't care about the environment; false branding as shills for Big Oil, tobacco companies or other non-existent sponsors; severe professional career penalties including unwarranted exclusions of significant research findings by scientific journals; lost research funding and promotion opportunities; employment terminations and sometimes even threats upon their personal safety and lives.

Fred Singer introduced me to vast sources of research information regarding climate influences and facts, as well as to a broad network of reliable sources with levels of expertise in a wide variety of related disciplines. None of these individuals have the slightest doubt that climate changes. It has clearly done so for millions of years. Nor do they question that the Earth has been warming since the mid-1800s, when the "Little Ice Age" ended and before the Industrial Revolution introduced smokestacks and other sources of carbon dioxide emissions.

The larger issue has to do with any notion that a "settled science" indicates that we are at the cusp of a climate change calamity and the claim that anyone who finds no evidence to support such alarmism is a "climate change denier." Such assertions are both grossly misleading and fundamentally anti-science.

Such defamatory charges fail to take into account readily confirmable facts. For example, whereas physics suggests that, all other things being equal, carbon dioxide would indeed warm the climate, the atmosphere is an almost infinitely complex mechanism that is far from fully understood. This fact is made evident by grossly failed predictions of computer models which have invariably exaggerated warming trends.

Yes, climate change is real, occurring with regular and irregular cycles, and for lots of reasons. Scientists know about many of them, but much less about how these dynamic causes and effects interact, or what combined results will occur at any given time.

Paleontology indicates that over millions of years there have been warmer and cooler periods that appear to have little or no correlation with CO_2 concentrations. The Jurassic warm period, major ice ages, the Medieval Warm Period a thousand years ago, and the "little ice age" that ended during the mid-1800s occurred without any human influences. Solid evidence suggests that other climate influences, including sun spot cycles and oscillations in the Earth's orbit, are at least as important as CO_2...a trace gas that comprises roughly 400 parts per million (0.04 percent) of the Earth's atmosphere.

Climate history reveals that Earth's present climate is not any warmer than during past periods when life flourished— times when agriculture was abundant, pyramids and cities were built and world citizens became connected in trade and culture. If any worry is warranted, think about the next overdue Ice Age that scientists predicted but a few decades ago. Worry that the cooling period we are currently experiencing will only be brief and that realistic initiatives to meet our fossil energy needs will not be disrupted by global warming hysterics.

Is this all a conspiracy? Probably not, at least not in the conventional sense where a diabolical network of people and organizations unite together to hatch intentionally malevolent plans. Let's assume that most of the entities and individuals discussed in this book truly believe they are pursuing righteous causes, even when we happen to strongly disagree with their viewpoints and priorities.

But then, what about when those people and institutions we rely upon for important public information knowingly violate our trust? They do so by perpetrating unwarranted fear campaigns and by politically attacking and marginalizing those who challenge and expose factual errors, omissions and uncertainties we need to know about.

No one, not anyone, can even begin to reliably predict what Earth's global climate will be in a decade or in multiple decades hence, much less determine the influences of human activities, for better or worse, upon such forecasts.

The stark reality is that climate science has become a big

and very profitable business for government agencies, universities and environmental benefactors. Some of the strongest proponents of human-caused climate change theories in Congress, for example, are among the strongest supporters of those funding programs. Government agencies that receive and distribute these funds find it necessary to demonstrate that threats are real and urgent in order to justify budgets and demonstrate public benefits.

Sadly, for many of "space guys and gals," a NASA entity known as the Goddard Institute for Space Studies (GISS) is no exception. Most people might imagine that if any organization could be trusted to get the data right it would be the agency that launches satellites and put humans on the Moon.

The public news media has routinely featured alarmist statements released by GISS typically reporting "NASA says is the warmest year/month/day since…". What most people don't realize, however, is that the Goddard Institute for Space Studies, which ironically is named after the great American father of rocketry, is only a small climate modeling shop housed in a midtown Manhattan office building which relies upon surface station data (not the far more accurate satellite measurements).

The Right Climate Stuff: Correcting the Records

Much of the most informed and persistent criticism of compromised climate science conducted by NASA GISS and other organizations is being voiced by individuals who actually travelled to the Moon and got them there. Included is a volunteer research team organized as The Right Climate Stuff (TRCS) comprised of more than 20 retired NASA manned space program scientists, engineers and astronauts.

As TRCS member Harold "Hal" Dorian, who worked on

NASA's Apollo program, explained:

> *At NASA, we have a policy: You can't make a design decision on a spacecraft or rocket that is not validated...You don't make critical decisions based on 'garbage in, garbage out.' Yet our government has been doing that with respect to climate alarm, because too many academics in universities are writing papers, drawing conclusions from models that don't agree with physical data.*

Dorian and his NASA veteran colleagues emphasize that they don't belong to any special interest group that would cloud their objectivity. His own interest in the politically contentious issue was prompted by suspicions that alarmist climate model-based claims couldn't be trusted. After all, at NASA he'd used computer models to develop the landing gear for the lunar module and "knows a thing or two about them."

He added:

> *So we validated the model before we used it for any design decisions. And the current climate models are not validated...I don't think we're using anything close to a rational process to deal with this concern about global warming.*

On April 10, 2012, 49 NASA scientists and astronauts sent a letter to NASA Administrator Charles Bolden admonishing the agency to stop GISS Director Hansen from making unsupportable climate claims based upon highly theoretical models while neglecting contrary empirical evidence. The group included seven Apollo astronauts and two former directors of NASA's Houston Johnson Space Center.

The letter stated:

Larry Bell

March 28, 2012
The Honorable Charles Bolden, Jr.
NASA Administrator
NASA Headquarters
Washington, D.C. 20546-0001

Dear Charlie,

We, the undersigned, respectfully request that NASA and the Goddard Institute for Space Studies (GISS) refrain from including unproven remarks in public releases and websites. We believe the claims by NASA and GISS, that man-made carbon dioxide is having a catastrophic impact on global climate change are not substantiated, especially when considering thousands of years of empirical data. With hundreds of well-known climate scientists and tens of thousands of other scientists publicly declaring their disbelief in the catastrophic forecasts, coming particularly from the GISS leadership, it is clear that the science is NOT settled.

The unbridled advocacy of CO_2 being the major cause of climate change is unbecoming of NASA's history of making an objective assessment of all available scientific data prior to making decisions or public statements.

As former NASA employees, we feel that NASA's advocacy of an extreme position, prior to a thorough study of the possible overwhelming impact of natural climate drivers is inappropriate. We request that NASA refrain from including unproven and unsupported remarks in its future releases and websites on this subject. At risk is damage to the exemplary reputation of NASA, NASA's current or former scientists and employees, and even the reputation of science itself.

Walter Cunningham: Restoring Public Trust

My good friend and Apollo 7 astronaut Walter Cunningham, who signed the letter, has summed up unacceptable consequences:

> Those of us fortunate enough to have traveled in space bet our lives on the competence, dedication, and integrity of the science and technology professionals who made our missions possible...In the last twenty years, I have watched the high standards of science being violated by a few climate scientists, including some at NASA, while special interest opportunists have dangerously abused our public trust.

Cunningham, who earned undergraduate and graduate degrees in physics and completed all course work for a doctorate in that field, points out:

> The Apollo program relied on quality data and objective interpretation to advance knowledge in areas of science and technology that had never before been explored. All of us had complete trust in the competence, integrity and accountability of those we worked with to create the systems and hardware we depended on in the most extreme environment.

Col. Cunningham emphasizes that:

> The aerospace culture is comprised of technically sophisticated problem-solving professionals who work together to connect the dots so that what they create can be verified to work...We didn't expect our

Larry Bell

scientists and engineers to know everything, or that their hypotheses would always be right. Hypotheses are ideas to be challenged, and ultimately be proven or disproven by empirical evidence.

Walt continues:

The biggest problems I see with the sorry state of 'climate science', as the public comes to know it through the media, are the alarmist claims unsupported by empirical data and history, being presented as facts.

Instead of NASA being in the forefront of science...

Unfortunately, it is becoming just another agency caught up in the politics of global warming, or worse, politicized science. Advocacy and support for the White House agenda is replacing objective evaluation of data, while scientific data is being ignored in favor of emotions and politics.

He observes:

Over the years, NASA has slowly, but inexorably changed their culture and filled management positions with those compatible with the new culture. They absorbed their 'new ways of thinking, new people, and new means. They have contributed to a society that is becoming less and less capable of measuring up to the motivation, inspiration, challenge, risk acceptance and accomplishments of Apollo.

Thinking Whole

Walter concludes,

> *With the right leadership, with the right science, and with the right commitment to excellence and integrity, we will go much farther. And it's high time to do so.* [364]

As with previous climate changes which have occurred over billions of years without help from humans, we can never be certain when they will occur, which direction temperatures will shift, how severe they will be or how long they will last. While NASA satellites and expertise have important roles to play in alerting us for preparedness, we must be able to trust them to separate science from politics.

Bill and Melinda Gated Foundation CEO Dr. Sue Desmond-Hellmann warns us to be skeptical of those who treat science as an ideology. Writing in the Wall Street Journal, she reminds us that skepticism is the lifeblood of scientific progress:

> *Whereas skepticism and uncertainty have always been at the heart and soul of science, confidence and certainty are the coin of the realm in much of today's public discourse. Unquestioning confidence is deeply troubling for the scientific community because it is not the currency we trade in, and it has led the people in America and around the world to question scientific enterprise itself. We should all be troubled when science is treated as if it were an ideology rather than a discipline.* [365]

Pointing out that skepticism and uncertainty have always been the heart and soul of science, Desmond-Hellmann states that it follows that scientific knowledge is always provisional:

> *Scientists talk about skepticism to assert that nothing should be accepted or rejected without considerable evidence. The point of science is not to produce doctrine, but to collect and test evidence that points toward conclusions, which in turn inform approaches, treatments and policies based upon rigorous research.*

She advises:

> *At a time when people of all ideological stripes are seeking definitive sources of truth, we should all embrace our inner skeptics and turn to the scientific method for a fresh approach to resolve our differences.*

Applying her sage advice to claims of "settled science" regarding climate change (e.g., assertions of a looming global warming crisis), let's hope that cooler heads finally prevail.

The Innovators

Burt Rutan: Flying High

OBJECTIVE SCIENCE IS a prerequisite that has propelled many innovative geniuses my life has been enriched to know. One, Burt Rutan, who is broadly regarded as being among the world's most innovative and renowned aircraft designers, has also devoted great attention to climate research.

First, by way of brief introduction, Burt Rutan designed "Voyager," the first aircraft to fly around the globe without stopping or refueling, along with the Virgin Atlantic "GlobalFlyer," which broke Voyager's 9-day time for a non-stop solo flight around the world by accomplishing this in 2 days and 19 hours.

Burt also designed "SpaceShipOne," financed by Microsoft co-founder Paul Allen, which won the $10 million Ansari X-Prize in 2004 for becoming the first privately-funded manned craft to enter the realm of space twice within a two-week period. Voyager, along with three other Rutan-designed aircraft, are on display at the National Air and Space Museum in Washington, DC. Voyager is featured in the main hall in the historic company of the "Wright Flyer," "Spirit of St Louis" and the "Bell X-1."

Born on June 17, 1943 in Estacada, Oregon, Burt developed an early interest in aviation. By age eight he was designing and building model aircraft, and soloed at age 16. Between 1965 and 1972, after graduating third in his class with a BS degree in aeronautical engineering from California Polytechnic University, he worked as a civilian flight test engineer for the U.S. Air Force at Edwards Air Force Base. His many projects including developing LTV's "XC-142" vertical/short take-off and landing (V/STOL) transport plane, and conducting spin tests of the McDonnell Douglas "F-4 Phantom" fighter.

Burt left USAF civilian service to become the director of development for Bede Aircraft in Newton, Kansas. He tested the concept for a canard pusher-prop design for a two-seat "VariViggin" using a model rigged atop his station wagon and measured forces while driving on empty roads. His popular "VarieEze" (pronounced *"very easy"*), flown by his brother Dick set, a world distance record in the under 500kg (1,100 lb) class, followed by a "Long-EZ," which doubled that range to 2,010 miles.

Many of Burt Rutan's innovative designs pioneered mold-less glass-reinforced plastic construction. In 1982, he founded Scaled Composites, LLC, which became one of the world's pre-eminent aircraft design and prototyping facilities headquartered in Mojave, California. Beechcraft contracted the company to refine and build the design for a "Starship."

Inspired by SpaceShipOne, Virgin Group founder Sir Richard Branson established Virgin Galactic and engaged Scaled Composites to develop and produce a line of commercial spaceships to fly the public ("SpaceShipTwo"). In 2012, Paul Allen announced "Stratolaunch Systems" with Burt on the board of directors.

My wife Nancy and I enjoyed a couple of great days visiting

with Burt Rutan and his wife Tonya at their beautiful new home in Coeur d'Alene, Idaho following his retirement from Scaled Composites in 2011. He was developing a new project at the time, a bi-pod hybrid gasoline-electric flying car with a 32-foot wingspan which can fit into a single-space garage. The removable wings are stored between the pods when parked.

Four-cycle 400 cc engines with generators in each pod power electric motors which spin propellers in flight, while separate motors drive wheels on the road. Lithium-ion batteries in the nose of each pod power take-off and emergency back-up for landing. Carrying 18 gallons of fuel, the craft cruises at speeds of 100 mph with 760-mile range, with capabilities to fly at 200 mph for up to 530 miles. Alternatively, the flying car can be driven 820 miles on the road...35 miles on electricity alone. Flight controls are in the right pod, steering wheel and brakes on the left.

Our visit with Burt and Tonya afforded an opportunity to discuss a variety of common interests, climate included. Some following excerpts taken from these conversations draw upon a more comprehensive September 9, 2012 Forbes article I wrote titled *A Cool-Headed Climate Conversation with Aerospace Legend Burt Rutan*. Burt has maintained a very expansive website addressing climate facts and issues which can be accessed at www.burtrutan.com. When I asked Burt what got him interested in this topic, he replied:

> *Even though I've been very busy throughout my entire career developing and flight-testing airplanes for the Air Force, I've always pursued other research hobbies in my time away from work. Since I'm very accustomed to analyzing a lot of data, about three or four years ago many alarmist claims by some climate scientists caught my attention. Since this is such an important topic, I began to look into it firsthand.*

Larry Bell

Burt was particularly concerned that widely reported media claims that the entire planet is heading towards a human-caused climate catastrophe were leading to proposed solutions which will have enormous impacts upon costs of energy, which of course, will increase costs of everything. Accordingly, he decided to investigate whether or not such assertions were supported by ethical science and solid facts. He reported:

> ...I always like to look at both sides of things that I take special interest in. So when I decided to look closely at the anthropogenic [man-made] global warming crisis claims, I avoided focusing on media reports, and instead, went directly to available raw climate data. The intent was to see if that data might just as reasonably be interpreted differently.

That search for credible raw data led to suspicions that it was either being withheld or didn't exist:

> I was shocked to find that there were actually climate scientists who wouldn't share the raw data, but would only share their conclusions in summary graphs that were used to prove their various theories about planet warming. In fact I began to smell something really bad, and the worse that smell got, the deeper I looked.

He observed:

> This was frankly astonishing because analyzing data is something I'm very good at. All my professional life I have been analyzing complex flight test data, interpreting it and presenting it. Something that I always did in flight test is to make a chart that shows every bit of the data, and only then, decide later on

346

the basis of real observed results which parts of the
data were valid.

The data Burt was able to obtain did not match or justify
alarmist findings. He noted:

> *Tragically, policymakers have thrown horrendous*
> *amounts of taxpayer money needed for other purposes*
> *at solving an unsubstantiated emergency*
> *...meanwhile, that alarmism has generated billions*
> *of dollars more to finance a rapidly growing climate*
> *science industry with budgets that have risen by a*
> *factor of 40 since the early 1990s. I consider this*
> *failure for honest scientists to speak up just as*
> *unethical as the behavior of those who put out the*
> *false catastrophic claims.*

Burt pointed out:

> *Actually, looking back over the past 11,000 or so*
> *years since Earth began to recover from the last big Ice*
> *Age, we're experiencing a very moderate and stable*
> *climate stage. And going back nearly half of the past*
> *million years, a long Ice Age occurred about every*
> *90,000 years or so with a large percentage of the*
> *planet uninhabitable. We're talking about ice as*
> *much as a mile or more thick covering large portions*
> *of North America and Europe. Any local warming*
> *that alarmists talk about is only a brief and tiny blip.*

He added:

> *There's certainly nothing alarming about the stable*
> *period we currently enjoy. I was struck by claims that*

we are experiencing unprecedented warming caused by
Man, where data clearly shows that our recent
warming isn't unprecedented...Another important
thing that caught my attention was that the increased
atmospheric CO_2 that all this alarmism centers on is
of huge benefit for agriculture. Green houses actually
supplement CO_2 to make plants grow better. So I'm a
very confused as to what's wrong with CO_2. It's the
food plants need to grow and feed all animals,
including us.

Burt first decided to present the results of his climate data studies on the occasion of receiving a lifetime design achievement award at the Pasadena Art College in July 2009. This topic focus was entirely unexpected by the audience, which was primarily interested in transportation design, a theme which prompted entertainer Jay Leno to bring a very rare and beautiful steam-powered vehicle to the event. As Burt recalled:

I had previously been on his [Leno's] show twice,
appearances related to our SpaceShipOne
program. The audience had obviously expected me to
present my designs and my philosophy...discuss how I
approached creative design. So I did that for maybe
five minutes, and then I launched into showing what I
have found with my climate hobby. I included chart
after chart of data that clearly showed there was
fraud and cherry picking bias used by alarmists
presenting climate data in order to try to make their
point...namely that the Earth faces a catastrophe
because of emissions into the atmosphere by Man.

Although Burt really didn't really know what to expect, he described looking out into the audience and witnessing what he described as "stunned silence." That response included Jay Leno who rushed onto the stage, took him to the side and told him that he didn't know that the global warming calamity subject was even debatable.

Burt was really surprised that someone who reaches millions of people every evening could be so totally insulated from any skeptical views on what the alarmists were trying to sell as a future catastrophe. He said:

> What shocked me most is that I had originally been thinking that the average viewer was at least aware that there are two sides to the issue, rather than almost universally accepting alarmist positions as absolute truth.

Burt's high-profile critical views regarding any unsupportable scientific basis for the supposed climate calamity continue to draw flak from detractors. Some challenge how an airplane designer can have the temerity to disagree with their views of science. Other attacks are very personal, denigrating his intelligence and accusing him of bias. As he told me:

> I have no reason to have any bias. Some said I was obviously being paid for by oil companies, which seemed like a joke. If you go through and read my responses you will find that I did so with hard data that alarmists will not publish. But they don't hesitate to publish personal attacks.

Burt is encouraged that even prominent former global warming doomsayers are finally seeing the light of reason. As he reported:

> One is my good friend James Lovelock who once said that within the next 50 years or so the few remaining

humans will be huddled up in high latitudes to escape the heat of the lower latitudes. He has recently said the alarmists were wrong, and has moved to a new coastal home, unafraid of rising seas.

Burt is encouraged about the future of aviation and space as well. His website states:

Manned spaceflight is not only for governments to do. We proved it can be done by a small company operating with limited resources and a few dozen dedicated employees. The next 25 years will be a wild ride; one that history will note was done for everyone's benefit.

And the future for Burt Rutan? I asked him about that too. He replied:

Larry, after working an average of 60 to 70 hours a week for 46 years, having a lot of fun starting in flight testing Air Force airplanes during the Vietnam War, and then developing some 45 new airplane types, I decided that I wanted an enormous change in retirement.

He continued:

I have now cleared my calendar entirely, even deemphasizing golf, so that I am free to investigate and do absolutely whatever interests me the most. However, after designing 372 new types of aircraft, of which 45 have been built and taken through flight test, I realize I can't quite get that urge out of my system. So right now I'm designing a [hybrid car] seaplane, just for myself, which I can use to explore the hundreds of small lakes and rivers around this beautiful area of north Idaho where I now live.

Burt concluded with an obvious whole-brain promise:

You can bet that it will be very different than any standard seaplane. Hell, if I wanted something conventional, I would just buy a Super Cub on floats.

Max Faget: A Genius Behind Apollo

Five and one-half decades have now passed since a young President John Kennedy rallied a nation behind a bold challenge to send an American to the Moon and safely back before the end of that decade. We did this, and even better...putting four of our citizens on the lunar surface and returning them by 1969, plus delivering two more into lunar orbit who returned with them. Within three more years, eight others had walked on the Moon on successful round-trip voyages, along with four more orbital companions.

The 45 years that have passed since American's last left footprints on the Moon have taken a mortal toll on half of the 28 astronauts who walked them and orbited above, along with thousands of dedicated scientists, technical innovators and system development contractors who got them there.

My life has been honored and enriched to know many of these wonderful individuals, including good friends and colleagues who are no longer alive. One, whose legendary behind-the-scenes contributions made Apollo possible, exemplifies and personifies the American character and spirit that created that legacy.

Maxime "Max" Faget, who served as the first Chief Engineer at NASA's Johnson Spaceflight Center, was a technical genius who developed many of the innovative concepts that were incorporated into all manned U.S. spacecraft. Included are the characteristic gum drop capsules for projects Mercury, Gemini, Apollo and the straight-winged design of the Space Shuttle.

Following his retirement from NASA, Max became my partner in a private space venture that will be discussed later. Very fortunately, Jim Slade at NASA conducted and recorded a June 1997 interview with Max for a *NASA Johnson Space Center Oral History Project* which provides direct quotations that bring back wonderful memories of his voice and times.

Born in British Honduras on August 26, 1921, Max trained in mechanical engineering at San Francisco Junior College and Louisiana State University before doing submarine duty off the coast of Vietnam during World War II. In 1946, following naval service, he was hired by the Pilotless Aircraft Division at the National Advisory Committee for Aeronautics (NACA) Laboratory at Langley Field, Virginia which later evolved to become NASA. NACA's head, Robert Gilruth, later became the first director of NASA Johnson Space Center in Houston.

Max's interest in aeronautics can be traced back to childhood.

He recalled:

> *I was the second son, my brother is two years older than I am, and we both got interested in model airplanes. Of course, he, being older, was always kind of the leader in breaking new ground. So we were very, very enthusiastic model airplane builders. When I [entered college] majoring in mechanical engineering, I minored in aero[nautics]...There were very few colleges at that time that dealt with a strict aeronautics degree.*

Max and his brother, both avid sailing enthusiasts, also built model submarines:

> *These were rubber-band-powered submarines that would submerge in the swimming pool that we had access to. After they'd stay down for several minutes, they'd come floating back up when the propeller stopped running. They were a lot of fun to build.*

Max's early NACA work involved solving aerodynamic problems to enable aircraft to fly faster and higher and led to the design of the hypersonic X-15, which achieved Mach 6. These activities later shifted to the design of ballistic missiles.

The Russians had large launch vehicles at that time, whereas the United States, which had developed a small atomic device, hadn't needed them. Our only realistic launch system capable of reaching Earth orbit, the Atlas, was much lighter, with an extremely thin steel skin that was only supported by internal pressure.

NACA was engaged with planning Project Mercury when the Soviet Union launched a big surprise…the first human in space. As Max commented in a June 1997 NASA interview: "I think higher management was probably aware of the fact that the Russians were making progress…but it never trickled down to the level of the troops in the trenches, that's for sure."

Max continued:

> *Nevertheless, we were able to get our first flight off with [Alan] Shepard just a matter of weeks after Yuri Gagarin went into orbit, and I really think that timing made it possible for the President [Kennedy] to jump on the fact that we were in a race with the Russians and that he wanted to win.*

As the NASA Johnson Space Center's top engineer, Max carried the one-man Mercury project through to a two-person Gemini and three-person Apollo capsule along with a two-vehicle Lunar Module landing and ascent system. Gemini was critical to develop and test sophisticated orbital rendezvous and docking and extravehicular activity capabilities which made Apollo possible. Max observed:

> *I'm convinced we would never been able to make the landing in Kennedy's decade without the training and operations development that Gemini provided.*

President Kennedy's commitment to extend human presence to the Moon within a decade presented endless scientific and engineering challenges which were both daunting and exciting.

As Max reflected:

> *I'm not a scientist, but I really got involved in that. It really sparked the imagination. The engineering problems that were involved has this scientific aspect to them. In other words, it was conjectural science data.*

Max believes imaginary problems required real solutions:

> *We didn't know what kind of Moon we were going to land on. We didn't know what the radiation environment would be like near the Moon. Just a whole host of things like that we didn't really know, and we had to move ahead anyway.*

That early progress developed rapidly. The Mercury-Atlas 6 spacecraft which carried John Glenn on America's first orbital flight on February 20, 1962, was shipped to the Cape only six to eight months before we actually flew it. That occurred only two and one-half years after McDonnell Douglas had cut the first piece of metal.

Planning for the Shuttle along with early thoughts about creating a Space Station began during the second or third Apollo mission to the Moon. Max reported that it seemed like an obvious thing to do:

> ...to have a laboratory in space where people could work and we could understand microgravity effects both on people as well as physical processes than on tiny capsules. Then later—as we got deeper into planning for a Space Station—we also needed a better and more reusable vehicle to service it. Gemini and Apollo were too small, and Saturn was too expensive.

Around the end of the 1960s and beginning of the 1970s, Max led a small group at the NASA Johnson Space Center in planning for an orbital laboratory where people could work to understand microgravity effects both on people and physical processes. That activity led to the development of the Space Shuttle Program.

As envisioned at the time, the vehicle was to be quite small, with a total cargo capacity of 3,000 pounds at most. The Air Force, however, wanted something much bigger. And although the final Shuttle design was a technological masterpiece, it never developed as an entirely economical or reusable vehicle.

Max was critical of a NASA decision to attach small relatively propulsion-inefficient 12-foot-diameter segmented solid-fuel booster rockets rather than use larger ones. This non-optimal design was dictated by transportation limitations imposed by shipping them through railroad tunnels from Utah. He also strongly faulted NASA for not fully recognizing and avoiding the cold weather solid rocket seal hazard that resulted in the tragic launch failure of Space Shuttle Challenger.

Reflecting back on the event, Max said:

> *They [NASA] had every warning sign not to make that launch, and the time constant between the people down in the trenches and the people who were running the Shuttle was too long to stop the launch.*

Upon retiring from NASA, Max joined with me and two other partners, Gilllermo "Gui" Trotti and James Calaway, to privately develop and operate a Shuttle-delivered Earth-orbiting commercial "Industrial Space Facility" (ISF) for weightless experiments. The company, Space Industries International, was later headed (after Max) by five-mission Shuttle astronaut Joe Allen. Our board members included Robert Gilruth, Apollo 11 astronaut Neil Armstrong, and other very distinguished individuals.

Max commented about the ISF plan during the *NASA Oral History Project* interview:

> *It was a good idea. Actually, I think it was a wonderful idea. The basic idea was that we built something that could be launched on the Shuttle that had a pretty good amount of volume...[It] was completely capable of doing everything. Nothing had to be added to it. Bring it to orbit, turn it loose, and it would work for 30 to 90 days, or maybe 120 days, you go up and rebuilt it, resupply it, leave it up in orbit, and the thing would work. So it was man-tended.*

Max continued:

It had an internal volume that was kept pressurized. Man [or woman] can enter it. They would live off the life support system on the Shuttle simply by transferring air between it and the Shuttle, so we didn't have to put lots of life support in there, and when you wanted to make it bigger, you just add another unit to it.

After two or three launches, each unit would be independent of the other. One of the units could be equipped with a life support system to clean the air for all and provide a safe refuge in case of a pressure failure for all of the others. Max explained:

...you could get up to maybe six or eight of these things all attached together, and you'd have the equivalent to a Space Station. You would do it where, after the first launch, you're being productive, so you would grow at the same time you would produce. It's a great idea.

NASA had its own plans for a Space Station. As Max noted:

...and if this thing ever got up there and we started adding onto it, people would say, 'Why do we need the Space Station? Why don't we just keep going this way?' It represented a major threat to the continuance of the Space Station Program. It had to be killed, and they did kill it.

Although the ISF was never built, the high-tech company grew through mergers and acquisitions to employ more than 8,000 professional employees. Entirely by coincidence, I also served with Max on the board of another company that developed enormously large high-altitude balloons used for edge-of space weather recordings.

Max was asked during the NASA interview why go to space at all—why the spark—"do we go for practical business reasons, or is there something more important lurking there in your mind?"

He responded:

> Man's curiosity is the big driver behind all things that happen, behind all progress. The trouble is, of course, that most leaders in any country don't have a great deal of curiosity. They have a great need to maintain the status quo. They're sitting where they want to be, so why rock the boat? But there's always going to be people who have curiosity, and they have to be supported. The same way we've supported the arts, we've got to support the curious.

Max also emphasized the importance of maintaining a playful spirit:

> I look at my life, and the way I approach things, everything has been a toy with me. My toys were things that worked, things that flew, dove under the water, little race cars. I always liked things like that, and it was just a hell of a lot of fun to make these things work. And then I grew up and my toys got bigger, more interesting, and I still like to play with toys. So I think the world will always have men that never grow up, and that will do things that, for reasons that no one ever dreamed of. So that's the way it goes.

To me, Max Faget's wisdom and creative spirit will always speak as the smartest technical voice in any room.

358

The Explorers

Buzz Aldrin: Beyond Footprints and Flagpoles

MANY PEOPLE WORLDWIDE know of Buzz Aldrin as the second human to walk on the moon during the historic Apollo 11 mission in 1969 with companion Neil Armstrong and Mike Collins, who orbited above. I prefer to regard him as one of the first two people to walk on the Moon. I have personally known both of them.

Fewer are aware of Buzz's major contributions to making that mission possible as the Gemini 12 mission pilot in 1966. I'll briefly discuss this later.

I have known Buzz in a far broader context as a brilliantly creative and passionately motivated professional colleague and close personal friend over four decades. His inclusion here as a whole-brain thinker is truly a no-brainer. His is a rich life of experiences and achievements well worth sharing.

To begin, Buzz Aldrin was born in 1930 in Montclair, New Jersey to Eugene and Marion Aldrin. Perhaps providently, his mother's maiden name was Moon.

His father, Eugene, was an engineer and aviation pioneer who inspired Buzz to pursue dreams of flying. Eugene, a personal friend of Charles Lindbergh and Orville Wright, had flown coast-to-coast for Standard Oil, and later served with the Army Air Corps during WWII. He had attended Clark University in Worcester, Massachusetts where one of his professors was Robert Godard, the renowned father of liquid-fueled rocketry. Eugene also attended MIT, where he came to know another famous classmate, Jimmy Doolittle, who led the first carrier-based bomber attack on Tokyo on April 18, 1942 off the USS Hornet.

Although his dad had urged him to attend the Naval Academy, some friends influenced Buzz, then 17 years old, to choose West Point instead. Upon graduation during the Korean War, he entered the U.S. Air Force and trained as an F-86 swept-wing fighter pilot. Buzz flew 66 combat missions, and shot down two MiG-15 aircraft over the Yalu River. *Life Magazine* featured a picture showing the pilot having ejected out of the first Soviet-made MiG he destroyed.

Following the Korean War, Buzz was sent to Germany flying F-100s that carried nuclear weapons. It was during the late 1950s when the Cold War was escalating between the Soviet Union and United States when he first learned of the Russians launch of the first artificial satellite in October 1957. That orbiting 184-pound chirping sphere called "Sputnik" initiated a space race.

Sputnik was followed on April 12, 1961 by a 108-minute-long mission flown by cosmonaut Yuri Gagarin in a Vostok 1 spacecraft. Then, only weeks later on May 5, an American Mercury-Redstone 3 rocket delivered astronaut Alan Shepard on a 15-minute suborbital flight to the edge of space.

That first U.S. suborbital launch, in turn, was immediately followed by President John Kennedy's bold commitment twenty days after that to deliver a U.S. citizen safely to the Moon and back before the end of that decade. As Buzz has recounted, with only 15 minutes of suborbital experience at the time, the know-how to accomplish this simply didn't exist.

While stationed in Germany, Buzz decided to pursue a doctorate of science in astronautics at MIT, the same university that his father had attended. His thesis, *Guidance for Manned Orbital Rendezvous,* applied his experience as a fighter pilot in intercepting enemy aircraft to develop orbital techniques which would enable spacecraft to meet in space.

As he later recalls:

> *US Air Force training, experience and mental focus on the challenge at hand greatly benefitted me as a prelude to Gemini and Apollo. Yes, and lots of good luck helped as well.*

Although Buzz became interested in becoming an astronaut, his lack of test pilot experience, which was prioritized at the time, worked against him during two initial applications. In 1963, a successful third try won out for admittance to a third group of Gemini-Apollo astronauts thanks to his fighter pilot record and the topic of his doctoral study. He became known by fellow team members as "Dr. Rendezvous," a title which was not regarded by anyone as a compliment.

Project Gemini served as a fundamental stepping stone between the one-person Mercury and three-person Apollo programs to test equipment and to do trial runs of rendezvous and docking scenarios in Earth's orbit. Buzz did his first spaceflight on November 11, 1966 as pilot of Gemini 12 alongside James Lovell, mission pilot.

During that 4-day mission, Buzz established a record-long five and one-half hour-long tethered spacewalk which drew upon both his MIT research and his extensive recreational scuba diving experience. He subsequently introduced underwater "weightlessness" training as a standard astronaut protocol in a special underwater buoyancy facility at NASA's Johnson Space

Center.

As my friend NASA Chief Scientist Max Faget observed:

> We didn't know what kind of Moon we were going to
> land on. We didn't know what the radiation
> environment would be like near the Moon. Just a
> whole host of things like that we didn't really know,
> and we had to move ahead anyway.

Buzz and Neil Armstrong, another friend, led the way to this unknowable place. Buzz recalls:

> Before we left Earth, some alarmists considered the
> lunar dust as very dangerous…in fact pyrophoric
> (explosive)…capable of igniting spontaneously in air.
> The theory was that the dust had been so void of
> contact with oxygen that as soon as we re-pressurized
> out lunar module it might heat up, smolder, and
> perhaps burst into flames. At least that was the worry
> of a few. A late July fireworks on the Moon was not
> something anyone wanted!

Although it fortunately didn't explode, that lunar dust did become a lasting memory:

> One of the strangest sensations I recall is the smell of
> the Moon. Neil and I reentered the Eagle lunar and
> re-pressurized our little home away from home. Lunar
> dust soiled our suits and equipment, and it had a
> definite odor, like burnt charcoal or the ashes that are
> in a fireplace, especially if you sprinkle a little water
> on them.

Buzz reflects that while that first visit to the Moon was brief, the emotion it left has been long-lasting. Since no one really knew what to expect, they both had to be prepared to adapt their activities to special circumstances as they arose. As he remembers:

> *If Neil started to do the wrong thing, I wouldn't have known, because I wasn't following a particular order of what we were doing. In some ways, we were thrown out onto the surface and expected to perform a checklist from memory. Set up the flag. Open rock boxes. Put experiment in place.*

Buzz adds:

> *So it was very extemporaneous. There was a sense of, 'Well, we're here. Let's go do what we're supposed to do. But what is next?'*

The later Apollo moonwalkers had a little more time to get used to the lunar environment. With enormous world attention directed to what was recognized to be a risky mission, along with national pride riding on its success, the Nixon White House prepared a secret statement for release just in case things went terribly wrong. The July 18, 1969 internal White House essay titled *In Event of Moon Disaster*, said:

> *Fate has ordained that the men who went to the Moon in peace will stay on the Moon to rest in peace.*

Went on to say:

> *There is no hope of recovery...*

...and added...

*In their exploration, they stirred the people of the
world to feel as one; in their sacrifice, they bind more
tightly the brotherhood of men.*

Most American's were keenly aware and concerned that space
represented a new frontier of international competition and
warfare threat involving the Soviet Union, in particular, as great
potentials for peaceful progress. Buzz observed from his fighter
pilot days:

> *In Korea we knew we were really fighting the Soviets
> as well as the North Koreans, and a strong sense of
> competition on our part carried into the space race.
> We were determined not to let the 'Ruskies' beat us in
> Korea, and we certainly weren't going to let them get
> the upper hand in space.*

During the early 1980s Buzz told me that he believed that the
Russians had active plans at that time to land their own people
on the Moon. I confirmed this when I was among the first
American visitors to be invited to Russia following the collapse
of the Soviet Union. I was allowed to see a mockup of a lunar
lander that they had developed. I was surprised by the module's
rather large size and the fact it incorporated some interior
elements made of wood.

Buzz now believes that another space race back to the
Moon would be counterproductive. Instead, the United States
should chart a course toward global leadership without huge
expenditures of taxpayer money to put and support people
there:

> *Let me be up front on this point. A second race to the
> moon is a dead end, a waste of precious resources, a
> cup that holds no national glory nor a uniquely*

American payoff in either commercial or scientific terms. How do we frame our collaboration or international effort to get to the Moon again? Let me reemphasize: Certainly not as a competition. We have done that, and to restart that engine is to rerun a race we won. Let's take a pass on that one.

He adds:

Going back to the Moon is not visionary in restoring space leadership for America. Like its Apollo predecessor, it will prove to be a dead end littered with broken spacecraft, broken dreams and broken policies. While the lunar surface can be used to develop advanced technologies, it is a poor location for homesteading. It is a lifeless, barren world. Its stark desolation matched by its hostility to all living things. Replaying the glory days of Apollo will not advance the cause of American space leadership or inspire the support and enthusiasm of the public and the next generation of space explorers. I'm not suggesting that America abandon the Moon entirely...but only that we forgo it as a destination priority in competition with other countries.

Buzz advocates that the United States must set its next trajectory on Mars, not just as a place to plant more footprints and flagpoles, but as a permanent destination. In doing so, the Moon will provide an excellent testbed to practice and perfect technologies and operational techniques on the Mars surface. Additionally, ice crystals in lunar polar regions can provide a valuable source of water, which can be split into liquid oxygen rocket fuel for space operations which include Mars applications.

Why go to is Mars? As Buzz explains:

Mars represents a new world of opportunity and discovery. Science about the planet has proceeded ever since 1960 telescope-driven talk about life has been augmented by voyages of numbers of automated spacecraft sent there by multiple nations have flown by, orbited, smacked into, radar-examined, rocketed onto, bounced upon, rolled over, shoveled, drilled into, baked, and even laser-blasted it...but has never been stepped on. The first footfalls will mark a historic milestone.

Buzz continues:

Robotic exploration of Mars has yielded tantalizing clue about what was once a water-soaked planet. Deep beneath its surface may lie trapped frozen water, possibly with traces of still-extant primitive life forms. The best way to study Mars is with two hands, eyes and ears of a geologist, first at a moon orbiting Mars...and then on the surface.

Buzz envisions Mars as home to new generations of colonists. He points out:

We need to begin thinking about building permanence on the Red Planet, not just have voyagers do some experiments, plant a flag and claim success. Having them go there, repeat this, in my view, is dim-witted. Why not stay there?

This is far different than Apollo expeditions to the Moon. Since great distance between Mars and Earth makes the window within which it is feasible for humans to return is very narrow, it makes sense to transport people there who plan to stay.

Who will these volunteers be? According to Buzz, they will have to be a pretty adventurous breed:

> *No doubt about it. One-way Mars travelers will be 21st-century pilgrims, pioneering a new way of life. That will indeed take a special kind of person. Instead of the traditional pilot / scientist / engineer, Martian homesteaders will be selected more for their personalities…flexible, inventive and determined in the face of unpredictability. In short, survivors.*

I have had the good fortune to know Buzz over a period of four decades, and have marveled at other of his numerous contributions that are far less well-known. One example is his innovative proposal for a "Mars Cycler" transportation trajectory, whereby spacecraft perpetually cycle between Earth and Mars, conserving huge amounts of propellant fuel in the process.

We have applied this approach in many of our mission planning concepts at my SICSA center at the University of Houston.

The Aldrin "Cycling Pathways to Mars" concept proposes an interplanetary system of fully reusable long-haul deep-space cruisers along looping pathways to transport people and cargo. Much like railroads and roadways that have formed transportation backbones throughout vast expanses of terrestrial wilderness, the cyclers will endlessly glide along "space expressways" within the inner Solar System. And like airlines, the strategy doesn't throw away spacecraft after reaching destinations.

The Cyclers also offer major cost economies over traditionally proposed one-shot Mars launch approaches by efficiently taking advantage of gravitational forces of the Earth and Moon to sustain the special orbit trajectory.

Larry Bell

As Buzz describes this concept:

> We can create 'space expressways' of beautiful
> simplicity that use gravitational forces to route
> Cyclers back and forth between two worlds—Earth
> and Mars—and points in between. The first transit
> from Earth to Mars will be an unmanned
> demonstration. Later transits will deliver pioneering
> homesteaders who will stay. Every time a Cycler
> swings past Earth it will be met by a supply ferry, and
> boarded by a fresh group of pioneering crews destined
> for the Mars surface or one of its moons.

Buzz has also been actively involved with us and others in broad
aspects of the planning and design of orbital and lunar/planetary
space habitats. I have had the occasion to discuss many concepts
with him during very late-night calls and early breakfast
conversations... he obviously requires much less sleep than I am
accustomed to. His commitment to space development is
uncompromising, and his scope of interests and knowledge are
expansive.

Greatly to his credit, Buzz has also overcome difficult
personal hardships throughout his life. He lost his close friend Ed
White along with fellow Apollo astronauts Gus Grissom and
Roger Chaffee in a January 27, 1967 Command Module test fire
accident, and his mother committed suicide the year before he
went to the Moon. Following that historic mission, Buzz went
into a deep depression and became addicted to alcohol.

Buzz got his life back together and stopped drinking in
1978. As he candidly wrote in *Magnificent Desolation: The Long
Journey Home from the Moon*: "I have a lot of frailties, a lot of
shortcomings, but I am a much more productive person now
than I ever was at the peak of my astronaut career." [366]

As for the future, Buzz urges that it's high time to raise our vision and commitment to loftier, more far-reaching goals:

> *We are at an important inflection point in human history. The decision is whether to look upwards and gain strength from vision and commitment to worthy goals beyond ourselves—beyond the here and now.*

That future will depend upon national leaders with bold visions. Unfortunately, Buzz observes:

> *In my frequent travels, around the world, I observe with sad irony that American leadership in space is appreciated more in foreign lands than it is within our own country. Many people I meet ask why we should invest huge sums of money going to space at times when there are so many important serious problems and needs at home.*

Buzz then reminds us:

> *My friends, there always have been such problems and needs, and there always will be. Great nations, great people, have always faced them, confronted them and triumphed over them. That is the bold spirit and confidence that made them great. That is the true character that defines America.*

Finally, why go to space at all? As Buzz sees it:

> *It reminds the public that nothing is impossible if free people work together to accomplish great things. It captures the imagination of our youth, it fuels the American workforce and economy with high technology jobs, and it fosters peaceful and beneficial*

international collaborations to ensure US foreign policy leadership.

He concludes:

America must once again dare to pursue big dreams. Although space exploration progress has slowed, it is my great hope that a new generation of leaders and doers will once again boldly venture where no one has gone before. Our Apollo days were a time when we did bold things, achieving leadership. Now is our time to be bold again in space.

Neil Armstrong: Testing Limits of Flight

Following his retirement from NASA, Apollo 11 astronaut Neil Armstrong served on the boards of several companies, including that of Space Industries Inc., an organization I co-founded along with former NASA Johnson Space Center Chief Engineer Max Faget and two other partners. This remembrance is taken from a *Forbes* magazine tribute feature I posted about Neil's life following his death on August 25, 2012.

As I then reported, Neil Armstrong has now been inducted into history's loftiest celestial ranks. He is greatly honored not only for what he accomplished, but fundamentally because of the inspirational spirit of exceptionalism he exemplified after America's psyche was badly jolted by unexpected Cold War events. Those shock waves began on October 4, 1957 when a tiny Soviet satellite chirped alarming evidence of technological superiority. Then, only three and one-half years later, a young cosmonaut named Yuri Gagarin leant his human face to a new extraterrestrial space era that threatened to leave the United States behind.

America immediately responded. On May 25, 1961, only a

few weeks after Gagarin's orbital flight, President John Kennedy upped the ante, committing the United States to send a man to the moon and return him safely before the end of that decade. He rallied the country to that cause, saying:

> ...no single space project in this period will be more impressive to mankind, or more important for the long-range exploration of space; and none will be so difficult or expensive to accomplish...in a very real sense, it will not be one man going to the moon—if we make this judgment affirmatively, it will be an entire nation. For all of us must work to put him there.

And the remarkable clincher:

> Let it be clear—and this is a judgment which the Members of the Congress must finally make—let it be clear that I am asking the Congress and the country to accept a firm commitment to a new course of action, a course which will last for many years and carry very heavy costs...If we are to go only half way, or reduce our sights in the face of difficulty, in my judgment it would be better not to go at all.

That historic Apollo 11 landing wasn't Neil's first space cowboy rodeo. As Gemini 8 Command Pilot, his March 16, 1966 mission with Pilot David Scott entailed complex rendezvous and docking maneuvers with an unmanned Agena target vehicle which ultimately required recovery from a harrowing, out-of-control spacecraft roll. As NASA Flight Director Gene Krantz later reported:

> ...the mission planners and controllers had failed to

realize that when two spacecraft are docked together,
they must be considered one spacecraft.

Neil Armstrong's story confirms opportunities for common citizens to realize uncommon goals in America. Born in Wapakoneta, Ohio on August 5, 1930, an early fascination with aviation began when, at the age of two, his father took him to the Cleveland Air Races. He experienced his first airplane flight in a Ford Tri-motor "Tin Goose" four years later. By age 15 he had earned a pilot flight certificate. That was before he had a driver's license.

In 1947 Neil enrolled in an aerospace engineering program at Purdue University as the second member of his family to attend college. He had also been accepted to MIT, but decided that it wasn't necessary to go all the way to Cambridge, Massachusetts to get a good education. Under conditions of a scholarship requirement, he interrupted his study after two years to serve three years in the U.S. Navy, returning to earn a BS in aeronautical engineering in 1955. He then went on to acquire an MS in aerospace engineering from the University of Southern California in 1970.

Arriving for about 18 months of flight training at the Pensacola Naval Air Station on January 26, 1949, Neil became qualified as a Naval Aviator for carrier landings two weeks after his 20th birthday. He was soon assigned to an all-jet squadron, making his first flight in an F9F-2B Panther on January 5, 1951. Six months later he achieved his first jet carrier landing on the USS Essex which then set sail for Korea.

Neil's F9F Panther was hit by anti-aircraft fire while making a low bombing run at about 350 MPH near Wonsan. While attempting to regain control, his aircraft collided with a 20-foot-high pole that sliced off about three feet of his right wing. Although he managed to fly back to friendly territory, he was forced to eject over an airfield near Pohang where he was picked up in a jeep driven by his flight school roommate. Following 78 Korean missions with 121 hours in the air, Neil received the Air Medal for 20 combat missions, a gold Star for another 20, and the Korean Service Medal.

After returning and graduating from Purdue, Neil applied to become a test pilot at the National Advisory Committee for Aeronautics High-Speed Flight Station at Edwards Air Force Base. Since they had no open positions, they forwarded his application to the Lewis Flight Propulsion Laboratory in Cleveland where he began working in March 1955. Four months later, a position at Edwards opened up, and he took it. His first rocket plane flight in the Bell X-1B experienced a nose gear failure on landing. He later flew the North American X-15 seven times, ultimately reaching an altitude of 207,500 feet.

Neil's X-15 incidents are legendary. On an April 20, 1962 flight achieving an altitude of 207,000 feet, he held the nose up too long during descent, causing the craft to bounce off the atmosphere back up to 140,000 feet. This caused him to fly 40 miles past the landing field at Mach 3 (2,000 MPH) before turning back, and only narrowly missing some trees. Then, four days later, flying touch-and-go landings in a Lockheed T-33 Shooting Star with Chuck Yeager, the wheels became stuck in a lake bed made wet by recent rain and Armstrong and Yeager waited there to await rescue.

On still another occasion, Neil misjudged his altitude in a Lockheed F-104 Starfighter during emergency landing tests, also not realizing that his landing gear wasn't fully extended. As he touched down, the gear began to retract. He applied full power to abort the landing, but the vertical fin and landing gear door struck the ground, releasing hydraulic fluid which, in turn, caused the tail-hook to deploy. Upon returning to base and landing, he caught an arresting wire attached to an anchor chain, dragging it along the runway.

In 1958 Neil Armstrong was selected for the U.S. Air

Larry Bell

Force's "Man in Space Soonest" program, and in November 1960, he was chosen as part of a consultant group for Boeing's X-20 Dyna-Soar military space plane. In March 1962, he was named as one of six pilot-engineers who would be first to fly it.

At that time, NASA was seeking applications for a second group of astronauts for the Apollo program. Although Neil's application arrived about a week after the June 1, 1962 deadline, Dick Day, who had worked closely with him at Edwards, reportedly slipped his late application into the pile before anyone noticed. Deke Slayton contacted Neil on September 13, asking him if he would be interested in joining the NASA Astronaut Corps as part of what the press dubbed "New Nine." The rest is history.

Neil Armstrong was an ardent adventurer and a reluctant hero. He never sought the celebrity he would win, or the honors a grateful nation bestowed upon him: The Presidential Medal of Freedom, the Congressional Space Medal of Honor or the Congressional Gold Medal to name a few. Instead, he returned back from space to devote his life to a more personal American dream of husband, father, university professor and provider of professional service. He served on the boards of several companies, including Marathon Oil, Learjet, Cinergy, Taft Broadcasting, United Airlines, Eaton Corporation, AIL Systems, Thiokol, and Space Industries, International. He also served on the Rogers Commission, which investigated causes behind the Space Shuttle Challenger tragedy.

During his later years, a growing concern about his country's continuing leadership in space sufficiently overcame his strongly private nature. He became an outspoken proponent for returning Americans back to the moon. Speaking to a Congressional House committee in 2010 he observed:

> ...after all, they say we have already been there. I find that mystifying. It would be as if 16th-century

monarchs proclaimed that we need not go to the New
World, we have already been there.

Eternal imprints of Neil Armstrong's "one small step for man, one giant leap for mankind," along with footprints left by Buzz Aldrin and other brave members of his elite group are now immortalized in a very special place in our human experience. They, and those who provided the roadmaps and means, inspired us to realize that courage, dedication, education and worthwhile, ambitious dreams simply await action. Let their example and lesson never be forgotten.

Bonnie Dunbar: An Adventurous Mind

My enormously dedicated and accomplished educator colleague and five Space Shuttle mission flight astronaut, Dr. Bonnie J. Dunbar, very fortunately disregarded comments from anyone who said that "space is not for women."

Growing up in a rural community of post-World War II veterans, many of whom were homesteading for the first time, she was encouraged to aim high and value her freedoms. Any discouragement she might have received for studying engineering or expressing a desire to become an astronaut, if actually stated to her, was infrequent. In any case, she ignored them, instead spending her time with the teachers, friends, and university professors who encouraged and mentored her. She prudently warns: "If you let cynics take up your brain space, you're wasting it."

Bonnie comes from stout moral stock and exemplifies determined family grit. At age 19, her Scottish immigrant grandfather, Charles Cuthill Dunbar chased the American dream a century ago to New York's Ellis Island to break horses near Syracuse. He later settled on a homestead in Condon, Oregon. Bonnie fondly remembers his mastery of playing Scottish folk tunes by ear on his fiddle, and that "He was never one to take charity or poke fingers."

Her father, Bob Dunbar, who graduated from a one room school house, had his own dreams delayed. When WWII began, he volunteered for the Marines, turning down a Union Pacific Railroad scholarship for a University in Oregon. After leaving the Marine Corps, he and wife Ethel forged a working farm and cattle ranch homestead near Outlook, Washington, out of dry, rocky, desert sage brush land. There, side by side, her parents raised Bonnie and her three siblings with values and discipline to ensure that the next generation of Dunbars would use their "God-given talents and lead good, productive lives."

Following in his father's footsteps, Bonnie's younger brother, by 16 months, Bobby, went to war. His short life ended in 1970 on a Vietnam battlefield. Bonnie painfully recounts that terrible personal and family loss:

> At 19, he was one of the youngest squad leaders in Vietnam. While on patrol, he stepped on a land mine, crawled out of the danger area, refusing to have anybody help him because he didn't want to put the rest of his squad at risk. For that, he received the Bronze Star with V for Valor.

Tragically, her other younger brother, Gary, died 16 years later in a house fire.

By age nine, Bonnie and her two brothers drove tractors, worked in the fields, and measured time by the season. Every spring they picked up rocks and tossed them into an old trailer bed to free up land for plowing and planting. The family split their time between farming of sugar beets, mint, alfalfa, and field corn, and herding cattle through ranchland of Central Washington's Yakima valley. Her hobbies included reading voraciously (without TV) and raising 4-H steers. When more funds were needed, she, her mom and her brothers would get up before dawn to cut asparagus for neighbors.

She recalls joining her family and friends singing as they huddled around the campfire after a roundup and a big cook-out, and experiencing an enriching sense of small community neighborliness and responsibility "that money just can't buy." She reminisces:

> There was something magical and inspiring about the togetherness out on the ranch. There was great satisfaction in seeing what you can do with a day, working hard and working together.

Life was not easy, but then, none of the Dunbar family expected it to be. In 1949, Bonnie's first-time-pregnant mother had been living in a tent until just months before she was born. The young family then took up residence in "two sheep herder huts pushed together" which were slowly towed in from Condon—about 124 miles away. They lived without running water and other modern conveniences for several years. By high school age, Bonnie had seen only two theater movies.

The Dunbar children were taught to be self-reliant. Bonnie took school gun safety courses when she was 9, observing:

> It can get cold, you can get lost, you can hurt yourself when you are on horseback in the hills. You're out at the base of the Rattlesnake Mountains, there are coyotes. There are rattlesnakes.

Those early memories are steeped in contact with nature, the discovery of scenic wonders of the Yakima Valley countryside witnessed on horseback, and the fresh fragrant mix of spearmint, peppermint, and grapes wafting through the open windows of the school buses every fall.

Bonnie's parents regarded education to be a greatly valued gift. There were always books in their home, the first being a full set of 1956 Encyclopedias, and the children were exposed to classical music, compliments of 33RPM records her mother ordered from the mail. Bonnie started playing piano at 9 years of age, but was too shy to participate in class when her mother tried to enter her into tap dance and ballet.

Her father sometimes acted in the local community theater (with a memorable experience in the "Hatfields and the McCoys"), and was active in the leadership of farm bureau and the cattleman's association. Social Activities were community centered, including picnics on the 4th of July, rodeos, and the local livestock fair where they showed their livestock. During the cold winters, entertainment was often family and ranch limited with spirited games of pinochle and scrabble and homemade popcorn.

Bonnie recalls:

> As a child, I read all the time. I learned through biographies that we all face obstacles, and that there will always be those who doubt we can succeed. People who are successful learn to ignore them and stay focused on reaching their goals. One saying that has always stayed with me is 'it's not what happens to you, but how you react to it that matters.'

She particularly enjoyed reading science fiction, imagining herself as a character in stories of Jules Verne, popular English author H.G. Wells, and Arthur C. Clarke who wrote her all-time favorite short story, "The Star".

Bonnie was also captivated by real science, an interest which was kindled by "Mr. Wizard", a phenomenally popular national television program which debuted in 1951. Perched in a tree house she fashioned together out of spare wood and big burlap sacks on the Dunbar property she dreamed of being in a spaceship rocketing to orbit.

Bonnie was eight years old when the Russian "Sputnik" astonished the world. She remembers following her parents outside to scan the vast Eastern Washington skies for traces of the small satellite. She remembers: "People tuned in to their radios listening for the sound of beep, beep, beep."

That experience intensified Bonnie's interest in pursuing what had previously been only fictional fantasies: "When I was growing up, young people were encouraged to study science because the Space Race was on."

No one around her questioned her sincerity or ability. As she happily notes, "The fact that I was a girl, never came up."

Nor did Bonnie's active science interest limit her engagement in extracurricular activities. She made the debate team and the Honor Society, became a cheerleader, and was voted most athletic girl in her Sunnyside High School class. She reflects: "I wanted to be everything I could be."

Bonnie's science interest and overall high school performance earned her a National Defense Education Act college scholarship that set her life on a provident trajectory. The NDEA program was initiated in 1958 to financially support academically qualified students to study science and engineering in the post-Sputnik space race competition with the USSR. She gratefully remembers:

> I was fortunate to start the math track with algebra in 9th grade, and really loved geometry, trigonometry, physics and chemistry. I could apply all of those subjects on the ranch. When I took the SAT test, I scored well enough in math and 'spatial ability' to be accepted into Engineering.

Enrolling at the University of Washington in 1967 as the first member of her family to attend college, Bonnie selected ceramic engineering as her major focus. This field includes research and development of inorganic materials to make everything from snowboards, to airplanes, to the thermal protection tiles needed to shield Space Shuttles she would later fly on from high temperatures they would encounter reentering the Earth's atmosphere.

As a freshman, Bonnie fortunately came to know Dr. I. Mueller, chair of the Ceramic Engineering Department, who was a Principal Investigator on a special NASA research project to develop those ceramic tiles. Dr. Mueller became her advocate and friend. She recalls:

> When I told him my freshman year that I really wanted to become involved with NASA and be an astronaut, he didn't laugh, he didn't try to dissuade me. He just promised that I would be able to meet NASA engineers if I joined his department. After that, he was true to his word.

Bonnie subsequently earned a Bachelor of Science Degree in Ceramic Engineering in 1971, and a Master of Science in Ceramic Engineering, also at the University of Washington, in 1975. Later, in 1983, she earned a doctorate at the University of Houston in Mechanical/Biomedical Engineering.

While Bonnie was only 13 years old, a charismatic young President John F. Kennedy made a bold announcement. Speaking at Rice University in September of 1962, he said: "We choose to go to the Moon in this decade and do the other things, not because they are easy, but because they are hard."

Nearly seven years later, when she was an undergraduate at the University of Washington, Apollo 11 roared into orbit atop a Saturn IV rocket with my friends Neil Armstrong and Buzz Aldrin aboard to accomplish exactly that.

Bonnie credits her life-long passions and achievements to Kennedy's inspiring words, and also to her science and engineering education. She reminds us:

> *When we went to the Moon, the whole world watched. We should be proud that we invested so much into education, technology, and the industries we have today. It has benefitted our society and improved our quality of life. We should never underestimate the role that science and technology has had in every major civilization since the dawn of time.*

Bonnie has applied and expanded her science and technology interests through a variety of professional experiences. In 1973 she tested her systems analysis problem-solving capabilities as a computer systems analyst with the Boeing Computer Sciences Company. She points out:

> *Computers don't have their own minds. We program them. If the computer follows the wrong instructions, it's because a human being wrote the wrong instructions. My job was to reverse engineering errors and to determine root causes.*

When later working on production of Space Shuttle tiles for Columbia at Rockwell International's Space Division in Downey, California, Bonnie applied to the NASA Astronaut Corps. Although not selected for the 1978 astronaut class (she was a finalist), she was offered a position in NASA's Mission Control. She became a Space Shuttle Payload Officer in Mission Control and a Guidance and Navigation Officer for the Skylab re-entry project (Skylab reentered July 11, 1979).

Bonnie was selected as a member of the second Space Shuttle astronaut class in the spring of 1980. In 1984, NASA called her to duty as the seventh American women to fly in space as a mission specialist aboard the Space Shuttle Challenger. Referred to as mission STS-61-A, it carried a Spacelab laboratory which orbited Earth in the Shuttle's payload bay as a joint U.S.-German venture. Over the next 18 months she trained tirelessly in the US and Germany, exercised at the gym and poured over mountains of training material.

In October 1985, her real childhood dream came true. NASA called Bonnie to duty as the seventh American women to fly in space as a mission specialist aboard the Space Shuttle Challenger. Referred to as mission STS-61-A, it carried a Skylab laboratory which orbited Earth in the Shuttle's payload bay as a joint U.S.-European venture.

As Bonnie describes her personal experience:

> You float up there in front of overhead windows that are now pointed at the direction you're flying. And I could only think about being on the deck of the Starship Enterprise. You know, going where no man or women has gone before.

Bonnie returned to space for her second flight in 1990 aboard the Space Shuttle Columbia Shuttle (STS-32). The mission involved chasing and deftly retrieving an orbiting research satellite (LDEF) that had been delivered in 1984 which was slowly falling out of orbit. Commenting upon the challenge of deftly nabbing it with a 50-foot-long robotic arm, she recalls:

> You're always excited before and after, but in the middle of performing, you're an athlete or race car driver or a pilot, you're really focusing on what you're doing. Everything you've done, in terms of training, must come into focus at that time it's like your finals. If you've been in the middle of a final,

> *are you thinking about your emotions at that time?*
> *Probably not. You are thinking about answering the*
> *question on the test.*

She adds:

> *You never think of making history while you're there.*
> *If you're doing that, you're not putting all your brain*
> *cells where they need to be.*

Her third voyage above Earth occurred in 1992 as Payload Commander aboard Columbia again (STS-50), a mission dedicated to more than 30 weightless or "microgravity" Spacelab life sciences, biotechnology, fluid physics, and material science experiments. The crew of seven operated around-the-clock over 13 days, traveling nearly eight million miles in 221 orbits around the Earth.

Bonnie's fourth spaceflight marked the 100th mission for the U.S. space program. It was also the first international orbital crew exchange in two decades whereby the U.S. Space Shuttle Atlantis (STS-71) was modified to dock with a Russian Mir Space Station. Bonnie returned to the U.S. from Russia for this flight, having trained for 13 months in Russia's Star City as back-up to another astronaut who flew to the MIR on the Soyuz 3 months earlier. Bonnie communicated with the MIR crew in Russian during the final docking sequence.

Again utilizing the Spacelab, Bonnie and other members of the U.S. crew performed medical evaluations on the returning Mir crew which included ascertaining the effects of weightlessness on the cardio/vascular system, the bone/muscle system, the immune system, and the cardio/pulmonary system.

Endeavor STS-89 in 1998 constituted Bonnie's fifth and final flight and accomplished the eighth Shuttle-Mir docking. The mission transferred more than 9,000 pounds of scientific equipment, logistics hardware and water to the Russian habitat. As Payload Commander, Bonnie was responsible for all payload activities, including the conduct of 23 technology and science experiments. The mission also delivered U.S. astronaut Andy Thomas to the Mir, and returned with American David Wolf.

Bonnie retired from NASA in 2005 to become president and CEO of the Museum of Flight in Seattle. There, she established a new Space Gallery, and expanded its K-12 science, technology, engineering and mathematics (STEM) education offerings. She later returned to her alma mater at the University of Houston's Cullen College of Engineering to head its STEM and graduate Aerospace Engineering programs.

I am most grateful that Bonnie agreed to succeed me after three decades as Director of the Sasakawa International Center for Space Architecture (SICSA) throughout the organization's 2014 administrative transfer from the College of Architecture and transition to the College of Engineering.

Following her own subsequent transfer to Texas A&M University, as professor and Director of its Institute for Engineering Education and Innovation (IEEI), Bonnie continues serve as a senior SICSA advisory officer.

In 2002, Dr. Bonnie Dunbar was elected to the prestigious the U.S. National Academy of Engineering, and was selected into the Astronaut Hall of Fame in 2013. Endowed with a bedrock foundation of family and community values, personal dedication to excellence, and perseverance essential to achieve ambitious quests, her simple advice is well worth heeding:

Measure success by how far you progress into your own goals. If you know you've worked for it and earned it, that's how you build confidence.

Part Six: Living Mindfully

HUMANIST PSYCHOLOGIST ABRAHAM Maslow's influential 1943 paper titled *A Theory of Human Motivation* emphasized the importance of attending to and developing the "whole" person with regard to all aspects of ourselves that make us human—the physical, emotional, intellectual and spiritual qualities.

He synthesized these desirable attributes into a famous pyramid-shaped hierarchical needs chart ranging from basic physiological needs at the lowest foundation level to self-actualization at the apex. His top level provided for morality, creativity, spontaneity, problem solving, lack of prejudice and acceptance of facts.

Maslow's theory identified common self-actualizing talents and other characteristics he attributed to selected individuals of exceptional accomplishment including Abraham Lincoln and Albert Einstein. Key among these tendencies were: abilities to tolerate uncertainties; acceptance of themselves for who they were; good senses of humor; creativity; genuine concerns for the welfare of humanity; appreciation for basic life experiences such as enjoying a country walk; deep satisfactions of interpersonal relationships with a few people; and strong moral and ethical standards.

Maslow postulated that many people never realize high levels of their full potential or "self- actualization" because they view life through a negative lens until the first basic human needs are met, including a need to feel safe, sleep and eat, and to love and be loved. Maslow reasoned that until these fundamental needs are met it is difficult to focus our abilities and attention to higher matters. He theorized that only through attainment of these needs can an individual achieve true happiness and purpose. Moreover, at that stage, "A musician must make music, an artist must paint, a poet must write, if they are to be at peace with themselves. What a man can be, he must be."

Psychologist Abraham Carl Rogers recognized a sense of playfulness—fun, joy and amusement—to represent an important part of a self-actualized personality: "The quiet joy in being one's self...a spontaneous relaxed enjoyment, a primitive joie de vivre."

"Joie de vivre" (joy of living), a French phrase, is characterized by Robert's Dictionary as "sentiment exaltant ressenti par toute la conscience," a sentiment that involves one's whole being. According to the well-known early 20th century British philosopher, mathematician and essayist Bertrand Russell, experiencing that joy doesn't require enormous intelligence as scored on standardized tests. He observed:

> I've made an odd discovery. Every time I talk to a savant I feel quite sure that happiness is no longer a possibility. Yet when I talk to my gardener I'm assured the opposite.

We individuals measure our personal self-actualization, more typically characterized as "success," according to varying personal priorities and criteria which don't necessarily assure joyful lives. Some equate success with money and security, some with respect and recognition, some with professional interests and challenges and some with contributions they make to the lives of others. These measures, of course, are not mutually exclusive. Many influence the ways most people see themselves to some degree. For some, success might represent an elusive goal that motivates them to grow. Just when you think that you know what it means and are getting close, something, possibly yourself, moves the peg up a notch.

A big problem with defining personal success is that you often can't be certain when you have acquired it—at least not by comparing yourself to others. Of course, you can usually visualize that you have achieved more in some areas than most people have, but others might properly view you in the same light.

Then you, in turn, might look back at them and ask: "Yeah, but are they as happy? Are their children as wonderful as mine? Are they as popular as I am?"

Maybe recognizing success is a matter of maturity—an ability to recognize many forms of it you already enjoy, to apply what you have learned in the process of getting it, and to have the wisdom to appreciate it.

Many are likely to worry less about whether they are successful and happy when they believe their lives have purposes beyond quests for personal gratification.

Life satisfactions are often most fully revealed when we are too consumed in contributing to events around us to think about how the outcomes will serve larger purposes. Real happiness typically has much more to do with liking and respecting who we are, rather than getting what we want.

I once had a somber occasion to contemplate purposeful live priorities during a conversation with a very close family member who was then in hospice care. He was someone I regarded to have lived a fine one and I wished to communicate my appreciation of what this meant.

I told him that if one day I find myself reviewing my own achievements in the face of known near-term terminal realities, three questions will emerge above all:

1) Did I have any fun?

2) Did I do any good?

And...

3) Did I live my life with passion?

With regard to the first, it would be a terrible waste not to celebrate opportunities to enjoy the miraculous gift of life. Were my satisfactions a product of wholesome living? Were many joys shared with others? Were important ones the products of worthwhile goal achievements?

Doing good fundamentally prompts each of us to contemplate: can I be trusted to be a good spouse, parent and friend? Do I have a generous nature when it comes to sharing credit and effort which recognizes the worth and contributions of others? Have I touched the lives of others in a constructive way simply because I could? Am I comfortable with the person that inhabits my own skin?

That third item...the "passion" word, is what sets humans apart from other perfectly wonderful creatures. It should be apparent watching puppies and kittens play that experiencing joie de vivre is not by any means unique to humans. As for doing good, Darwin's theory attributing pursuit of reward or approval as a primary motive isn't entirely unique to our species either. My dog Crosby will work hard to please me for food any day.

The All-Important Passion Factor

THE HUMAN MIND possesses a boundless capacity to care deeply about things beyond self...preferably, lots of somethings and someones. These passions guide and motivate us to experience and express our highest human potentials: to set goals; to meet challenges and seek excellence that set exceptional examples; to create music, art and literature that lift our intellect and spirits; and to believe in the power of worthwhile ideas and our abilities to make them real.

Passions arise from many sources. Sometimes they arise from exposures to a wide variety of people, ideas and experiences. On other occasions, they come to light through problems and obstacles we confront. They often relate to talents and other qualities we acknowledge in ourselves and others. Many are contagious, and can be shared to forge bonds with kindred souls who share our values.

One big advantage of those who have passion about something is that they are often too preoccupied with what they care about to become sidetracked listening to experts who are all too willing to tell them otherwise. In fact, the very reason many people become successful is because they became interested in a possibility or discovery that nobody else paid much attention to or thought would work.

Pursuing passions stimulates our curiosity, inciting us to courses of inquiry and persistent action that reveal unexpected possibilities. In pursuit of new worlds of understanding, the late theoretical physicist and cosmologist Stephen Hawking observed: "Science is not only a discipline of reason, but also one of romance and passion."

Canadian rock guitarist Randy Bachman appears to have a strong sense of what this pursuit of fulfillment means to him:

> When one knows at an early age that their gift, talent use direction is musical, one tends to focus on that and let nothing interfere or impede the forward motion toward the end of that rainbow. And after 50-something rears of rockin' out, you still realize there is no end to that distant rainbow until one's last sunset.

Celebrity talk show hostess, actress and movie producer Oprah Winfrey attributes the driving energy force behind her achievements as passion, "the power that comes from focusing on what excites you."

Internationally acclaimed cellist Yo-Yo Ma emphasizes the importance of caring deeply about something. He has said: "Passion is the great force that unleashes creativity because if you're passionate about something, then you're willing to take more risks."

Passion's Persistent Drive for Purpose

When the recent message in my fortune cookie at a favorite neighborhood Chinese restaurant seemed to make no intelligible sense whatsoever, Nancy suggested I make one up for myself. After but a couple of seconds I did: "Passion gives the gift of persistence to purpose."

I might have said, "Passion: Don't leave home without it." Perhaps maybe I'll leave that for some future fortune cookie.

In her blog *The Motivated Mind: Where Our Passion & Creativity Comes From*, neuropsychology researcher Malini Mohana writes that "passion is what moves you to persevere at something despite fear, unhappiness or pain. It is the determination to push through suffering for the sake of an end goal. What is more— this kind of motivation has an actual source in the brain." [367]

Researchers have observed that the ventral striatum, in combination with the amygdala (known as the brain's emotional center), is activated in proportion to how motivated a person feels: the higher degree of motivation, the higher the activation level. Mohana notes that: "Motivation does not simply give you the energy to work, but allows you to entirely change your perception of everything that you do."

Referring to the brain's neuroplasticity, she adds: "Conversely, your change in perception will start to affect the types of long-term behavior in which you engage."

Malini Mohana urges us to remember, as we are constantly told, we can only succeed by doing what we love:

> The science is simple; when you enjoy something, you have a natural tendency to work at it and become better at it. By doing so you are effectively building new neural connections that keep multiplying as you keep working.

As American Civil War abolitionist and humanist Harriet Tubman urges us to recognize:

> Every great dream begins with a dreamer. Always remember, you have within you the strength, the patience, and the passion to change the world.

History reminds us that many of those people who have changed the world had to put their egos on the line and set disappointments behind them before their efforts were eventually rewarded.

President Abraham Lincoln urged us to "Always bear in mind that your own resolution to success is more important than any other thing." He drew upon personal experience on this matter, having previously been defeated before winning a seat in the Illinois legislature, then later being passed over twice in nomination bids for the U.S. Congress.

The late African anti-apartheid revolutionary leader Nelson Mandela encourages us to set our passion goals high. He advises: "There is no passion to be found in playing small—in settling for a life that is less than one you are capable of living."

It is not selfish to expect everything possible in life. When we deny ourselves, we may also diminish our abilities to enrich others. In this regard, Mandela prompts us to make best advantage of opportunities afforded to constantly learn, grow, create and to transform passions into actions.

Have fun with your passions. Value them, nurture them and yes, apply them for good. A well-lived life deserves no less.

Gifts of Unconditional Caring

The ability to care is both our greatest human gift and reward. It is most rewarding when there are no conditions and we expect nothing back in return. We care because we care. It is as simple as that.

- We support charities because we care that they help people who need support.

- We care about the natural environment because it holds the future.

- We care about animals and other creatures because we

are capable of being kind.

- We care about our parents because we love them.

- We care about our children because we feel responsible for them and they represent our unselfish hopes and dreams.

- We care about lovers and friends because they have touched our lives.

In business, as well as personal relationships, people put greatest trust in those who subordinate their own private agendas to achieve the greatest benefits for a partnership. Those who succeed at the expense of others are likely to experience hollow victories and empty lives.

I have observed that people who practice caring relationships develop a habit of bringing that character into all of their endeavors. Others trust them, and for good reasons. They have developed the capacity to focus their minds and energies upon helping to create a worthwhile result for everyone rather than concentrating on ways they can receive the greatest benefit, including claiming the most credit.

Truly caring people are willing to contribute more than their share without keeping a ledger to demonstrate that they deserve more. Often, they don't have to. Their generosity is usually recognized and valued by recipients who reward them far beyond their greatest expectations.

As exemplified in the previous section, people I most admire typically have broad and deep capacities to care about issues and possibilities beyond personal gains. Through caring we experience life most fully. Caring provides motivations and rewards to love, seek, thrill, question, learn, solve, imagine, create, play, dare, feel, compete and commit.

Caring about self and others are not mutually exclusive. Both are vitally essential to our emotional and spiritual survival.

Yet as Irish playwright, novelist and poet Oscar Wilde warned, dangers lurk in temptations to compromise our highest life expectations in order to achieve societal conformity:

> *I won't tell you that the world matters nothing, or the world's voice, or the voice of society. They matter a good deal. They matter far too much. But there are moments when one has to choose between living one's own life, fully, entirely, completely—or dragging out some false, shallow, degrading existence that the world in its hypocrisy demands. You have that moment now. Choose!*

Nevertheless, all civilized societies are bound together by bonds of moral principles common to leading religions and civil societies throughout civilized history.

In 2000, Richard Kinner and Jerry Kernes in the Division of Psychology in Education at Arizona State University-Tempe, along with Phoenix counselor Therese Dautheribes, compiled *A Short List of Universal Values* taken from texts of major world religions. Included were Judaism (the *Tanaka*), Christianity (the *New Testament*), Islam (the *Quran*), Hinduism (the *Upanishads* and the *Bhagavad Gita*), Confucianism (the *Analects of Confucius*), Taoism (the *Tao Te Ching of Lao Tzu*) and Buddhism (the *Dhammapada*).[368]

The study also consulted with and reviewed materials of several secular organizations, including the American Atheists Inc. (*Atheist Aims and Purpose, Atheism Teaches That,* and *Introduction to American Atheists*), The American Humanist Association (*Humanist Manifesto I, 1933* and *Humanist Manifesto II, 1973*), and the United Nations (*The United Nations Declaration of Human Rights, 1948*).

Here's what they came up with:

- Commitment to something greater than self: To

recognize the existence of and be committed to a Supreme Being, higher principle, transcendent purpose or meaning to one's existence; and to seek the truth (or truths) and justice.

- Self-respect, but with humility; self-discipline; and acceptance of personal responsibility: to respect and care for oneself; to not exalt oneself or overindulge; to show humility and avoid gluttony or other forms of selfishness and self-centeredness; and to act in accordance with one's conscience and to accept responsibility for one's behavior.

- Respect and caring for others (i.e., the Golden Rule): to recognize the connectedness between all people; to serve humankind and be helpful to individuals; to be caring, respectful, compassionate, tolerant and forgiving of others; and to not hurt others (e.g., do not murder, abuse, steal from, cheat or lie to others.)

- Care for other living things and the environment.

Discovering Motivational Mojo

Being motivated is more a matter of choice than chance. We can decide if we want to be involved in the affairs and events of the world that surround us: if we are willing to take the risks that are attached to challenges; if we are prepared to accept the responsibilities that go along with relationships; and if prospects for a brighter future are within our control and worth working for.

When we simply wait for motivation to appear and seize us, we surrender our will and imagination to fate. Maybe it's time to get ahold of ourselves, get excited about something and shine!

Where can we find wellsprings of inspiration to raise us out of occasional doldrums, rekindle our enthusiasm about everyday events and encourage us to explore untested possibilities? We can begin by looking in familiar places: within ideas and examples of people we know that illuminate higher values to aspire to; among simple interests and pleasures that we take for granted and never fully recognize; and discover them connected to unresolved problems that cry out for innovative solutions.

There are occasions when its source may come from a realization that the path that we are on is unacceptable, and we must change it, even if we're not certain where to go. Nevertheless, every time we fail to act on something that we seriously intend to do, we break an agreement with ourselves. We are admitting that we can't trust ourselves to follow through on our bargains.

There are times in each of our lives when discouraging setbacks diminish goal expectations and deflate our resolve—if only for a while. As the late motivational speaker and author Zig Ziglar observed: "People often say that motivation doesn't last. Well, neither does bathing—that's why we recommend it daily."

Although motivation to accomplish something is a great beginning, good intentions don't really get rolling until deliberately acted upon. Or as the late American self-help author Napoleon Hill put it: "A goal is a dream with a deadline."

Procrastination becomes a real problem when we miss out on opportunities that aren't likely to come around again; when we don't fulfill commitments we have made; when we let people down who depend upon our performance; and when we feel harried and frustrated because responsibilities are piling up as we get farther behind schedule.

We can often make our situations much easier by being more selective and realistic about our intentions in the first place. Otherwise, the necessary time, energy and attention required to address them all will be consumed by other demands that invariably creep in. Initiatives deferred frequently become prerogatives lost.

As author and former Stanford University gymnastics director Dan Millman advises:

> *I learned that we can do anything, but we can't do everything...at least not at the same time. So think of your priorities not in terms of what activities you do, but when you do them. Timing is everything.*

But don't wait too long. As astrophysicist and science communicator Neil deGrasse Tyson observes: "The most successful people in life recognize they create their own love, they manufacture their own meaning, they generate their own motivation."

The biggest issue isn't whether something can be accomplished, but rather, whether it should be, and who will do it. Mark Twain urged us to consider that...

> *Twenty years from now you will be more disappointed by the things you didn't do than by the ones you did do. So throw off the bowlines. Sail away from the safe harbor. Catch the trade winds in your sail. Explore. Dream. Discover.*

Opportunities in the Here and Now

Why do some people always seem to be at the right place at the right time and enjoy more opportunities than others do? Maybe it's because they realize that every place and time is right for something good to happen, and they are creative enough to figure out some possibilities. They are also objective enough to understand which options make the most sense, motivated enough to act upon them and perceptive enough to recognize when they don't and move on to something else.

Most opportunities don't have neon lights attached to them that flash the words "Here I am!" Instead, they are often camouflaged to blend into the background of everyday circumstances, or are disguised to appear innocuous or even undesirable. Some opportunities have no form at all until new ideas shape them.

People who passively wait for opportunities to introduce themselves don't understand that the best ones usually don't behave that way. Being in popular demand, they seldom have to send out formal invitations, advertise in Want Ads or knock on doors to solicit interest. It takes a little bit of initiative to find them.

Really fine opportunities are personalized to fit our special interests and strengths. We're least likely to find these hanging around in settings that are dominated by assembly line mentalities—and which cater to one-size-fits-all aspirations. More often, they are discovered or created by individuals with discriminating opinions about who they are and what they expect. These people are selectively attuned to recognize possibilities that are most appropriate and accessible for them.

Opportunities frequently appear where they aren't anticipated and when they're not being sought. Sometimes finding them doesn't require any effort at all; we just open our minds, and there they are. This may seem unfair to people who work very hard, yet never seem to discover chances to get ahead. Perhaps they miss seeing them because their noses are too close to grindstones.

Big opportunities often come in deceptively small packages. Examples include chance meetings that introduce relationships and work prospects; satisfying hobbies that lead to new vocations; and casual observations that reveal exciting concepts to pursue.

These fortunate accidents can have profound influences over our lives. How can we prepare ourselves for these unforeseen developments? We can begin by realizing that everything we experience has potential importance.

Recognizing opportunities has as much to do with attitude as with aptitude. We can stand in place and complain when possibilities don't come our way, or steer our courses where the action is. We can lament conditions that are unsatisfactory, or seek ways to improve them a little at a time. We can make it a habit to avoid risks, or recognize that they are necessary investments for moving forward. We can allow discouragements to defeat us, or apply lessons of failed efforts to avoid future mistakes.

The process of living is an aggregation of opportunities—to experience, to grow, to contribute and to learn. So long as we're here, there's no good reason to miss out. Why not reach out instead?

Personal Insights and Outlooks

The conditions and opportunities we recognize in life depend much more upon vision than location. Wherever we are, what we see is influenced by the viewing angles we choose and the ways we focus our minds. How we interpret what we see also reflects ways that we view ourselves in those settings.

We can choose to see our personal world any way we wish...both from the inside out and from the outside in. We also have the power to change it through our priorities and vision.

Viewing ourselves and circumstances from the outside, we can begin to observe our relationships, opportunities and choices within more objective frames of reference. Then we might ask ourselves such questions as whether or not that person we are witnessing is cheerful and enjoyable to be around.

Does he or she appear to be interested and involved in what they are doing? Are they honoring friendships? Do they seem to be acting upon possibilities which are within arms' reach? Are they proactive; or rather do they appear to be sitting at life's sidelines waiting for opportunities to be presented by someone else?

As Leonardo Da Vinci observed:

> *It had long since come to my attention that people of accomplishment rarely sit back and let things happen to them. They went out and happened to things.*

Da Vinci also reportedly said...

> *I have been impressed with the urgency of doing. Knowing is not enough, being willing is not enough; we must do.*

Mindful Changes

SOMETIMES SURVIVAL IS not nearly enough to wish for. Consider the experiences of a small mollusk known as the sea squirt, for example. After swimming around early in life and eventually finding a permanent place such as a barnacle it can attach to, its thinking mission is then fully accomplished. The little squirt then absorbs its own brain which it no longer needs for nutrients to be rebuilt into other organs.

Even if no one, including ourselves, expects us to change the world, we do so every day by just taking up space. So while we're here, we might as well do something useful, interesting and stimulating that causes us to evolve...to make something of rich opportunities to become something more.

We all impact peoples' lives in ways we can't fathom. Some routinely do this through their work. Doctors make people well; teachers motivate and guide young minds; police and firefighters rescue people; employers enable people to support families and create personal and professional networks; attorneys help people get out of trouble; scientists, engineers and architects enhance our lifestyles; and elected officials influence circumstances of peace and war.

Unless we live alone on islands, we also affect lives of

others just by being our natural selves. We may intentionally or inadvertently introduce people to each other who fall in love and have families. We possibly influence people to relocate or change jobs as a result of our advice or assistance, causing their lives to take a whole new direction. And most assuredly, we touch and affect loved ones and friends in countless ways, large and small, on virtually a daily basis.

A lot of those interactive events—probably most—are similar to "Brownian Motion," where, like molecules, we randomly bounce off others, transfer energy and change our own trajectories and theirs at least somewhat with nearly every contact. If these experiences are sometimes a bit bruising, they do help to keep things lively.

Although the global world may scarcely notice, we can also change our personal worlds by releasing limitations we perceive in ourselves. Buddha erased all boundaries for these potentials teaching that "The mind is everything. What you think, you become."

As Jefferson once asked (and answered), "Do you know who you are? Don't ask. Act! Actions will delineate and define you."

William Shakespeare challenged us contemplate potentials far beyond our current selves..."We know what we are, but not what we may be."

Astrophysicist and science communicator Neil deGrasse Tyson observes: "The most successful people in life recognize that in life they create their own love, they manufacture their own meaning, they generate their own motivation."

Being bored might seem like a great gift to less fortunate people whose lives are full of turmoil and strife for reasons they can't control. They represent the majority of the world's population. Unlike them, most of us have other options, and boredom is a luxury we can't afford. Life is far too short and valuable to waste.

Each of us has our own ideas about the sort of lives that we wish to experience. For some of us, these desires and expectations may evolve as we go through different stages. We might occasionally envy those whose lives which have qualities we feel are missing in our own, yet realize in our more realistic moments that we will be more comfortable keeping things somewhat the way they are.

For instance, we might desire more adventure, but be unwilling to give up the security we presently enjoy to get it. The reverse can be equally true. Or maybe we make small compromises to accommodate our desires without abandoning what we care most about.

If you're really unhappy with your current life, you may want to do something more ambitious to change it. At least consider what a more ideal life would be like if you were to add a future chapter or more to a personal fictionalized autobiography.

Then, when you look at that character in the circumstances that you have portrayed, you can consider whether or not that person is someone you would trade your present situation to be—or just a fantasy to be enjoyed on that basis alone?

Your life is your book to write. Fact or fiction, it is all you have.

Dreaming Up Future Realities

Imagining the sort of futures we want should be regarded as more than idle fantasies. Dreaming up worthwhile futures can also energize us to make them become real.

Novelist Anais Nin, author of Delta of Venus, reminds us to remember that "We don't see things as 'they' are, we see them as 'we' are."

If we don't visualize what we really want out of life, we won't have any basis for setting our course in the right direction in order to avoid wasting time and energy on routes destined to nowhere.

Life is a voyage to meet a new person we are always in the process of becoming at each successive port along the way. Each leg of the journey offers challenges and lessons that change us. Meanwhile, near-term concerns often press us to concentrate on the present, and let future selves deal with tomorrow. For now, it may be all we can handle just getting to the next safe harbor.

Maybe we begin to question the value of visualizing that person we wish to eventually become, believing that such illusions will probably be dispersed by unpredictable winds and tides of fate anyway. Those sorts of dreams probably came easier in childhood.

That was before setbacks and other disappointments challenged our confidence, before we forgot how special we are and before magic was disproven. Maybe our expectations began to wither when our parents and teachers warned us about how difficult it is to convert hopes into realities, and stressed the importance of looking at life from a practical point of view.

Dreaming about the future may be a forgotten art we must relearn from our inner child-selves in order to rediscover what we truly value most in ourselves and our lives. Assuming that visions direct realities, and I believe they do, then dreaming is something that we can't afford to abandon or postpone. If we do, our ship of opportunity piloted by others may leave port without us.

Michelangelo purportedly warned:

> The greater danger for the most part of us lies not in setting our aim too high and falling short; but in setting our aim too low, and achieving our mark.

Six centuries later American media mogul and philanthropist Ted Turner offered similar advice: "Set your goals higher than you can achieve."

And as Walt Disney proved: "If you can dream it, you can do it."

Becoming Who We Really Are

As George Bernard Shaw noted, "Life isn't about finding yourself, it's about creating yourself."

"Being" is a constantly evolving state of awareness and development; an open-ended pursuit of understanding; a perpetual process of "becoming." Opportunities for progress are retarded when we cling to fixed outlooks, intractable viewpoints and simplistic preconceptions that are falsely construed to be natural consequences of aging.

In reality, the opposite is true. Those limitations are causes, not results, of getting "old." We don't grow old. We become old when we allow ourselves to stop growing.

Some people seem to confuse being with owning, and becoming with attaining even more. Warranted, it's fine to be ambitious: to seek financial security; to have nice things; to realize achievements and recognition; and to encourage exclusive relationships. Maturity and sensibility teaches us downfalls of carrying this too far—for example, when we become obsessed with accumulating material and social trophies, and then begin to treat people like personal possessions as well.

Others sell large portions of their lives in exchange for doing things that they don't enjoy, and sometimes even detest. We hear them tell us that they are overworked, underpaid and unappreciated; their job is boring, and their colleagues are offensive. Or they feel alone and neglected when others whom they haven't taken initiatives to reach out to haven't called or visited them.

Like all living organisms, when we cease to progress, we get into big trouble. Either we grow or stagnate—those are our only options. But unlike other less cerebral and self-actualizing creatures, we can exercise free will to determine which condition shall prevail. We can elect to be vital parts of the happenings around us—or we can passively submit to the forces of those events, whether they sweep us along or pass us by. In short, we can become involved, or we can become obsolete.

Few of us would consciously choose that second option. It is more fun to be productive and witness wonderful changes that we can bring about through our enterprises. It's gratifying to engage and cooperatively interact with people that we respect and enjoy. It's rewarding to realize that we are in control of our lives, not allowing ourselves to be dominated by circumstances that limit and misuse us.

Growth and vitality, vs. stagnancy and obsolescence, are matters for personal definition. Each of us must determine which progress indicators are appropriate. Some may attach such priorities as wealth and material possessions, popularity and recognition, work achievements and honors, activity levels and adventures, spiritual and intellectual understanding, compassion and service, qualities of relationships and triumphs over tragedies and hardships.

Most of us apply multiple criteria. The central issue has to do with how we visualize ourselves today relative to where we were and where we are heading. Take yourself for example. Are you moving in a direction you like? Are you moving at all?

If you're not pleased with your answer, consider some possible reasons:

1. Have you become either so comfortable with achievements or so beaten by failures that you lack motivation to move forward? Have you lost the willingness to accept reasonable risks for greater gains?

2. Do you cling to familiar ways of thinking and doing things without considering other alternatives?

3. Have you settled for marginally acceptable or even unsatisfactory circumstances and relationships, rather than exert the imagination and initiative to improve them?

4. Have you allowed yourself to be so out of touch with changing social, technical and business conditions that you feel disenfranchised from the world around you?

5. Is it becoming more and more difficult to get excited about events and possibilities due to feelings of déjà vu, cynicism, exhaustion, or other symptoms of psychological burnout?

We risk missed opportunities leading to obsolescence whenever we pigeonhole ourselves into limiting self-concepts. For example, when mothers wrap their entire identities around caregiving to children who will ultimately leave home and create lives for themselves...abandoning their own personal sense of self in the process. Personal growth and self-esteem can be stifled when workers view themselves exclusively in terms of highly specialized roles, and when prestigious office titles are vulnerable to termination or redefinition. Versatility and resilience are valuable safeguards.

We can never be obsolete so long as we recognize our strengths and can find ways to apply them. If we aren't entirely sure what those strengths are, then it's time to really start looking for challenging opportunities to discover them.

The longer these circumstances are permitted to continue, the more difficult it becomes to turn things around. And quoting a popular NASA mission planning adage, "The sooner you fall behind, the more time you'll have to catch up."

In putting off important changes, energy dissipates, confidence erodes, determination ebbs and hopes evaporate.

As another Chinese fortune cookie message I recently drew wisely advised: "If you wait too long for the perfect moment, the perfect moment will pass you by."

Or as American author H. Jackson Brown Jr. observes in Life's Little Instruction Book: "Opportunity dances with those who are already on the dance floor."

Inspirational Brainstorms

Creative thinking is not a talent, it is a skill that can be learnt. It empowers people by adding strength to their natural abilities which improves teamwork, productivity and where appropriate profits.
—Edward de Bono

So where do we find that inspiration?

Sometimes it sneaks up on us unannounced when we're not looking, or we miss it when we search in the wrong places. Sometimes it shows up within ourselves and we reflect it on others.

Inspiration assumes an infinite variety of definitions and forms:

- The *Merriam-Webster Dictionary* describes it as "Something that makes someone want to do something or that gives someone an idea about what to do or create."

- The *Open Dictionary* characterizes it as "A sudden feeling of enthusiasm, or a new idea that helps you to do or create something."

- According to the *Cambridge Dictionary* it is "Someone or something that gives you ideas for doing something."

- The *Free Dictionary* defines it as "A sudden good idea; the excitement of the mind or emotions to a high level of feeling or activity."

However incomplete and inadequate our attempts to define it, inspiration is something needed to fill an otherwise human void. It is something that guides our quest for understanding and practicing higher values. It is something that reveals forgotten beauty of nature and wisdom. It is something that provides examples of excellence we can aspire to and learn from, including generosity, courage, creativity, tenacity and true-life achievements. It is something that arouses our senses...something you feel when it touches you, sometimes prompting you to touch back.

Inspiration is all things we can imagine, and much, much more.

How do we recognize it?

Sometimes it arrives in our consciousness as a thunder clap of WOW!...or as a silent unexpected tear we shed when it softly touches our hearts. Sometimes it appears in the form of provident dreams upon which to construct marvelous thought castles of promise to house realities much larger than ourselves. Sometimes it is a force transmitted through bonds and connections of love and friendship that empower us...and often humble us as well.

Sometimes we are its agents. Without meaning to we inspire others through shared experiences and lessons. Sometimes inspiration transforms...other times it instructs. Sometimes it enriches a moment...at others, it influences a lifetime.

Oftentimes we let it inspiration find and recognize us.

Our charismatic High School band director, Irv Hansen, once told us: "Don't be afraid to blow a sour note...be prepared to make it a loud one everyone can hear. Otherwise, we will never make music." Those who know me will recognize that I continue to heed this wisdom.

Yet many years later, when I reminded him of this important advice, he said he didn't remember. Maybe he just didn't want to accept blame on my behalf.

It's great to receive gifts of inspirational wisdom and thoughtfulness from others with much experience and insight to share. I will pass along a just a few that you may appreciate as I do:

Keep love in your heart. A life without it is like a sunless garden when the flowers are dead.
—Oscar Wilde

The best and most beautiful things in the world cannot be seen or even touched—they must be felt with the heart.
—Helen Keller

Keep your face always toward the sunshine—and shadows will fall behind you.
—Walt Whitman

Clouds come floating into my life, no longer to carry rain or usher storm, but to add color to my sunset sky.
—Rabindranath Tagore

It's not what you look at that matters, it's what you see.
—Henry David Thoreau

Nothing is impossible, the word itself says 'I'm possible'!
—Audrey Hepburn

Perfection is not attainable, but if we chase perfection we can catch excellence.
—Vince Lombardi

There is only one corner of the universe you can be certain of improving, and that's your own self.
—Aldous Huxley

Wherever you are—be all there.
—Jim Elliot

Be happy for this moment. This moment is your life.
—Omar Khayyam

And finally...at least for this moment...

Today I choose life. Every morning when I wake up I can choose joy, happiness, negativity, pain...to feel the freedom that comes from being able to continue to make mistakes and choices—today I choose to feel life, not to deny my humanity but embrace it.
—Kevyn Aucoin

A Matter of Attitudes

Our attitudes have enormous influences upon what we expect out of life, the way we view ourselves and the importance we represent to those around us. Some people thrive on being needed, and routinely hold themselves accountable for more than their share of obligations. Others shun unnecessary entanglements, viewing life as a perpetual series of self-centered cost-benefit analyses.

We've all met people who often complain that their current situation or environment doesn't measure up to others that they knew before. For instance, they form negative judgments about a community that they have only recently relocated to, before they have made any effort to investigate its strong points of interest and opportunities. They do the same thing when it comes to evaluating new people that they meet, working conditions they enter into and organizations they participate in.

Sometimes this negative tendency reflects a fundamental unwillingness and inability to adapt, a typical problem for many as they grow older. Others may just tend to be critical and unhappy by nature. Whatever the reasons, they close out wonderful realities and possibilities that are all around them.

Bad things happen to all of us. When there may sometimes be an inclination to ask: "Why is this happening to me?" an objective answer may be: "Because you were there at the time, dummy!"

Viewing problems and injustices as affronts to our individuality drains precious psychological reserves and promotes victim complexes that are invariably counterproductive. Others are usually quick to recognize attitudes of blame and defeat we project and think less of us for it. While foolish errors and even incompetence may be forgiven, negativity and self-pity seldom are.

Every problem contains the seeds of opportunities that make at least one thing better for ourselves and others. That can involve shared experiences, contributions to wisdom or greater understandings of our own potentials.

There are always adversities and adversaries. Our challenges are to find the rewards embedded in them.

Positive changes in our lives are often most fully enjoyed when we are free of preconceptions that limit clear vision; when we are ready for new challenges; when we are confident and optimistic about our abilities to make contributions; and when we are prepared to release restrictive tethers to the past. This applies to routine everyday matters as well as to momentous developments that affect our lives in major ways.

Changing ourselves is often the most difficult challenge. It can require us to drop old and comfortable habits, embrace risks with uncertain rewards and abandon prejudices that filter the way we see things as well as the way others view us.

Yet there is much to gain in the process. Changes offer us chances for fresh new starts and opportunities to reach higher experiences and goals.

As John F. Kennedy noted: "Change is the law of life. And those who look only to the past or present are certain to miss the future."

Positive attitudes help to keep us looking forward, and to get our lives pointed in the right directions.

And apparently, life really does imitate art after all. It can be difficult to resist temptations to be influenced by hopeless pursuits of illusory perfection quests portrayed by glamorous magazine and TV idols and ads hawking weight reduction pills, diet plans and exercise equipment targeting our image insecurities. They urge us that we can pretty much kiss any real chances of social romance goodbye unless we buy their products, enroll in their fitness programs and pluck and tuck our bodies into molds that they prescribe.

We get swept up in fear that we aren't pretty enough, tall enough, thin enough. We aren't rich enough to buy those expensive vehicles, go on the luxury cruises or vacation in the most lavish resorts. And we obviously aren't smart enough to recognize that someone who isn't classically beautiful or doesn't have a corner office in the executive suite isn't likely to be missing all that much.

Canadian Jungian analyst and author of *Addiction to Perfection* Marion Woodman equates dangers of addiction to a need for perfection to dependencies upon drugs and other destructive obsessions. She warns:

> *Perfection is defeat...Perfection belongs to the gods:*
> *completeness or wholeness is the most a human being*
> *can hope for...it is in seeking perfection by isolating*
> *and exaggerating parts of ourselves that we become*

neurotic. The chief sign of the pursuit of perfection is obsession.

Woodman wisely observes:

> *...To move toward perfection is to move out of life, or what is worse, never to enter it. A problem arises when our external focus inhibits our ability to focus within, to develop our spiritual, mental and psychological selves.*[369]

So, like dealing with those old skinny clothes in your closet, it might be a good idea to consider discarding other false ideals of perfection that no longer fit as well.

When we grant license to occasionally be generous to ourselves, it becomes easier to acknowledge, accept and respond to that need in others who are close to us. Hopefully, they will answer in kind. These can be win-win situations, provided that the parameters of these reciprocal agreements are equitable and well understood by all parties.

Ideal timing is another big self-indulgence advantage. You can find creative ways to reward yourself whenever you need to—for instance, when your morale can stand a boost without having to wait for a special occasion, or depending upon someone else to come up with a cheering idea.

If all this sounds a little selfish, it is. That is what's so great about it!

We shouldn't need to come up with reasons to be nice to ourselves if it makes us feel better—even though others who are disposed with a less charitable nature may take issue with them.

Here are ten possible excuses to consider when you really feel a need to:

1. If I'm not happy, I'll probably make everyone else

miserable too.

2. I was looking around for someone equally deserving, but was alone at the time.

3. I wanted to get something that was exactly right, so that I wouldn't have to return it.

4. It's a personal incentive to work harder and be more successful.

5. It's a merit award for something good that I did that no one else noticed.

6. I offered wonderful opportunity to the best qualified person that I could find.

7. I was bored, and couldn't think of anything better to do.

8. I'm making up for the fact that someone forgot my birthday.

9. I wanted to try it out before I gave it to someone else.

10. I suffered from momentary insanity.

Or maybe you can simply admit that sometimes you feel like being selfish, and just let it go at that.

Choosing to Choose

LIFE IS QUITE often a confusing series of experiences. There are so many choices available to us that we can never be certain which option would turn out best.

David Eagleman and Anthony Brandt observe:

> *Although separated by hundreds of millions of years, the brains of primitive creatures and corporate CEOs have the same questions to ask: how do I best balance exploiting my knowledge against exploring new territories? No creature, or business, gets to rest on the laurels of past success: the world changes unpredictably. The survivors are those who stay dexterous, responding to new needs and opportunities.*[370]

We inevitably face situations which require us to make very difficult decisions that are important to ourselves and others. These circumstances often catch us completely off guard and unprepared. We may have little time or information to assess options and implications, and lack appropriate experience to direct us. Some of the choices may involve high-stakes gambles that we can't avoid, where lives, relationships or financial survival might hang in the balance.

The really tough decisions that we make reveal our true character. They force us to confront our worst fears, come to terms with fundamental values and take charge in the face of great uncertainties. Regardless of the outcomes, our responses to these challenges can teach us many important things about ourselves that we might otherwise never know, enabling us to develop, discover, test, understand and appreciate personal strengths that can be applied in the future.

Fortunately, most of the time, our decisions don't immediately seem to matter much. Just about the worst thing that can happen is that we wind up sitting through a boring or depressing movie, have a bad meal at a restaurant where the service is even worse, purchase something that breaks down shortly after the warranty expires, or experience other disappointments of that ilk.

Of course, negative consequences of more important decisions can be very serious. We might trust people who take advantage of us, sacrifice an excellent career opportunity for one that doesn't work out or invest a great deal of time or money in a losing "sure thing" venture. In extreme circumstances, such as selecting between critical medical treatment options, the decisions can even be life or death matters.

Try as we may to investigate all background information, or consult with experts and carefully weigh the data, we sometimes find that complexities only add to our confusion. There may not be enough recent and reliable information to support a decision necessary to provide any level of assurance.

Different decisions involve independent judgments on our part. We typically have to consider how much a particular opportunity or result is worth to us, how much of ourselves we are willing to invest in order to achieve success and how much influence we are likely to have in controlling the outcomes. In seeking answers to these questions, we must attempt to understand ourselves better and come to terms with our real interests—sometimes within the context of new situations that we have never before encountered.

Recognizing that each of our experiences are unique, what we can learn from them offer universal lessons that have been expressed by people with diverse perspectives. Here are a few notable quotables worth sharing:

I am sure it is everyone's experience, as it has been mine, that any discovery we make about ourselves or the meaning of life is never, like a scientific discovery, a coming upon something entirely new and unsuspected; it is rather, the coming to consciousness recognition of something, which we really knew all the time but, because we were unwilling to formulate it correctly, we did not hitherto know we knew.
—English poet, W.H. Auden Markings

Not what we experience, but how we perceive what we experience, determines our fate.
—Austrian writer, Marie von Ebner-Eschenbach.

You gain strength, courage, and confidence by every experience in which you really stop to look fear in the face. You are able to say to yourself, 'I lived through this horror. I can take the next thing that comes along.'
—America's first lady, Eleanor Roosevelt.

Character cannot be developed through ease and quiet. Only through experience of trial and suffering can the soul be strengthened, ambition inspired, and success achieved.
—Humanitarian Helen Keller

Given the choice between the experience of pain and nothing, I would choose pain.
—American writer, William Faulkner

Experience is never limited, and it is never complete; it is an immense sensibility, a kind of huge spider-web of the finest silken threads suspended in the chamber of consciousness, and catching every airborne particle in its tissue.
—American author, Henry James

You can't create experience. You must undergo it.
—French novelist, Albert Camus

And finally:

Some days are just bad days, that's all. You had to experience sadness to know happiness, and I remind myself that not every day is going to be a good day, that's just the way it is!
—Fashion designer, Dita Von Teese

Exercising Wisdom and Confidence

Walls full of important looking certificates and awards in my office should leave no doubt that I am learned and smart. That's why I hung them there. Hopefully these will qualify me to offer twelve important tips on my successes:

1. You are under no obligation to make the effort required to fully understand or excel at anything that you aren't responsible for or have no particular interest in.

2. If you don't understand what someone is talking about, there is a good possibility that they don't either, or they aren't explaining it very well.

3. If someone doesn't understand what you are talking about, the preceding lesson applies here also.

4. When you present yourself as an expert on anything, you are either being a fool, or are setting yourself up for a wonderful challenge from someone else who believes that they are.

5. The more that you focus on trying to know everything about a particular subject, the less you are likely to know or care how that information relates to anything else. That's a big problem with "higher education."

6. Being intelligent is an opportunity, not a gift. Like love, it only becomes meaningful when passionately acted upon.

7. Knowledge is benign without insight. Insight becomes impotent without use.

8. Some of the smartest people frequently don't seem to know that they are, or at least pretend not to. When you open your mind, you can find them in the most unexpected places.

9. Acting naïve is a useful excuse for asking dumb, probing and often insightful questions without any risk of embarrassment.

10. To learn rapidly, emulate the alertness, curiosity and excitement of a child.

11. Creativity and its resulting innovations are the products of child-like minds.

12. Cultivating the garden of wisdom requires constant weeding as well as generous amounts of natural

fertilizer.

Now that you know the fundamental precepts of my success, there is really no reason to get on the waiting list for the inspirational *Twelve Easy Steps to Being as Smart and Confident as I Am* instructional book and digital library series that I may put together someday soon.

Our Powers of Intuition

As I previously noted in Part Three, our memories record vast repertories of knowledge and skills acquired throughout our lifetime of practice which we apply through intuition to guide us through analogous circumstances and challenges. Accordingly, many successful people I have known have learned to trust internal voices speaking to them from positive and negative experiences, from successes and failures and from actions taken and avoided. In doing so, they have gained the courage and insights necessary to seize opportunities when others falter, and avoid temptations that have led others along treacherous paths of action.

Steve Jobs observed:

> You can't connect the dots looking forward; you can only connect them looking backwards. So you have to trust that the dots will somehow connect in your future. You have to trust in something—your gut, destiny, life, karma, whatever. This approach has never let me down, and it has made all the difference in my life.

Recognizing that intuition born of experience is vital, these winners apply very rational processes gained through experience as well. They get all the good advice they can, sensing whether or not particular possibilities are desirable and realistic early in the process. They look ahead to consider various implications of key choices.

I regard intuition to be our greatest intellectual resource...one that aggregates, integrates, correlates and guides almost everything that we think and do, whether consciously or not.

Intuition requires a foundation and scaffold constructed of lots and lots of experience and information to build upon. That construction process begins right after we leave the womb... and probably even much earlier than that.

So exactly what is intuition? That depends a lot upon who you ask.

The *Merriam-Webster Dictionary* defines it as "...a natural ability or power that makes it possible to know something without any proof or evidence."

The *Cambridge English Dictionary* describes it as "... an ability to understand or know something immediately based upon your feelings rather than facts."

Some characterize intuition as a "gut feeling"...an unconscious reasoning that propels us to decide or do something without necessarily telling us how. Some lightly characterize it as a merely a "hunch."

Those gut feelings are sometimes capable of making us hungry, or alternatively "sick to our stomachs."

International business consultant Francis Cholle, author of *The Intuitive Compass,* urges us not to disregard those hunches either. He observes:

> *We don't have to reject scientific logic in order to benefit from instinct...We can honor and call upon all these tools, and we can seek balance. And by seeking this balance we will finally bring all the resources of our brain into action.*

Cholle describes a dialog between those two different parts going something like...Conscious brain: "What should I wear today?" Unconscious brain: "Red". Conscious: "Red what?" Unconscious: "I don't know, just something red." [371]

As Sophy Burnham, bestselling author of *The Art of Intuition* described it:

> *It's different than thinking, it's different from logic or analysis...It's knowing without knowing.* [372]

Ivy Estabrooke, a program manager at the Office of Naval Research, told the *New York Times* in 2012 that intuition is a power the U.S. military is researching to determine the role it plays in helping troops make quick life-saving judgments during combat. He reported:

> *There is a growing body of anecdotal evidence, combined with solid research efforts, that suggests intuition is a critical aspect of how we humans interact with our environment and how, ultimately we make many of our decisions.* [373]

A 2013 study published in the journal *Perspectives on Psychological Science* indicates that intuition can be practiced by working on your "mindfulness" which is described as "paying attention to one's current experience in a non-judgmental way." [374]

Ultimately, intuition is challenging to describe and impossible to confine in a bounded box. It somehow unexplainably bridges between the conscious and nonconscious parts of our mind, and between instinct and reason.

Our intuition enables us to fill in blanks of conscious understanding; to perceive patterns and relationships between things that others may not recognize; to connect dots; to notice trends and assumptions that do and don't fit our world experience perspectives; to provide early warnings regarding which people and ideas to trust; to alert us to promising opportunities and warn us of hidden dangers; and to guide personal priorities that keep us focused on things that matter most.

Intuition is something very personal...something we have often earned the hard way through painful errors...something that deserves our respect. It is our inner voice speaking to us: loudly sometimes, and sometimes in a barely perceptible whisper. It is something that can appear as an inner sense of dark fear and foreboding, or as a bright flash of sudden insight. It can come over you unexpectedly as a cold chill, or a warm breath of promise.

Our intuition can be defiantly obstinate or fleetingly fragile when challenged by others who believe that they know better while offering little evidence of this. Our clarity on such matters can be clouded by strong agendas and emotions.

Intuition is the inspirational wellspring of creativity, and the ultimate arbitrator of differences between business winners and losers. Steve Jobs called it "more powerful than intellect."

Some will refer to intuition as common sense, but it isn't always all that common. Yours is unique to you...a major part of what makes you special.

Your intuition personifies you. Listen to yourself intently and intuitively.

Risking Successes

Big risk decisions often involve tradeoffs between desires for security and adventure. Since we can't have copious amounts of both, we typically try to hedge our overall bets so that we can expect to wind up with an acceptable balance. How much of either that we seek is influenced by a variety of personal factors, including: our histories of hardships and successes; our sense of responsibility for others who depend upon us; our general temperament, self-confidence and optimism; and our dreams and ambitions.

When we have too little security to meet basic needs, it is natural to be risk-averse. When we are comfortable and confident that those requirements are assured, then we can well afford to pursue more adventurous options.

Being too risk-averse, however, may jeopardize personal growth. As Neale Donald Walsch, American author of the series *Conversations with God* wrote: "Life begins at the end of your comfort zone."

In reality, there is no such thing as total security. Regardless how affluent and satisfied we are, mortality presents inescapable perils for everyone. And if we hope to achieve more security in life, we must almost always accept some risks and costs associated with the new initiatives required to gain it.

When we avoid worthwhile risks, we deny ourselves challenges that cause us to grow and to realize the excitement of experiencing fuller lives. Henry David Thoreau reminds us: "The price of anything is the amount of life you exchange for it."

Only you can determine which risks and costs are appropriate for you. When opportunities come along, no one else can evaluate whether the prospective benefits warrant necessary expenses and uncertainties of the gamble.

Before you decide, make it a habit to ask yourself what you have to lose both ways, and to remember that not taking a chance sometimes presents the greatest risk of all by. As hockey's "The Great One" Wayne Gretzky observed, "You miss 100 percent of the shots you don't take."

Personal Insights and Outlooks

The conditions and opportunities we recognize in life depend much more upon vision than location. Wherever we are, what we see is influenced by the viewing angles we choose and the ways we focus our minds. How we interpret what we see also reflects ways that we view ourselves in those settings.

We can choose to see our personal world any way we wish…both from the inside out and from the outside in. We also have the power to change it through our priorities and vision.

Viewing ourselves and circumstances from the outside, we can begin to observe our relationships, opportunities and choices within more objective frames of reference. Then we might ask ourselves such questions as whether or not that person we are witnessing is cheerful and enjoyable to be around.

Does he or she appear to be interested and involved in what they are doing? Are they honoring friendships? Do you seem to be acting upon possibilities which are within arms' reach? Are they proactive; or rather do they appear to be sitting at life's sidelines waiting for opportunities to be presented by someone else?

As Leonardo Da Vinci observed:

> It had long since come to my attention that people of accomplishment rarely sit back and let things happen to them. They went out and happened to things.

Da Vinci also reportedly said:

> I have been impressed with the urgency of doing. Knowing is not enough, being willing is not enough; we must do.

Viewing our lives from higher vantage points affords broader perspectives. Do you like the scenery where you are? Are you out in an open field, or enclosed in a canyon? Are you alone, or are you involved in a center of activity? Are there places in sight where you would rather be? Can you see any paths that lead there? What obstacles are in your way? Are you pointed in the right direction?

As you ponder your answers, perhaps consider the following points of view:

Seeing clearly often begins with introspection:

- It's unrealistic to expect anyone to understand what we don't reveal of ourselves.

- When we accept ourselves, compassion for others comes much easier.

- Understanding and appreciating someone else requires that we recognize ways that they are similar to us — yet also different and special.

Our realities are products of our perceptions:

- Each of us is continuously evolving into the person projected by our own perceived limitations, strengths and expectations.

- Shared dreams and goals offer opportunities to become more together than we can ever imagine alone.

- Pursuing only what we think we want often reveals our limits in knowing who we are and appreciating what is really possible.

With vision, we can always find options:

- To deny choices is to accept impotence.

- Future choices expand or contract with each decision we take.

- Vacancies for new opportunities are filled by compromises that we settle for.

Looking back at regrets obscures views of the road ahead:

- Dwelling on past errors consumes the confidence, energy and creativity needed to move forward.

- We can seldom be certain that previous decisions were wrong because the results of rejected alternatives may have been much worse.

- To embrace the future, we must release the past.

It's important to keep everything in perspective:

- Experience is no substitute for curiosity and imagination.

- Give yourself credit for trying.

- When your life is consumed by work, work to find satisfaction in everything you do.

Work to maintain a broad field of vision:

- Set your sights to interconnect foresight, insight and hindsight.

- Let your vision be illuminated and guided by values and virtues that you know to be true.

- Have your prescription lenses adjusted regularly. Focus upon what is most important around you now, and how to be a more active and effective part of it all.

Pay attention to traffic and road conditions:

- As time hurdles you forward, keep your eyes open and your hands on the steering wheel.

- Don't allow petty distractions of anger, avarice and the thoughtless actions of others to steer you into oncoming traffic.

- Don't be in a big rush to get to where you imagine to be heading. The best destination may be where you are now.

Believe in yourself:

- Having all you want and doing what you choose means very little if you can't accept who you are.

- Challenges are opportunities to grow. Your responses become you.

- The best thing you have going for you is you. If you aren't perfect, think about how boring life would be if you were.

Enjoying the Times of Our Lives

Nearly all of us realize that our time in this life is short. This awareness increases as it appears that our clocks are constantly speeding up.

Young people who seem to live in slower time are naturally less concerned. They take immortality for granted, and are too busy living and having fun to think beyond summer vacations, birthdays, Christmas or Hanukkah.

It is ironic that time seems to speed up the most when we are busiest and really enjoying ourselves, and to slow at a rate correlated with our levels of frustration and impatience for good things to happen. In dental offices, for example, time seems to stop altogether.

So, if "time flies," the other old adage *where has the time gone?* logically follows. How did we become this age already? How could the kids have grown up so fast? How can I possibly get everything done in time for "<u>fill in the blank</u>"?

One theory is that time seems to speed up as we age because adulthood is accompanied by fewer memorable events. That's because unlike children, we have less excitement about counting down until times when adults plan some wonderful events or gifts for them.

As we become older, familiar events appear to slip by unnoticed. Many emerge into life patterns that focus upon routine work, meeting deadlines, and raising necessary incomes to pay for those urchins and their presents.

In 1890 William James wrote in *Principles of Psychology* that time seems to speed up as we age because adulthood is accompanied by fewer memorable early experiences measured in terms of "firsts:" first day of school, first family vacation, first prom, first kiss, first car, first graduation, etc.

James morosely concluded that this circumstance causes "the days and weeks [to] smooth themselves out...and the years grow hollow and collapse."

According to a "ratio theory" we constantly compare time intervals with the amount of time we have lived. For a five-year-old, one year is 20 percent of their entire life, whereas at age 50, it represents only two percent.

Still another hypothesis suggests that our biological clock slows as we age like some sort of internal pacemaker. Relative to unstoppable clocks and calendars, external time is perceived to pass more quickly...like seeing something shrink in the rear-view mirror. That would be like witnessing our lives literally passing before our eyes.

Some studies indicate that time perceptions don't change with age nearly so much as we imagine.

A 2005 survey, conducted by Marc Wittman and Sandra Lehnhoff at Ludwig-Maximillian University in Munich, asked nearly 500 participants aged between 14and 94 how they gauged time passage—ranging from "very slowly" to "very fast." [375]

Another part of the study consisted of statements and metaphors where subjects were asked to quickly rate sentences ranging from 0 ("strong rejection") to 4 ("strong approval"). Here, the researchers found a weak correlation between age and perceptions of time speed…all, regardless of age, thought time was passing by quickly.

On the other hand, a question "How fast did the past 10 years pass for you?" did yield a tendency for time perception to speed up with age. This pattern peaked at age 50, and remained steady until the mid-90s. Shorter time perception intervals than a decade didn't appear to be age-related.

A follow-up to that study conducted in 2010 by William Friedman at Oberlin College and Steve Janssen at Duke University asked 49 undergraduate students and 50 older adults aged between 60 and 80 years old how well they remembered twelve newsworthy events that occurred during the past decade and to identify when they happened. [376]

As with the Wittman-Lehnhoff study, older groups tended to perceive that the past decade passed more rapidly while viewing shorter periods (hours, weeks, months) similarly. Yet while both age groups also had comparable memories of the events, younger adults did tend to underestimate when they occurred.

An extension of the Friedman-Jansssen study published in 2013 which included researcher Makiko Naka from Hokaido University in Japan found that experiencing significant time pressure made perceived short-term periods speed up. Those who felt time pressure over the previous decade perceived that period "passing in a flash" as well. This time pressure influence was determined to be cross-cultural, with similar study results among German, Austrian, Dutch, Japanese, and New Zealander participants.

If it's any consolation, time probably isn't speeding up after all. In any case, remember that we only live in one moment at a time. Through mindfulness to pay closer momentary attention there is still time to fill your schedule with life.

So meanwhile, rediscover childhood curiosity and wonderment. Explore and discover the world around you. Open your eyes and mind to new possibilities. Care and dare again...just because you still can.

Never forget that getting older is a privilege denied to many.

Savor the rich experiences before time passes you by.

Some Final Afterthoughts

FIRST AND FOREMOST, the time and thought I have
devoted to writing this book is a selfish gift to myself. Through
the process I have granted myself license and priority to explore
enormously broad and diverse aspects of intellect, creativity,
and purposeful value-seeking that I can contextualize and apply
as lessons for my own life.

Writing, something I do a lot, provides greatly valued
rewards. It incentivizes me through learning goals and deadlines
I put on myself to delve into subjects I wish to know more
about. It challenges me to sort out and connect what I discover
to realities and potentials within and far beyond my personal
world. It disciplines me to communicate important observations
and conclusions to others in order to objectify and express them
to myself.

The exploratory journey I have experienced throughout
this book project has been a wonderfully selfish mind-expanding
adventure. It has led me to discover and appreciate marvelously
wise, thoughtful and often humorous observations about basic
life lessons, values, travails, strategies and blessings which are
common to all times, cultures and individual human conditions.
It has prompted me to rediscover inspirational qualities in others

so that I can more deftly recognize and nurture them in myself. It has challenged me to determine and prioritize lessons that I can confidently present to you, so that I can share them with myself with the same confident assurances.

This journey began with a fundamental premise...namely, that through releasing self-imposed limitations about who we are frees us to embrace, explore and experience more fully enriched lives. In this regard, "logical" and "creative" thinking shouldn't be viewed as mutually exclusive. Our "whole brains" routinely do both.

The broader intent of the book is to stimulate each reader to consider if, and to what degree, they might self-identify as being predominately either right or left brain dominant. If they do, that's fine. Those who are entirely comfortable being exclusively one way or the other probably wouldn't have selected this book.

The essential "selves" that form our sense of identity, our aspirations, our inspirations and our progress towards realizing the sort of lives we imagine we most desire are a perpetual work in progress. We become more or less the person we truly wish to be through practice and habit.

Whether that person we are constantly in the process of becoming is the same individual we most admire and wish to emulate depends a lot upon whether we believe it is worth all the effort necessary to take on that burden of responsibility. Lessons from others we respect teach us the import role of persistence in prevailing over daunting obstacles and rebounding from setbacks.

The persistent will to succeed—to grow—to contribute—to innovate—reflects a large capacity to care deeply enough about somethings and someones to remain passionately energized and unflappably determined. The greatest rewards of caring come when our focus goes beyond self-gratification.

I will sadly conclude this gratifying contemplation

adventure with five general take-away lessons drawn from my own experiences:

Lesson One is that if you can't sit still, then really get moving! You can't rely entirely upon the swift current of events to carry you safely through all of the obstacles. Instead, you sometimes have to paddle like hell to take command of your options so that they aren't left to chance, or fall under the control of others.

People who constantly operate in a reactive mode are typically overwhelmed, confused and ineffective. Even though you may not have all of the desired knowledge and confidence, it is important to set some form of purposeful, yet flexible plan into action. Put yourself in charge of your own choices. They are too vital to delegate.

Lesson Two is to make it a practice to look at the *BIG PICTURE* so that you don't get lost in the details. In your personal life, try to be clear about what it is that you care most about. In a new job or position assignment, work to understand the broad priorities and scope of the business or service environment of the organization, and the ways that your designated role fits into and contributes to them.

Constantly strive to visualize your participation within the context of larger purposes and processes which will be impacted by your performance. Focus on things that are most important, and make certain that they are accomplished well and on time. Get and stay organized.

Lesson Three is to define your opportunities, responsibilities and prerogatives as ambitiously as possible. Push the boundaries of your personal expectations and job descriptions to the limit. Be more than anyone expects you to be.

Don't worry about what others might consider to be either

beneath or above your appointed station. Find ways to help friends and associates look good, and be an advocate for them. Think of any title or status that you have as an opportunity to take action rather than as a license to take credit. See yourself as a leader, and act like one.

Lesson Four is to value your own resources and abilities. If you don't know how to solve a problem someone else's way, then devise your own approach. Don't allow yourself to be intimidated by things that you don't immediately comprehend merely based on a lack of background information and experience. Just absorb what you can, and make it a point to later investigate points that you missed.

Learn to be patient with yourself. Don't be afraid to ask questions, but do this thoughtfully, especially when formal occasions warrant some discretion.

Heed Henry Ford's advice: "Whether you believe you can do a thing or not, you are right."

Lesson Five is to learn from others but be yourself. Everyone has their own unique strengths and styles. When you attempt to emulate others or compete with them on their terms, you are likely to fail. Doing that often tends to cloud your awareness of your own unique qualities, impairs natural creativity and keeps you off balance. Besides, being who you are can be a lot of fun once you get the hang of it.

You can't always buck the current and reverse direction, or even steer to a safe refuge on shore. So, you better learn to swim, get ready for that raging white water, do your best to stay clear of the boulders and submerged logs and be prepared to get your feet wet.

Dive in and enjoy the thrill.

About the Author

LARRY BELL IS an endowed professor of space architecture at the University of Houston where he founded the Sasakawa International Center for Space Architecture (SICSA) and its space architecture and aerospace engineering/space architecture graduate programs.

Prior to moving to Houston, Larry headed the industrial design graduate program at the University of Illinois, and he served as lead planner for a national crime prevention through environmental design demonstration program sponsored by the U.S. Justice Department in Washington, DC.

Larry is a former U.S. Air Force air traffic controller, a national award-winning inventor, and also a serious wood and stone sculptor who has exhibited his work in major one-person and group museum and gallery shows. In addition, he has published more than 500 articles on a wide variety of topics in Forbes, Newsmax and other national publications along with six books including one co-authored with Apollo 11 and Gemini 12 astronaut Buzz Aldrin.

Professor Bell's numerous professional honors include certificates of appreciation from NASA Headquarters, the

Larry Bell

Kyushu Sangyo University (Japan) *Space Pioneer Award*, and two of the highest awards granted by Russia's most prestigious aerospace society for his international space development contributions. His name was placed in large letters on the outside of the Russian Proton rocket that launched the first crew to the International Space Station.

[1] "Split Brains," Berit Brogaard, Psychology Today.com, November 6, 2012.

[2] "Left Brain, Right Brain? Wrong: This popular theory lacks basis in solid science. The story of an urban myth," Stephen M. Kosslyn and G. Wayne Miller, Psychology Today, January 27, 2014.

[3] "Consciousness, Personal Identity and the Divided Brain," Roger Sperry, Neuropsychologia, 1984.

[4] "Split Brains," Berit Brogaard, Psychology Today.com, November 6, 2012.

[5] "Despite what you've been told, you aren't 'left-brained' or 'right-brained,'" Amy Novotney, The Guardian, November 2013.

[6] "Sounds of Music in the Cerebellum," Dan Ferber, Science Magazine, November 1998.

[7] "BRAIN: Inside the organ and how it makes us who we are and how it Works," The Curious Mind Bookazine series, Future Publishing Ltd., 2017.

[8] "The Organization of Behavior: A Neuropsychological Theory," Publication Name, Donald O. Hebb, 1949.

[9] "BRAIN: Inside the organ and how it makes us who we are and how it Works," The Curious Mind Bookazine series, Future Publishing Ltd., 2017.

[10] "Consciousness and the Social Brain," Michael S.A. Graziano, Oxford University Press, 2015.

[11] "Facing Up to the problem of Consciousness," David Chalmers, Journal of Conscious Study, 1995.

[12] "Towards a neurological theory of consciousness," Francis Crick and Christof Koch, Seminars in Neurosciences, Vol 2, 1990.

[13] "The Intelligent Movement Machine," Michael Graziano, Medicine & Health Science Books, 2009.

[14] "The Tell-Tale Brain: A Neuroscientist's Quest for What Makes Us Human," V.S. Ramachandra, WW Norton & Company, 2011.

[15] "What Do We Mean by 'Thinking'?" Charles Fernyhough, Psychology Today, August 2010.

[16] "Thinking in Speech," Lev Vygotsky, Collected Works of L.S. Vygotsky, Vol. 1, 1934.

[17] "I Sing the Body's Pattern Recognition Machine," Diane Ackerman, New York Times, June 15, 2004.

[18] "Perception in Chess," Chase and Simon, Cognitive Psychology, 1973.

[19] "Temple Grandin on a New Approach for Thinking about Thinking," Temple Grandin, Smithsonian Magazine, July 2012.

[20] "Does Visual thinking Work in the mind of a person with Autism? A personal Account," Temple Grandin, Philosophical Transactions of the Royal Society, 2009.

[21] "Holism and Evolution," Jan Smuts, Greenwood Press, 1973.

[22] "General System Theory: Fundamentals, Development, Applications," Ludwig von Betlanffy, New York, George Braziller, 1968.

[23] "Introduction to Cybernetics," Ross Ashby, Routledge Kegan and Paul, 1964.

[24] "Industrial Dynamics-A Major Breakthrough for Decision Makers," Jay Forrester, Harvard Business Review, 1958.

[25] "What is talent — and can science spot what we will be best at?" Scott Barry Kaufman, The Guardian.com, July 6, 2013.

[26] Ibid.

[27] "Talent and its development: An emergenic and epigenetic model," Dean Keith Simonton, *Psychological Review,* July 1999.

[28] "Domain-general creativity: On producing original, useful, and surprising combinations," D. K. Simonton, J. C. Kaufman, J. Baer, and V. P. Glăveanu, *Cambridge handbook of creativity across different domains,* 2017.

[29] "What is talent — and can science spot what we will be best at?" Scott Barry Kaufman, The Guardian.com, July 6, 2013.

[30] "Psychologists Defend the Importance of General Abilities: Current Directions in Psychological Science," David Hambrick and Elizabeth Meinz, Journal of the Association for Psychological Science, October 20, 2011.

[31] Ibid.

[32] "Link Found Between Child Prodigies and Autism," Joanne Ruthsatz, Ohio State University Research and Innovation Communications, November 9, 2012.

[33] "The mind of the Prodigy," Scott Barry Kaufman, Scientific American.com, July 13, 2014.

[34] "Link Found Between Child Prodigies and Autism," Joanne Ruthsatz, Ohio State University Research and Innovation Communications, November 9, 2012.

[35] "Will We Ever Find the Next Einstein?" Jonathan Wai, Psychology Today.com, March 2, 2011.

[36] "Are Prodigies Autistic," Scott Barry Kaufman, Psychology Today.com, July 6, 2012.

[37] "Sources of human psychological differences: the Minnesota study of twins reared apart" Thomas J. Bouchard, Jr.; David T. Lykken; Matthew McGue; Nancy L. Segal; and Auke Telligen, Science, 1990.

[38] "8 Surprising Facts About parenting, Genes and What Makes Us Who We Are," Scott Barry Kaufman, HuffingtonPost.com, November 19, 2011.

[39] Ibid.

[40] "What is talent – and can science spot what we will be best at?" Scott Barry Kaufman, *The Guardian.com*, July 6, 2013.

[41] Ibid.

[42] "After Watching this, your brain will not be the same," Ted Talk, Lara Boyd, December 15, 2015.

[43] "The Cult of Personality Testing," Annie Murphy Paul, Simon and Schuster, 2004.

[44] "Personality Plus: Employers love personality tests. But what do they really reveal?" Malcom Gladwell, The New Yorker, September 20, 2014.

[45] "Why the Myers-Briggs Personality Test is Misleading, Inaccurate, and Unscientific," Drake Baer, Business Insider, June 18, 2014.

[46] Ibid.

[47] Ibid

[48] "Myers-Briggs Type indicator (MBTI): Some psychometric limitations," Gregory J. Boyle, Bond University publication, 1995.

[49] "Measuring the MBTI...And Coming Up Short," David Pittenger, Journal of Career Planning and Placement, 1993.

[50] "In the Mind's Eye: Enhancing Human Performance," D. Druckman, and R. A. Bjork, Rds. National Academy Press, 1991.

[51] "Why the Myers-Briggs Personality Test is Misleading, Inaccurate, and Unscientific," Drake Baer, Business Insider, June 18, 2014.

[52] "It takes more than IQ to describe how our brains work," Roger Highfield, The Telegraph, December 20, 2012.

[53] "Confidence Matters Just as Much as Ability," Scott Barry Kaufman, Psychology Today, December 8, 2011.

[54] "Where are the Gender Differences? Male Priming Boosts Spatial Skills in Women," Tuulia Ortner and Monika Sieverding, Springer.com, August 2008.

[55] "Confidence Mediates the Sex Difference in Mental Rotation Performance," Zachary Estes and Sydney Felker, Archives of Sexual behavior, December 2011.

[56] "Math-Gender Stereotypes in Elementary School Children," Dario Cvencek, Andrew N. Meltzoff and Anthony G. Greenwald, Child Development, 2011.

[57] "Talent is made, not born: Is innate intelligence highly over-rated in our society?" InpaperMagazine, ThriveWork Staff, Dawn News, January 15, 2011.

[58] "The Talent Code: Unlocking the Secret of Skill in Sports, Art, Music Math, and Just About Everything Else," Daniel Coyle, Bantam, 1st Edition, May 13, 2009.

[59] Ibid.

[60] "Talent is Overrated: What Really Separates World-Class Performers from Everybody Else," Geoff Colvin, Penguin, 2008.

[61] "The Hedgehog and the Fox," Isiah Berlin, Wiedenfeld & Nicholson, 1953.

[62] "What Makes a Renaissance Man?" Olivia Goldmill, The Telegraph, December 2014.

[63] "Aristotle on Memory and Recollection," David Bloch, BRILL, Leiden-Boston, 2007

[64] "A History of the Association Psychology," Howard Warren, Charles Scriber's Sons, 1921, The University of Chicago Press Journals, ISBN-13: 978-0521716314 , ISBN-10: 0521716314

[65] "The Book of Memory: A Study of Memory in Medieval Culture," Mary Carruthers, Second Edition: New York university and All Souls College, Oxford, 2007.

[66] "Aristotle's Life" in A Companion to Aristotle - Aristotle's Life," Wiley-Blackwell, Georgios Anagnostopoulos, 2009.

[67] "A Companion to Aristotle - First Athenian Period," Wiley-Blackwell, Georgios Anagnostopoulos, 2013.

[68] "Alexander of Macedon," Peter Green, University of California Press Ltd., 1991.

[69] "Aristotle's Syllogistic," Lynne E. Rose, Springfield: Charles C Thomas Publisher, 1968.

[70] "Aristotle Politics," Translated by Ernest Barker and revised with introduction and notes by R. F. Stalley, Oxford: Oxford University Press, 2009.

[71] "Athenian impiety trials: a reappraisal," Jakub Filonik, Dike, 2013.

[72] "Aristotle's Syllogistic," Lynne E. Rose, Springfield: Charles C Thomas Publisher, 1968.

[73] Aristotle-Philosopher,Biography.com https://biography.com/people/aristotle-9188415, 2018.

[74] "Alexander of Macedon," Peter Green, University of California Press Ltd., 1991.

[75] "The Birth of Modern Science," Paolo Rossi, Blackwell Publishing, 2001.

[76] "Leonardo da Vinci," BBC History, 2018.

[77] "Leonardo da Vinci, Artist, Inventor and Universal Genius of the Renaissance," History.com, 2018.

[78] "The notebooks of Leonardo da Vinci," Jean Paul Richter, Dover, 1970.

[79] "Leonardo da Vinci: Italian Artist, Engineer and Scientist," Encyclopedia Britannica, 2018.

[80] Ibid.

[81] "The Life and Times of Leonardo," Liana Bartolon, Paul Aamlyn, 1967.

[82] "Thomas Jefferson and the New Nation; a Biography," Merrill D. Peterson, University Press, 1970.

[83] "Thomas Jefferson: Reputation and Legacy," Francis Cogliano, Edinburgh University Press, 2008.

[84] "Thomas Jefferson: A Life," Willard Sterne Randall, Harper Collins, 1994.

[85] Ibid

[86] "Adams vs, Jefferson: The Tumultuous Election of 1800," George Tucker, Oxford University Press, 1837.

[87] "Thomas Jefferson," Richard B. Bernstein, Oxford University Press, 2003.

[88] "Thomas Jefferson: Reputation and Legacy," Francis Cogliano, Edinburgh University Press, 2008.

[89] "Martha Wayles Skelton Jefferson," White House Archives, 2018.

[90] "Slavery at Monticello – Property Slavery at Monticello FAQ – Property," Gordon-Reed, Thomas Jefferson Foundation, 2008.

[91] "Thomas Jefferson and Slavery," Thomas Jefferson Foundation, 2018.

[92] "Setting the World Ablaze: Washington, Adams, Jefferson, and the American Revolution," John Ferling, Oxford University Press, 2000.

[93] "Making the American Self: Jonathan Edwards to Abraham Lincoln," Daniel Walker Howe, Oxford University Press, 2009.

[94] "Thomas Jefferson: The Art of Power," Jon Meachum, Random House LLC, 2012.

[95] "Thomas Jefferson: An Intimate History," Fawn Brodie, W. W. Norton & Company, 1974.

[96] "The Hemingses of Monticello: An American Family," Gordon-Reed, W. W. Norton & Company, 2008.

[97] "Thomas Jefferson: The Art of Power," Jon Meachum, Random House LLC, 2012.

[98] "The Hemingses of Monticello: An American Family," Gordon-Reed, W. W. Norton & Company, 2008.

[99] "The Jefferson Image in the American Mind," Merrill D. Peterson, University of Virginia Press, 1960.

[100] "Evading the Ordinance: The Persistence of Bondage in Indiana and Illinois," Paul Finkelman, Journal of the Early Republic, 1989.

[101] "Thomas Jefferson: The Art of Power," Jon Meachum, Random House LLC, 2012.

[102] "Native America, Discovered and Conquered: Thomas Jefferson, Lewis & Clark, and Manifest Destiny," Robert Miller, University of Nebraska Press, 2008.

[103] "President Jefferson and the Indian Nations," Thomas Jefferson

Foundation, 2018.

[104] "Gathering Voices: Thomas Jefferson and Native America," American Philosophical Society, 2018.

[105] "The Encyclopedia of the Wars of the Early American Republic, 1783–1812 A Political, Social, and Military History. Santa Barbara, California," James Scythes and Tucker Spencer, ABC-CLIO, 2014.

[106] "Benjamin Franklin: American Author, Scientist and Statesman," Theodore Hornberger and Gordon S. Wood, Encyclopedia Britannica, 2018.

[107] Ibid

[108] "Benjamin Franklin," Carl Van Doren, *Viking,* 1938.

[109] "Benjamin Franklin: An American Life. New York," Walter Isaacson, Simon & Schuster, 2003.

[110] "Words of the Founders: Selected Quotations of Franklin, Washington, Adams, Jefferson, Madison and Hamilton," Steve Coffman, NC Jefferson, McFarland, 2012.

[111] "Benjamin Franklin: American Author, Scientist and Statesman," Theodore Hornberger and Gordon S. Wood, Encyclopedia Britannica, 2018.

[112] Ibid

[113] "Benjamin Franklin's Printing Network: Disseminating Virtue in Early America," Ralph Frasca, University of Missouri Press, 2006.

[114] "Benjamin Franklin and Lightning Rods," Philip Kriderr, Physics Today, January, 2006.

[115] "A Companion to Benjamin Franklin," David Waldstreicher, Wiley-Blackwell, 2011. ISBN: 978-1-405-19996-4

[116] "The Life of Benjamin Franklin," J. A. Leo Lemay, Volume 2: Printer and Publisher, 2005.

[117] "The library: an illustrated history," Stuart A.P. Murray, New York: Skyhorse Pub, 2009.

[118] "Benjamin Franklin: An American Life. New York," Walter Isaacson, Simon & Schuster, 2003.

[119] "Benjamin Franklin: American Author, Scientist and Statesman," Theodore Hornberger and Gordon S. Wood, Encyclopedia Britannica, 2018.

[120] "Science and Medicine," Colonial America Reference Library,

2016.

[121] "History of Science, Technology, and Philosophy in the Eighteenth Century," A. Wolf, National Archives, Founders Online, "The Kite Experiment," 1939.

[122] "Benjamin Franklin and Lightning Rods," Philip Kriderr, Physics Today, January, 2006.

[123] "Benjamin Franklin: American Author, Scientist and Statesman," Theodore Hornberger and Gordon S. Wood, Encyclopedia Britannica, 2018.

[124] "The First Congress," Fergus M. Bordewich, Simon & Shuster, 2016.

[125] "Runaway America: Benjamin Franklin, Slavery, and the American Revolution," David Waldstreicher, Hill and Wang, 2004.

[126] "Benjamin Franklin: American Author, Scientist and Statesman," Theodore Hornberger and Gordon S. Wood, Encyclopedia Britannica, 2018.

[127] Ibid

[128] Ibid

[129] Ibid

[130] "Autobiography of Benjamin Franklin; Forward," Benjamin Franklin, Frank Woodworth Pine, ed. Henry Holt and Company via Gutenberg Press, 1916.

[131] "Benjamin Franklin: An American Life. New York," Walter Isaacson, Simon & Schuster, 2003.

[132] "Einstein, His Life and Universe: the Basis for Genius," Walter Isaacson, Simon and Schuster Paperbacks, 2017.

[133] Ibid

[134] Ibid

[135] "Einstein as a Student (Unpublished paper)," Dudley Herschbach, Provided to the Author, 2005.

[136] "Einstein, His Life and Universe: the Basis for Genius," Walter Isaacson, Simon and Schuster Paperbacks, 2017.

[137] Ibid

[138] Ibid

[139] Ibid

[140] Ibid

[141] Ibid

[142] Ibid

[143] Ibid

[144] "Naturwissenschaftliche Volksbucher," Aaron Bernstein, Howard and Stachel, 2000.

[145] "Einstein, His Life and Universe: the Basis for Genius," Walter Isaacson, Simon and Schuster Paperbacks, 2017.

[146] Ibid

[147] Ibid

[148] Ibid

[149] Ibid

[150] Ibid

[151] Ibid

[152] Ibid

[153] Ibid

[154] Ibid

[155] Ibid

[156] Ibid

[157] "Why Do They Hate the Jews?" Einstein, Colliers, November 26, 1938.

[158] "Einstein, His Life and Universe: the Basis for Genius," Walter Isaacson, Simon and Schuster Paperbacks, 2017.

[159] Ibid

[160] "A Machine to End War: Nikola Tesla," George Sylvester Viereck, PBS.org, February 1937.

[161] "My Inventions: The Autobiography of Nikola Tesla," http://www.teslaautobiography.com, 2018.

[162] Ibid

[163] "My Inventions: The Autobiography of Nikola Tesla," http://www.teslaautobiography.com, 2018.

[164] Ibid

[165] Ibid

[166] Ibid

[167] Ibid

[168] "About Nikola Tesla," Society of USA and Canada, 2018.

[169] "My Inventions: The Autobiography of Nikola Tesla,"

http://www.teslaautobiography.com, 2018.

[170] "A Machine to End War: Nikola Tesla, "George Sylvester Viereck, PBS.org, February, 1937.

[171] "My Inventions: The Autobiography of Nikola Tesla," http://www.teslaautobiography.com, 2018.

[172] Ibid

[173] Ibid

[174] "The Freethinker," G.W. Foote & Company, 1970. Freethought Archives, http://www.ftarchives.net/index.html

[175] "No Immortality of the Soul," Thomas A. Edison, New York Times, October 2, 1910.

[176] "Edison: A Life of Invention," Israel Paul, John Wiley & Sons, 2000.

[177] "The Education of Thomas Edison," Jim Powell, Foundation for Economic Education, February 1, 1995.

[178] "Edison: A Life of Invention," Israel Paul, John Wiley & Sons, 2000.

[179] "The Education of Thomas Edison," Jim Powell, Foundation for Economic Education, February 1, 1995.

[180] Ibid

[181] "For Sesquicentennial, Cooper Union Puts Artifacts on View", November 30, 2009, (http://cityroom.blogs.nytimes.com/2009/11/30/for - sesquicentennial-cooper-union-puts- artifacts-on-view/?_r=0. The New York Times.)

[182] "Edison," Matthew Johnson, McGraw Hill, 1959.

[183] "Edison: Inventing the Century," Neil Baldwin, University of Chicago Press, 2001.

[184] "The Education of Thomas Edison," Jim Powell, Foundation for Economic Education, February 1, 1995.

[185] Ibid

[186] Ibid

[187] Ibid

[188] "Curie, Maria ze Skodowskich," Tadeusz Estreicher, Polski slawnik biograficzny, 1920.

[189] "Radiant Marie: Mother of Modern Physics," Futurist, September

9, 2012.

[190] "Obsessive Genius: The Inner World of Marie Curie," Barbara Goldsmith, Great Discoveries, 2005.

[191] "Marie Curie: And the Science of Radioactivity," Naomi Pasachoff, Oxford Portraits of Science, 1997.

[192] "Marie Curie," New World Encyclopedia, 2018.

[193] "Marie Curie-Student in Paris (1891-1897) Part 1," American Institute of Physics, 2018.

[194] "Marie Curie," New World Encyclopedia, 2018.

[195] "Madame Curie: A Biography," Eve Curie, Cambridge Press, 2001.

[196] "Marie Curie," New World Encyclopedia, 2018.

[197] "Marie Curie," Robert William Reid, New American Library, 1974.

[198] "Churchill: A Life," Martin Gilbert, An eight-volume biography begun by Randolph Churchill, 1992.

[199] "World War One: History In An Hour: Winston Churchill and the First World War," Rupert Colley, Harper Press, 2018.

[200] "Winston Churchill and his 'black dog' of greatness," Nassir Ghaemi, The Conversation; Academic rigor, journalistic flair, January 23, 2015.

[201] "Churchill: A Biography," Roy Jenkins, Farrar, Straus and Giroux, New York, 2001.

[202] "Who Won the Battle of Britain? London," Hubert Raymond Allen, St Albans : Panther, 1976.

[203] "Winston Churchill Biography Online," www.biographyonline.net, 2018.

[204] Winston Churchill and his 'black dog' of greatness," Nassir Ghaemi, The Conversation; Academic rigor, journalistic flair, January 23, 2015.

[205] "Who Won the Battle of Britain? London," Hubert Raymond Allen, St Albans : Panther, 1976.

[206] "Churchill: A Biography," Roy Jenkins, Farrar, Straus and Giroux, New York, 2001.

[207] "Churchill's Black Dog, Kafka's Mice, and Other Phenomena of the Human Mind," Anthony Storr, Grove, 1990.

[208] Winston Churchill and his 'black dog' of greatness," Nassir

Ghaemi, The Conversation; Academic rigor, journalistic flair, January 23, 2015.
[209] "Stephen Hawking; I'm happy if I have added something to our understanding of the Universe," Radio Times, December 7, 2013.
[210] "Stephen Hawking: His Life and Work," Kitty Ferguson, Transworld, 2011.
[211] "Stephen Hawking: A Biography," Kristine Larsen, Greenwood Biographies, 2005.
[212] "Stephen Hawking: His Life and Work," Kitty Ferguson, Transworld, 2011.
[213] Ibid
[214] "Stephen Hawking: A Life in Science," Michael White and John Gribbin, The National Academies Press, 2002.
[215] Ibid
[216] "Stephen Hawking: His Life and Work," Kitty Ferguson, Transworld, 2011.
[217] "Stephen Hawking: A Life in Science," Michael White and John Gribbin, The National Academies Press, 2002.
[218] "Stephen Hawking: His Life and Work," Kitty Ferguson, Transworld, 2011.
[219] Ibid
[220] "Stephen Hawking: A Life in Science," Michael White and John Gribbin, The National Academies Press, 2002.
[221] "Stephen Hawking: His Life and Work," Kitty Ferguson, Transworld, 2011.
[222] "Stephen Hawking: A Life in Science," Michael White and John Gribbin, The National Academies Press, 2002.
[223] "Stephen Hawking: His Life and Work," Kitty Ferguson, Transworld, 2011.
[224] "Stephen Hawking: A Biography," Kristine Larsen, Greenwood Biographies, 2005.
[225] "Stephen Hawking: A Life in Science," Michael White and John Gribbin, The National Academies Press, 2002.
[226] "Stephen Hawking: His Life and Work," Kitty Ferguson, Transworld, 2011.
[227] Ibid

[228] "Stephen Hawking: A Life in Science," Michael White and John Gribbin, The National Academies Press, 2002.

[229] "Relativity in Curved Spacetime: Life Without Special Relativity," Eric Baird, Chocolate Free Books, 2007.

[230] "Stephen Hawking: His Life and Work," Kitty Ferguson, Transworld, 2011.

[231] "Stephen Hawking's explosive new theory", Roger Highfield, June 26, 2008, The Telegraph

[232] "Multiverses and Blackberries: Notes of a Fringe-Watcher," Martin Gardner, Skeptical Inquirer, September/October 2001.

[233] "THE EVERETT FAQ," Michael Clive Price, Washington University- St Louis, Dept. of Physics, February 1995.

[234] "Stephen Hawking: A Life in Science," Michael White and John Gribbin, The National Academies Press, 2002.

[235] "Stephen Hawking: His Life and Work," Kitty Ferguson, Transworld, 2011.

[236] "Stephen Hawking: A Life in Science," Michael White and John Gribbin, The National Academies Press, 2002.

[237] "Traveling to Infinity; My Life With Stephen," Jane Hawking, Alma, 2007.

[238] "Stephen Hawking's Religion and Political Views," Hollowese; The religions and political views of the influential, 2018.

[239] "I'm an Atheist: Stephen Hawking on God and Space Travel," Alan Boyle, NBC, September 23, 2014.

[240] "The Dancing Wu Li Masters: An Overview of the New Physics," Gary Zukav, HarperCollins, 2001.

[241] "The Evolution of Physics," Albert Einstein and Leopold Infeld, Simon and Shuster, 1961.

[242] "S-Matrix Interpretation of Quantum Theory," Henry Stapp, Lawrence Berkeley Laboratory, June 22, 1970.

[243] "Physics and Philosophy," Werner Heisenberg, Harper Torchbooks, 1958.

[244] Ibid

[245] "Across the Frontiers," Werner Heisenberg, Harper & Row, 1974.

[246] "Philosophiae Naturalis Principia Mathematica," Isaac Newton, Sir Isaac Newton's Mathematical Principles of Natural Philosophy and His

System of the World, 1946.

[247] "Proceedings of the Royal Society of London, Correspondence of R. Bentley," Gary Zukav, HarperCollins, 2001.

[248] "Physics and Philosophy," Werner Heisenberg, Harper Torchbooks, 1958.

[249] "S-Matrix Interpretation of Quantum Theory," Henry Stapp, Lawrence Berkeley Laboratory, June 22, 1970.

[250] "The Dancing Wu Li Masters: An Overview of the New Physics," Gary Zukav, HarperCollins, 2001.

[251] "S-Matrix Interpretation of Quantum Theory," Henry Stapp, Lawrence Berkeley Laboratory, June 22, 1970.

[252] "The Evolution of Physics," Albert Einstein and Leopold Infeld, Simon and Shuster, 1961.

[253] "The Dancing Wu Li Masters: An Overview of the New Physics," Gary Zukav, HarperCollins, 2001.

[254] "S-Matrix Interpretation of Quantum Theory," Henry Stapp, Lawrence Berkeley Laboratory, June 22, 1970.

[255] "The Dancing Wu Li Masters: An Overview of the New Physics," Gary Zukav, HarperCollins, 2001.

[256] "Mind, Matter and Quantum Mechanics: The Copenhagen Interpretation," Henry Pierce Stapp, SpringerLink, 2018.

[257] "The Dancing Wu Li Masters: An Overview of the New Physics," Gary Zukav, HarperCollins, 2001.

[258] "Judgment Under Uncertainty: Heuristics and Biases," Amos Tversky and Daniel Kahneman, Science, 1974.

[259] "Thinking Fast and Slow," Daniel Kahneman, Farrar, Strauss and Giroux, 2011.

[260] Ibid

[261] "Pupillary Stroop Effects," Bruno Laeng et al., Cognitive Processing, 2011.

[262] "Thinking Fast and Slow," Daniel Kahneman, Farrar, Strauss and Giroux, 2011.

[263] Ibid

[264] Ibid

[265] "Polya's Problem Solving Techniques: How to Solve It," George Polya, 2nd ed., Princeton University Press, 1957. ISBN 0-691-08097-

6.

[266] "Thinking Fast and Slow," Daniel Kahneman, Farrar, Strauss and Giroux, 2011.

[267] Ibid

[268] "Rationality and the Reflective Mind," Keith Stanovich, Oxford University Press, 2010.

[269] "Thinking Fast and Slow," Daniel Kahneman, Farrar, Strauss and Giroux, 2011.

[270] Ibid

[271] Ibid

[272] "Easy Does It: The Role of Fluency in Cue Weighting," Anuj K. Shah and Daniel M. Oppenheimer, Judgment and Decision Making, January 2, 2007.

[273] "Thinking Fast and Slow," Daniel Kahneman, Farrar, Strauss and Giroux, 2011.

[274] "On Understanding Nonliteral Speech: Can People Ignore Metaphors?" Sam Glucksberg, Patricia Gildea, and Howard G. Bookin, Journal of Verbal Learning and Visual Behavior, 1982.

[275] "Thinking Fast and Slow," Daniel Kahneman, Farrar, Strauss and Giroux, 2011.

[276] Ibid

[277] Ibid

[278] Ibid

[279] Ibid

[280] Ibid

[281] Ibid

[282] "Demystifying Intuition: What It Is, What It Does, How It Does It," Seymore Epstein, Psychological Inquiry, 2010.

[283] "Thinking Fast and Slow," Daniel Kahneman, Farrar, Strauss and Giroux, 2011.

[284] "Conditions for Intuitive Enterprise: A Failure to Disagree," Daniel Kahneman and Gary Klein, American Psychologist, 2009.

[285] "Thinking Fast and Slow," Daniel Kahneman, Farrar, Strauss and Giroux, 2011.

[286] "Task Switching," Stephen Monsell, Trends in Cognitive Sciences, 2003.

[287] "Thinking Fast and Slow," Daniel Kahneman, Farrar, Strauss and Giroux, 2011.

[288] Ibid

[289] "Decision Making and the Avoidance of Cognitive Demand," Wouter Kool et al., Journal of Experimental Psychology, 2010.

[290] "The Impact of Anticipated Demand on Attention and Behavioral Choice," Brian Bruya, Bradford Books, 2010.

[291] "Thinking Fast and Slow," Daniel Kahneman, Farrar, Strauss and Giroux, 2011.

[292] Ibid

[293] "Ego Depletion and the Strength Model of Self-Control: A Meta-Analysis," Martin S. Hagger et al., Psychological Bulletin, 2010.

[294] "Thinking Fast and Slow," Daniel Kahneman, Farrar, Strauss and Giroux, 2011.

[295] Ibid

[296] Ibid

[297] "The Pursuit of happiness: Bringing the Science of Happiness to Life," Mihaly Csikszentmihalyi, 2018.

[298] "Where machines could replace humans- and where they can't (yet)," Michael Chui, James Manyika, and Mehdi Miremadi, *McKinsey Quarterly*, July 2016.

[299] Ibid

[300] "Rise of the Robots," Stephen Moore, Newsmax, October 2017.

[301] As related in *AI as Servants or Spies?*, John Edwards, *Newsmax*, October 2017.

[302] "AI as Servants or Spies?" John Edwards, Newsmax, October 2017.

[303] "Quantum Computing May Outsmart All Cyber Defenses," Larry Bell, Newsmax, November 12, 2017.

[304] "Algorithms With Minds of Their Own," Curt Levy and Ryan Hagemann, Wall Street Journal, November 13, 2017.

[305] "Post-quantum cryptology – dealing with the fallout of physics success," Daniel J. Bernstein and Tanja Lange, National Science Foundation/European Commission, April 9, 2017.

[306] "We'll Need Bigger Brains Keeping Up With the Machines," Christof Koch, Wall Street Journal Review Section, October 28-29, 2017.

[307] Ibid

[308] "Creativity," http://psychology.wikia.com/wiki/Creativity, 2018.

[309] "The Evolution of Imagination," Stephen T. Asma, University of Chicago Press, 2017.

[310] Ibid

[311] "The Age of Insight: The Quest to Understand the Unconsciousness in Art, Mind, and Brain: from Vienna 1900 to the Present," Eric Kandel, Random House, 2012.

[312] "The Evolution of Imagination," Stephen T. Asma, University of Chicago Press, 2017.

[313] "Descent of Man," Charles Darwin, Penguin Classics, 2004.

[314] "The Evolution of Imagination," Stephen T. Asma, University of Chicago Press, 2017.

[315] Affective Neuroscience: The Foundations of Human and Animal Emotions," Jaak Panksepp, Oxford: Oxford University Press, 2004.

[316] "The Evolution of Imagination," Stephen T. Asma, University of Chicago Press, 2017.

[317] Ibid

[318] "Neocortex Size as a Constant on Group Size in Primates," Robin Dunbar, Journal of Human Revolution, 1992.

[319] "Understanding Primate Brain Evolution," R.I.M Dunbar and Susanne Shultz, Philosophical Transactions of the Royal Society of London B: Biological Sciences, 2007.

[320] "The Evolution of Imagination," Stephen T. Asma, University of Chicago Press, 2017.

[321] "The role of the prefrontal Cortex in Dynamic Filtering," Ralph Adolphs, Psychology, 2000.

[322] "Behavioral and Neural Correlates of Delay of Gratification 40 Years Later," B.J. Casey et al., Proceedings of the National Academy of Sciences, 2011.

[323] "The Evolution of Imagination," Stephen T. Asma, University of Chicago Press, 2017.

[324] Ibid

[325] "The Evolved Apprentice," Kim Sterelny, MIT Press, 2012.

[326] "The Age of the Spiritual Machines," Ray Kurzweil, Viking, 1999.

[327] "The Runaway Species: How Human Creativity Remakes the

World," Anthony Brandt and David Eagleman, Canongate Books Ltd., Great Britain, 2017.

328 Ibid

329 "The Evolution of Distributed Association Networks in the Human Brain," Randy L. Buckner, Trends in Cognitive Sciences, 2013.

330 "The Evolution of Imagination," Stephen T. Asma, University of Chicago Press, 2017.

331 "The Age of Insight: The Quest to Understand the Unconscious in Art, Mind and Brain: From Vienna to the Present," Eric Kandel, Random House, 2012.

332 "The Evolution of Imagination," Stephen T. Asma, University of Chicago Press, 2017.

333 "An Early Bone Tool Industry from the Middle Stone Age at Blombos cave, South Africa; Implications for the Origins of Modern Human Behavior, Symbolism and Language," C.S. Henshilwood, F. d'Errico, C.W. Marean, R.G. Milo, and R. Yates, Journal of Human Evolution, 2001.

334 "The Evolution of Imagination: An Archaeological Perspective," Steven J. Mithen, SubStance 30, 2001.

335 "The Evolution of Imagination," Stephen T. Asma, University of Chicago Press, 2017.

336 Ibid

337 Ibid

338 Ibid

339 "The Runaway Species: How Human Creativity Remakes the World," Anthony Brandt and David Eagleman, Canongate Books Ltd., Great Britain, 2017.

340 Ibid

341 "The Evolution of Imagination," Stephen T. Asma, University of Chicago Press, 2017.

342 "Flow and the Psychology of Discovery and Invention," Mihaly Csikzentmihalyi, Harper Collins, 1996.

343 "The Runaway Species: How Human Creativity Remakes the World," Anthony Brandt and David Eagleman, Canongate Books Ltd., Great Britain, 2017.

344 Ibid

[345] "The Runaway Species: How Human Creativity Remakes the World," Anthony Brandt and David Eagleman, Canongate Books Ltd., Great Britain, 2017.

[346] Ibid

[347] Ibid

[348] "Engineering of Jihad: The Curious Connection between Violent Extremism and Education," Diego Gambetta and Steffen Hertog, Princeton University Press, 2016.

[349] "Free Play: Improvisation in Life and Art," Stephen Nachmanovitch, Jeremy Thacher/Putnam, 1990.

[350] "The Runaway Species: How Human Creativity Remakes the World," Anthony Brandt and David Eagleman, Canongate Books Ltd., Great Britain, 2017.

[351] "The Philosophies of Royce, James and Dewey in their American Setting," George Herbert Mead, International Journal of Ethics, 1930.

[352] "The Runaway Species: How Human Creativity Remakes the World," Anthony Brandt and David Eagleman, Canongate Books Ltd., Great Britain, 2017.

[353] "Edison: A Life of Invention," Paul Israel, John Wiley, 1998.

[354] "The Runaway Species: How Human Creativity Remakes the World," Anthony Brandt and David Eagleman, Canongate Books Ltd., Great Britain, 2017.

[355] Time Magazine, 20 October 20, 1980

[356] "No Innovator's Dilemma Here: In Praise of Failure," James Dyson, Wired, April 8, 2011.

[357] "The Runaway Species: How Human Creativity Remakes the World," Anthony Brandt and David Eagleman, Canongate Books Ltd., Great Britain, 2017.

[358] "55 Quotes To Inspire Creativity, Innovation and Action", Psychology Today, 2010.

[359] "Linus Pauling Quotes." BrainyQuote.com. Xplore Inc, April 2, 2018. https://www.brainyquote.com/quotes/linus_pauling_163645

[360] "The Runaway Species: How Human Creativity Remakes the World," Anthony Brandt and David Eagleman, Canongate Books Ltd., Great Britain, 2017.

[361] "The chimpanzees of Gombe: patterns of behavior," Jane Goodall,

Belknap Press of Harvard University Press, 1986.

[362] "A researcher in her prime," Jane Goodall, Associated Press, 1997.

[363] Princeton Architectural Press, 2018. *ISBN-10: 161896612, ISBN-13: 978-1616896614.*

[364] "A Conversation with Apollo Astronaut Walter Cunningham about a Vital Need to Restore Climate Science Integrity," Larry Bell, Forbes, August 6, 2013.

[365] "Be Skeptical of Those Who Treat Science as an Ideology," Sue Desmond-Hellman, Wall Street Journal, January 20-21, 2018.

[366] "Magnificent Desolation: The Long Journey Home from the Moon," Buzz Aldrin, Telegraph Books, 2018.

[367] "The Motivated Mind: Where Our Passion & Creativity Comes From," Malini Mohana, PsccgCentral, May 17, 2016.

[368] "A Short List of Universal Values," Richard T. Kinnier, Jerry L. Kernes and Therese M. Dautheribes, Wiley Online Library, 2000.

[369] "Addiction to Perfection: The Still Unravished Bride: A Psychological Study," Marion Woodman, Studies in Jungian Psychology by Jungian Analysts Series, 2018.

[370] "The Runaway Species: How Human Creativity Remakes the World," Anthony Brandt and David Eagleman, Canongate Books Ltd., Great Britain, 2017.

[371] "The Intuitive Compass – why the best decisions balance reason and instinct," Francis Cholle, *HRZone*, 2011 .

[372] "The Art of Intuition: Cultivating Your Inner Wisdom," Sophy Burnham, Penguin Publishing Group, 2011.

[373] "U.S. Navy Program to Study How Troops Use Intuition", Joseph Channing, Newyorktimes.com, March 27, 2012
https://www.fbo.gov/index?s=opportunity&mode=form&tab=core&id=be0a1ab47e05fe0f9c2bd0ffd5e40b1a&_cview=1

[374] "Know Thyself: How Mindfulness Can Improve Self-Knowledge," Perspectives on Psychological Science, 2013.

[375] "Why Does Time Fly as We Get Older? Time seems to pass more and more quickly as we age. Why is this?" Jordan Gaines Lewis, Psychology Today, December 18, 2013.

[376] Ibid